ALEXIS S. TROUBEZKOY was born in Paris in 1934 into a
Russian princely family. At an early age he emigrated to the
United States. He is the author of *Imperial Legend: The
Mysterious Disappearance of Tsar Alexander I* and *The Road
to Balaklava*. He lives in Canada.

Other titles in this series

A BRIEF HISTORY OF

THE
CRIMEAN WAR

The causes and consequences
of a medieval conflict
fought in a modern age

ALEXIS S. TROUBETZKOY

CARROLL & GRAF PUBLISHERS
New York

Carroll & Graf Publishers
An imprint of Avalon Publishing Group, Inc.
245 W. 17th Street, 11th Floor
New York NY 10011-5300
www.carrollandgraf.com

AVALON
publishing group incorporated

First published in the UK by Robinson,
an imprint of Constable & Robinson Ltd, 2006

First Carroll & Graf edition, 2006

ISBN-13: 978-0-78671-830-6
ISBN-10: 0-7867-1830-7

Printed and bound in the EU

To the peacemakers,
the famed and the faceless.

What has happened will happen again,
and what has been done will be done again,
and there is nothing new under the sun.

Ecclesiastes 1:9

CONTENTS

ACKNOWLEDGEMENTS

Of the numerous authorities consulted in the course of writing this book, I am especially indebted to professors J.S. Curtiss, G.P. Gooch, C. Grünwald, V.J. Puryear, E.V. Tarle and H.W.V. Temperley, from whose works I have drawn liberally. Of the more recent accounts of the war itself, I have relied strongly on Trevor Royle and on Ian Fletcher-Natalia Ishchenko. No study of the Crimean War or its causes is possible without recourse to A.W. Kinglake's nine-volume history of the war or to Russell's contemporary reports, and for these sources I am also thankful.

The dates given herein are according to the Julian calendar. Conversations reported in this work are authentic, as recorded by contemporary witness. Transliteration of names has been done according to the *New York Times* form.

I wish to thank the staff of the following libraries for patient assistance and cooperation in making available the materials listed in the Bibliography: Columbia University, the British Library, University of Toronto, McGill University, the Bodleian Library (Oxford), Library of the City of New York. I am grateful also for advice and encouragement offered by Dr George Ignatieff, Canadian diplomat and quintessential 'peace monger', now deceased; Dr Hereward Senior, Professor of History, McGill University; my dear friend and critical reader, Douglas C. Robertson; and Bill Hanna, my agent from Acacia House. Above all, I thank my wife, Hélène, for her benign toleration of scores of unsociable days and nights spent in the development of this work.

PREFACE

A century and a half ago, the Crimean War was fought, and by the time it had ended over a half million men lay dead. They fell – both Russians and allies – on the battlefields, at sea, in hospitals and in the steppes. The horrendous losses closely match the combined military deaths suffered by the United States in both World Wars. It was a bizarre war, or in the words of H.A.L. Fisher, a 'contest entered into without necessity, conducted without foresight and deserving to be reckoned from its . . . tragic mismanagement rather among medieval than modern campaigns'. A judgement that today gives pause for reflection.

Tennyson wrote, '. . . the soldier knew / Some one had blunder'd,' adding quickly, 'Their's not to reason why, / Their's but to do and die.'

Why the Crimean War? For that matter, why any war? Why are the threads of warfare so firmly and conspicuously woven into the fabric of history?

The answer is that human nature ineluctably dictates warfare. Simply put, our propensity for war is embedded in us. How so? The answer varies. The ethnologist would argue that it is matter of the 'territorial imperative' of the animal world – the primitive of defence against intrusion into one's breeding or feeding ground. Man, this scientist will go on to explain, is afflicted with the instinct of pugnacity which is driven by the same primeval forces that cause certain animals to butt heads and others to mark their terrain – aggressiveness in the exercise of possession.

The sociologist will argue that man is not merely an individual, but an integral part of society – of a clan, a state or a nation. As such, he acts and reacts differently in different social circumstances. The seeds of war, the sociologist will argue, emanate from societal structures. These lie not only in the internal formations of states but also in the international organizations within which they operate. In contemporary terms, the likes of the Tamils and the Chechens within Sri Lanka and Russia; and the failures of the United Nations in strife-torn Africa.

The psychologist – perhaps the most revealing of all – will contend that it is a matter of the psychological maladjustments of leaders. And, he or she will add, of the skewed perceptions they hold of other countries and their leaders. In the first instance, hark back to such lovelies as Hitler, Pot Pol and, more recently, Saddam Hussein. In the second, consider George III and the American colonists, or Napoleon following his escape from Elba.

Whatever the cause, war is the unalterable stuff of history. Its underlying causes are one thing, and these invariably find root in conflict over resources or in clashing ideologies or in power struggles. Warfare is a last-resort outcome of these diverging interests or ambitions.

But what factors actually precipitate the explosion – the triggering mechanisms, as it were? It may be a need to exploit or manipulate the perceived weaknesses of a neighbour, or it may be in the defence of a felt injustice. It may be the unbridled aspirations of a lone individual, or it could originate in a societal stand taken on some high moral ground. As more recent history demonstrates, it might be a pre-emptive strike for reasons of security. Carl von Clausewitz, the iconic strategic theoretician and thinker on war, focuses concisely on the matter: 'War is an act of force to compel our enemy to do our will.' And that well may be driven by fear or hatred, by ambition, greed or injured pride, by misunderstanding or even a sense of duty – the strong shall aid the weak. Most pathetic of all: it may be the fanatical conviction that war must be had 'in the name of the Almighty'. Whatever the condition, the reasons for wars are wildly varied.

The causes of the Crimean War – 'the world's most curious and unnecessary struggle' – are so convoluted that they defy simple definition. Perhaps in this instance, fate draws together the ethnologist, sociologist and psychologist. Certainly all the other elements are there: exploitation, manipulation, diverse interests, unbridled aspirations, injured pride, societal stands and, above all, power struggle. 'The war and its causes,' observed Frederick Engels, the socialist writer, 'was a colossal comedy of errors in which at every moment the question was asked, "Who's being swindled here?"'

What is little appreciated of the Crimean War is that it was not something that took place exclusively on a remote peninsula of the Black Sea. Engagements were fought on the Danube, along the Persian border and in the Caucasus. Naval battles of magnitude took place in the Baltic and gunfire was exchanged in the high Arctic, a few miles from the Norwegian frontier. In the Pacific, British Columbia, Hong Kong, Calcutta and Australia prepared defences, while on Siberia's Kamtchatka Peninsula, Petropavlovsk suffered invasion by the British navy. In a way, it was a global war.

Much has been written about the Crimean War, particularly of its battles and its heroes. This present work does not set out to review what is generally familiar. The aim here is twofold: first, to trace the manifold causes, events and results of the war and, secondly, to sketch a fleeting picture of an age which made it possible. In bygone days of teaching, I strove to impress on students that the critical aspects of historical events are not primarily to do with *when* they happened or through *whom*, or in the details of *what* transpired. The pith of history lies in an understanding of *why* they happened, and what the *results* were.

The lessons of history are offered us, but how successfully do we learn from them? Surveying the lamentable list of twentieth and twenty-first century wars, both great and small, one wonders why any one of them was not prevented. As Ecclesiastes cautions, 'What has happened will happen again, and what has been done will be done again, and there is nothing new under the sun.'

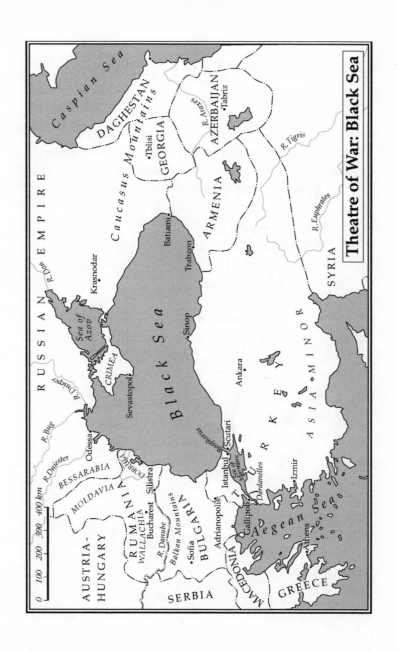

Theatre of War: Black Sea

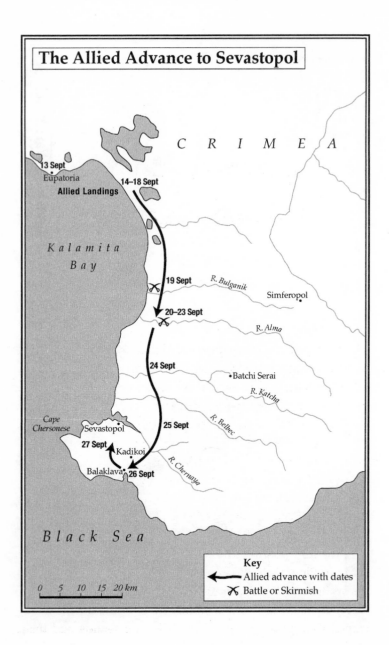

The Allied Advance to Sevastopol

C R I M E A

13 Sept
Eupatoria

14–18 Sept
Allied Landings

Kalamita Bay

19 Sept

R. Bulganik

Simferopol

20–23 Sept

R. Alma

24 Sept

• Batchi Serai

R. Katcha

Cape Chersonese

Sevastopol

25 Sept

R. Belbec

27 Sept

Kadikoi

Balaklava

26 Sept

R. Chernaya

Black Sea

0   5   10   15   20 km

Key
← Allied advance with dates
✗ Battle or Skirmish

1

1844 AND THE STRAITS

The twenty-one saluting guns roared their welcome, shattering the stillness of Woolwich's humid summer evening. The three steamers dropped anchor in the Thames, and a small armada of light vessels pulled away from the jetties to meet them. From the mast of the Cyclops, flew the imperial standard of the black double-headed eagle on a field of orange. This was the personal insignia of His Imperial Majesty Emperor Nicholas I, Tsar of All the Russias. Ten minutes to ten, Saturday 1 June, 1844. At the invitation of his royal cousin, Her Britannic Majesty Victoria, Queen of the United Kingdom and Ireland, the Russian emperor had arrived in England to begin a state visit.

In the lead boat that hastened towards the anchored ships sat Lord Bloomfield, British ambassador to St Petersburg, and Baron Brunov, Russian ambassador to the Court of St James. A score of other officials followed in other tenders. The emperor cordially greeted Bloomfield and Brunov and then, accompanied by his suite, which included Prince Wassiltchik-off, Prince Radizvill, Count Orloff and General d'Adlerberg, made his way to shore. By midnight the imperial party was comfortable installed in Ashburnham House, the mansion of the Russian embassy on Dover Street, and there the emperor retired for the night.

At 9:30 the following morning, Prince Albert called on the tsar. Nicholas met the prince consort midway down the main stairs and embraced him warmly. Albert remained for an hour and a half and then departed so that the emperor might attend Liturgy at the Russian chapel on Welbeck Street. At 1.30 pm, the prince consort returned to Ashburnham House with a couple of carriages and escorted the emperor and his suite to Buckingham Palace.

The invitation to visit Britain had been extended to Nicholas in early March. When he accepted, the British court began elaborate preparations for his reception. During the weeks that followed, however, the emperor kept postponing his departure from St Petersburg. His youngest daughter Alexandra – 'Adina' as she was familiarly called, then in the fourth month of pregnancy, had developed an undiagnosed illness, tubercular by nature. By mid-May the condition of the young grand duchess had improved considerably, and her father's anxiety diminished.

At the same time, world events far from the palaces of St Petersburg were unfolding in an unexpected sequence. In Tahiti, the French Admiral Dupetit-Thouars drove out the English missionary Pritchard and then took possession of the islands. Conflict ensued, and by 18 May Britain and France were distinctly at odds over the issue. In North Africa the French were fitting out an expedition against Morocco, and this was perceived by the British as a threat to their interests in Tunis. More serious, however, was the publication of a curious brochure by Prince de Joinville, son of Louis Philippe and a Vice Admiral in the French navy, in which he advocated the attack and destruction of British coastal towns. The British press howled the public's anti-French sentiment.

For years the tsar had sought to ally his country with Britain, and now he grasped at the opportunity offered by the deteriorating condition of Anglo-French relations. Characteristically, at a moment's notice, Nicholas departed St Petersburg, leaving even some of his ministers unaware of his sudden plans. As he embarked for England, a special courier was dispatched to the British capital to notify the queen of his imminent arrival. Victoria had barely twenty-four hours to prepare for the tsar's reception. The timing was entirely inconvenient. A few days earlier the King of Saxony had arrived in England, and was at that very moment in residence in Buckingham Palace. The young queen, furthermore, was in her seventh month of pregnancy.

The imperial cortège arrived at Buckingham Palace and the queen received the tsar in the Great Hall. The two embraced and exchanged kisses. The King of Saxony was presented, following which the three monarchs went in to lunch. In the late afternoon, Nicholas made brief visits to the Duke and Duchess of Cambridge, the Duke of Gloucester, Princess Sophia (an aged daughter of George III) and the Duke of Wellington, hero of Waterloo. He then returned to the Russian embassy for a rest. That evening a grand banquet was held at Buckingham Palace and for the first time the emperor came face to face with members of the government – Sir Robert Peel, the prime minister; Lord Aberdeen, the foreign secretary; and others. The occasion was strictly social, and no record has come down of diplomatic discussions having been taken place on that particular evening.

The following morning was spent at leisure. Nicholas

strolled through Regent's Park and the streets of London. He stopped at Messrs Mortimer and Hunt, jewellers, and there he made purchase to the sum of £5,000. The Duke of Devonshire, Britain's extraordinary ambassador at the tsar's coronation in 1826, was invited to the Russian embassy for lunch. In the afternoon, the tsar paid a formal courtesy call on the prime minister. Then, accompanied by Baron Brunov, Nicholas left London by the Great Western Railway for Windsor. The queen, Prince Albert and the King of Saxony had departed earlier that day. At Slough station, the imperial party was met by Albert and, in a series of carriages and four, the tsar and his suite arrived at Windsor Castle. The emperor was to spend four days here and during that time he acquired a great fondness for the royal residence. 'It is worthy of you,' he remarked to the queen.

On Tuesday afternoon, Prince Albert took the emperor and the Saxon king to the Ascot races. The queen remained at the castle. It was a windless day, clear and warm, ideal for the opening of the races. Disappointingly, the attendance at the heath was not as great as in the preceding years but the stands were 'tolerably well filled'. Shortly after one o'clock, the imperial cortège entered the grounds, led by Lord Rosslyn, the Master of the Buckhounds.

The first carriage conveyed the emperor and the king, and opposite them sat Prince Albert. The tsar was dressed in a plain blue coat, void of decorations. The King of Saxony was also in civilian dress, but he wore the riband of the Order of the Garter. In the carriages that followed came the Duke of Wellington, Sir Robert Peel, Lord Aberdeen and numerous other dignitaries of the three courts. The illustrious visitors were cheered and warmly applauded.

When the tsar and the king appeared at the windows of the royal stand, the cheering became louder and widespread. The

Duke of Wellington then stepped forward and the noise reached a crescendo. The races then started. Throughout the events the tsar was in animated conversation with Albert, from whom he received a running commentary on the nature of the sport. At the conclusion of the afternoon's highlight, the Queen's Cup race – won by a filly named 'Alice Hawthorne', a 3 to 1 favourite – the imperial party went to the turf to examine the winner. The emperor was cheered lustily and the police had a difficult time in restraining the eager crowd. On the uniform of an attending police officer, Nicholas spotted the Waterloo Medal and he immediately inquired as to which regiment the veteran had belonged, in what portion of the battle he had been engaged and other questions pertaining to Wellington's great victory.

Then to the astonishment of those attending, Nicholas deserted his suite, plunged into the crowd and shook hands with many of the eager spectators. Count Orloff and Baron Brunov tried in vain to follow. The tsar obviously enjoyed it all and, after returning to his party and perceiving the many concerned faces, he asked, 'What's the matter with you? These people wish me no harm.' The Englishmen within the party remained silent, leaving their fears unexpressed. England at the time was a haven for hundreds of Polish exiles who had fled their homeland after the Russian emperor suppressed their revolution. Most of the unhappy exiles were fanatic nationalists – one never knew what attempt might be made on the tsar's life.

That evening a grand banquet was held in the castle's Waterloo Gallery. The centre of the long table was decorated with exotic flowers interspersed among magnificent gold ornaments. In the middle stood an immense candelabrum, a sculptured gold masterpiece of St George and the Dragon. The gallery was illuminated by numerous gold chandeliers. The band of the Scots Fusilier Guards – Prince Albert's regiment – played the fashionable tunes of the time, including waltzes, polkas and selections from Romberg and Bellini. However, there was no dancing, as the court was in official mourning for Prince Albert's father, the Duke of Saxe-Coburg-Gotha.

After that evening's dinner and the one of the following day, the tsar held his most serious discussions with the prime minister and members of cabinet. Nicholas did not leave his ailing daughter to journey 1,700 miles (2,750 kilometres) across Europe in order to attend races and state dinners. The emperor had long dreamed of drawing Britain into agreement on the question of Turkey. In particular, he wished for approval and accord on Russia's policy concerning the sultan's empire.

Fifteen years earlier, the emperor had established a seven-man commission to recommend a national policy respecting Turkey. Since the days of Catherine II, Russians had dreamed of fulfilling their 'historic mission' – to precipitate the dissolution of the Turkish empire and to gain control of Constantinople and the Straits, 'the gates to our house'. The Duke of Argyll in 1854 best described the significance of the Straits:

There is no feature in the physical geography of our globe so peculiar in its political significance as that which consists in the two channels of the Bosphorus and the Dardanelles, with the Sea of Marmora between them. Nowhere else in the world is there a vast inland sea, more than 700 miles [1,125 kilometres] broad, that washes the shore of two separate quarters of the world, and yet opens with a mouth as narrow as a neck of a bottle, so that the Power possessing it must have irresistible facilities of attack from a position altogether impregnable in defence. If this imperial dominion were to be added to what Russia already has, the Black Sea would be a Russian lake, the

Danube would be a Russian river, and some of the richest provinces of Eastern Europe and of Western Asia would give to Russia inexhaustible resources of men, in money and in ships. With these, together with a unique position of geographical advantage, she would possess inordinate power over the rest of Europe.

The tsar's commission on Turkey, presided over by Count Victor Kotchubey, was composed of some of the empire's highest functionaries, including Count Nesselrode, the chancellor. 'We have to decide,' wrote Nesselrode, 'is the preservation of the Ottoman government hurtful or useful to Russia? . . . The idea of hunting down the Turk out of Europe and re-establishing the worship of the one true God in St Sophia is certainly very fine, and, if realized, would make us all live in history. But what will Russia gain by it all? Glory undoubtedly, but at the same time she would lose all real advantages offered by being a neighbour to a state weakened by a fortunate series of wars, and she would have inevitable struggles with the chief powers in Europe.'

Kotchubey's group met in secret and after prolonged discussion came to a unanimous conclusion – it was in Russia's interests to maintain Turkey for as long as possible as a weak power. The committee contended that any division of the Ottoman empire would inevitably involve Austria, Britain and France. Each would lay claim to a share of the Turkish dominions. Russia would then have three strong neighbours with whom to contend, rather than one weak power. Furthermore, it was argued, an annexation of Constantinople might cause Russia's southern provinces to gravitate away from St Petersburg. The Ukraine, Georgia and Bessarabia could well look to Constantinople as a new political centre, and if this were to happen the Russian empire might find itself divided.

The maintenance of the status quo in Turkey should be continued.

The Kotchubey committee furthermore recommended that if Turkey should some day dissolve through its own internal weakness, Russia should not strive to restore it. On the contrary, Russia should lose no time in opening negotiations with the other European powers to settle amicably the problem of succession and to effect a peaceful disposition of Ottoman territories and population. These recommendations were accepted by Nicholas and became the basis of imperial government policy toward Turkey until the outbreak of the Crimean War.

The adoption of such a policy by the tsar was an internal matter, a unilateral decision having no international basis. Nicholas was now determined to bring the policy to international agreement.

The revolutionary events of 1830, which helped to shake the foundations of the old order throughout Europe, drew Russia and Austria closer together. These two imperial powers were bastions of conservatism and reaction. Austria, furthermore, shared an extensive border with the Ottomans and for centuries had been directly active in Turkish affairs. It was logical that, if international agreement over Turkey were to be reached with other powers, Austria ought to stand first.

By the early 1830s, the internal affairs of Turkey had increasingly deteriorated. Rebellion within the Ottoman dominions had reached an alarming state. In Egypt, Mehemet Ali, a former Albanian tobacco dealer, had succeeded in securing control over that Turkish protectorate. He now threatened to occupy Constantinople and to establish a new regime. The possibility of a vigorous Egyptian empire on the shore of the Bosphorus was certainly not in the best interest of Russia. Mehemet, furthermore, was actively supported by

France, and to have a French dominant power in Constantinople was equally odious. Austria shared these fears with Russia.

In January 1833, Nicholas sent Count Tatischev, Minister of War, as a special envoy to Vienna in order to sound out the Austrian chancellor. Metternich was quick to appreciate the advantages of an Austro-Russian accord, and after some negotiation the Treaty of Münchengrätz was signed. By the agreement, the two countries pledged not only to co-operate fully in supporting the existing regime in Turkey, but to maintain their union in the ultimate partition of the Ottoman empire, should Mahmud II fall. Nesselrode considered Münchengrätz 'a brilliant diplomatic victory', for now he felt assured that in any contingency, 'Austria will be with us and not against us.' Metternich, too, was pleased, for not only were Russia's Eastern objectives for the future successfully checked, but now Austria was assured a healthy slice of Turkey on the latter's demise.

The Austro-Russian alliance in which Prussia pledged co-operation was a splendid step forward in the tsar's scheme for a great power accord on Turkey. However, to assure a complete guarantee of a pacific settlement to any succession of the Ottoman dominions, Nicholas realized the unqualified necessity of a further alliance with one of the two great Western European powers, France and Britain.

France, the cradle of revolution, was Europe's greatest opponent of conservatism. Nicholas, the fervent anti-revolutionary, was champion of the *ancien régime*. The French, furthermore, had encouraged and supported the Egyptian revolt against Mahmud II that now threatened the peace. Britain, on the other hand, possessed the world's greatest fleet, which could do great harm to Russia. Or it could effectively abate possible international discord over Turkey. The imperial government set out to draw Britain into an alliance – that was why Nicholas now found himself in Windsor.

After the splendid banquet was over, the guests filed out of the Waterloo Gallery and adjourned to the neighbouring rooms. Most of the ladies and gentlemen gravitated to the Great Hall where her majesty's private band waited to entertain. The tsar, Sir Robert Peel and Lord Aberdeen, however, sought the seclusion of a private study where they closeted themselves for some hours.

The queen retired early to her private quarters and there wrote an intimate letter to her favourite uncle, King Leopold of the Belgians, in which she gave some impressions of the tsar and of his visit:

> My beloved Uncle . . . a great event and a great compliment the Emperor's visit is, and the people here are extremely flattered at it. He is certainly very striking; still very handsome; his profile is beautiful and his manners most dignified; extremely civil – quite alarmingly so, as he is so full of attentions and politesse. But the expression of his eyes is formidable, and unlike anything I ever saw before . . . he seldom smiles, and when he does the expression is not a happy one. He is very easy to get on with. Really, it seems like a dream when I think that we breakfast and walk out with this greatest of all earthly Potentates . . . The Emperor amused the King of Saxony and me by saying he was so *embarrassé* when people were presented to him, and that he felt so 'gauche' *en frac*, which certainly he is quite unaccustomed to wear . . . ever your devoted Niece, VICTORIA R.

Some days later, after Nicholas had departed from England, the queen continued this letter with further impressions of the tsar:

I got to know the Emperor and he to know me. There is much about him which I cannot help liking, and I think his character is one which should be understood, and looked upon for once as it is. He is stern and severe – with fixed principles of duty which nothing on earth will make him change; very clever I do not think him to be, and his mind is an uncivilized one; his education has been neglected; politics and military concerns are the only things he takes great interest in; the arts and all softer occupations he is insensible to, but he is sincere, I am certain, sincere even in his most despotic acts, from a sense that that is the only way to govern . . . He is, I should say, too frank, for he talks openly before people, which he should not do, and with difficulty restrains himself. His anxiety to be believed is very great, and I must say his personal promises I am inclined to believe; then his feelings are very strong; he feels kindness deeply – and his love for his wife and children, and for all children, is very great. He has a strong feeling for domestic life, saying to me, when our children were in the room: '*Voilà les doux moments de notre vie*' . . . my angel, Albert, thinks that he is a man inclined too much to give way to impulse and feeling, which makes him act wrongly often. His admiration for beauty is very great, and put me much in mind of you when he drove out with us, looking out for pretty people . . . *pour finir*, I must say one more word or two about his personal appearance . . . he is bald now, but in his Chevalier Garde uniform he is magnificent still and very striking. I can not deny that we were in great anxiety when we took him out lest some Pole might make an attempt, and I always felt thankful when we got him safe home again. His poor daughter is very ill, I fear . . . ever your devoted Niece, VICTORIA R.

2

NICHOLAS AND VICTORIA

Nicholas was the eighth of ten children. His eldest brother, Emperor Alexander I, dominated the family scene, just as he dominated Europe in the years immediately following Napoleon's catastrophic retreat from Moscow in 1812. Alexander's education was supervised by his brilliant grandmother, Catherine the Great, who wished to give the future tsar an education in conformity with the enlightened ideas of the French *philosophes*. The youngster's tutor was the Swiss republican, Frederick La Harpe. Nicholas, younger by nineteen years, never knew his grandmother. His education was much neglected, entrusted to General Lamsdroff, a rough man who relied heavily on the rod as the principle means of instilling learning. 'In my lessons,' wrote Nicholas, 'I learned only coercion and I had no pleasure in learning. I was often blamed for laziness and inattention, probably wrongly; but it was not rare for Lamsdroff to give me very painful blows with a cane at lesson time.'

Unquestioning obedience and strict subordination was inculcated in the boy from earliest years. As a sixteen-year-old, Nicholas witnessed Napoleon's campaign from the sidelines, too young to participate. Virtually all his military experience was limited to the parade square. Resplendent in his uniform, which he rarely shed in later years, the grand duke derived much pleasure in reviewing countless parades. From the troops he demanded the highest precision of drill and a flawless turn out of dress. A special room in the palace was set aside for his enormous collection of military miniatures. Even after he acceded to the throne, Nicholas occasionally found fleeting moments to closet himself in this room given over to wooden soldiers. As emperor, it has been suggested, he so drilled the army that all evidence of fire and spirit was crushed.

Nicholas' accession to the throne was a most curious episode, and the circumstances left an indelible impression on the new monarch. It coloured his thirty-year reign.

In November 1825, Emperor Alexander I died under peculiar circumstances in the remote Black Sea town of Taganrog, at a premature age of forty-eight.[1] Three years earlier, Grand Duke Constantine, Viceroy of Poland and next in line to the throne, had renounced his right to it. This arrangement, however, was not communicated to Nicholas, who was next in line after him. When news of Alexander's death reached St Petersburg, Nicholas promptly proclaimed Constantine the next tsar. Almost simultaneously, Constantine in Warsaw proclaimed Nicholas the new emperor. For three anxious weeks couriers sped to and fro between St Petersburg and Warsaw, as Nicholas tried in vain to persuade his brother to return to the capital and make a formal act of abdication. During this brief period Russia was without a ruler.

For months prior to Alexander's death, an underground

group known as the Northern Society plotted to overthrow the established order in the empire. It sought to bring about a constitutional monarchy with an elected constituent assembly and a federal form of government. The startling news of Alexander's death, and the confusion that enveloped Russia that December, offered the group a sudden window of opportunity – more correctly, perhaps, forced its hand – and their members determined to act. It was precipitously decided to block the senate from publishing a proclamation of succession and to force its members to issue instead a revolutionary manifesto. To lead them, the conspirators looked to Prince Sergey Troubetzkoy, whom they elected 'provisional dictator' in the new order. Troubetzkoy came from one of Russia's oldest and most noble families, whose members over the centuries had played prominent roles in its history. After the failed revolution, Nicholas was shocked to discover Prince Sergey among the arrested rebels. 'What was in that head of yours, when you, with your name and family, got involved in such an affair?' demanded the infuriated emperor. Then, tapping his forefinger against the young officer's forehead, he added, 'Colonel of the Guards, Prince Troubetzkoy! Have you no shame for having joined with such rabble!'

In the early hours of 14 December, the revolt was launched and by eleven o'clock the Moscow Regiment took its station in Senate Square. At this point, everything that could go wrong for the conspirators did go wrong. The guardsmen slated to seize the Winter Palace failed to do so, and no other troops arrived to support the Moscow Regiment. Worst of all, Troubetzkoy forsook the rebel cause and failed to appear to lead the insurgent troops that morning. Action came to a grinding halt – long enough for Nicholas to grab the initiative. By four o'clock, thirty-two artillery pieces had been placed along the perimeter of the square. Seven rounds of gunshot were fired at the mass of rebels and the Decembrist forces scattered. The revolt was ended.

In the months which followed, arrests were carried out throughout Russia. Scores were sentenced to hard labour in Siberia – including Troubetzkoy – while others were sent to serve as private soldiers in the Caucasus. On 13 July 1826, five of the ringleaders were executed and the curtain fell on 'the first Russian revolution'. On 3 September, Nicholas was crowned Emperor of All the Russias. Whatever might be, vowed the young ruler, insidious societies such as the Decembrists would never again be given opportunity for insurrection. His vow was ruthlessly kept.

The Emperor Nicholas stood apart from other sovereigns of Europe. While the flame of revolt burned under most thrones, the overwhelming majority of the Russian people venerated their tsar. His authority was boundless, limited only by the Divine; there was no parliament to curb it. The clergy recognized him as the spiritual leader of the Church. The tsar's power was a really an amalgam of old-time despotism, Byzantine theocracy and military dictatorship. His physical stature and commanding presence embodied the actual power of the state. The few intellectuals and liberals who dared to utter against him – some even attempting palace revolts – inevitably found themselves lamenting their folly in one or another remote Asiatic outpost of the huge empire. The tsar was bound by nothing – what he chose to do, he did.

But Nicholas was of a simple character, and Queen Victoria quickly saw through it – honest, firm and determined. He did not lack nobility and he could 'make others feel the prestige of his dignity'. The tsar invariably showed reserve and distrust of others, but when he was friendly, the 'frankness of his manner had an irresistible charm'. He evidenced no mercy with the Polish rebels of 1830, and his severity made him the dread object of hate to millions. At the same time, this sternness enhanced his presence, and significantly increased the delight of being with him, when he was in a good mood. He was a man of his word, one in whose personal honour most European statesmen placed their faith. All that was fair and honourable, Nicholas held, was exemplified in the English concept of gentleman; diplomatic negotiations with the British were often sealed by a mere handshake and the *parole de gentleman*.

Nicholas had boundless energy and a developed sense of duty. He effectively took on a vast share of the actual business of governing. Contrary to the practice of his predecessors, he appointed Russians to the principle posts of the empire, and surrounded himself with a coterie of capable and talented advisors. Dimitri Dashkov was appointed minister of justice, a person 'incorruptible in the face of temptations and who combined great erudition with an absolute passion for work'. The tsar entrusted Count E.F. Kankrin the gargantuan task of codifying the laws, which eventually appeared in forty-five indexed volumes. Count Alexander Benkendorf received the infamous Third Section, which had as its objective the protection of 'the peace and rights of citizens [lest they be] violated by the pernicious aims of evil-minded men'. Never had Russia been so thoroughly administered. The tsar's admiration for Prussian military order and precision was manifest in every department of government. Reports, commissions: paper, paper and more paper. Soon an official government commission became necessary 'to seek ways of diminishing unnecessary correspondence'.

Before half a decade had passed, events in Western Europe wrought a new page in Russian history. In 1830, Charles X was overthrown and Louis Philippe became not the King of France, but the King of the French. Louis' father, Philippe Egalité, had voted some years earlier for the execution of his cousin, Louis XVI. The new regime was a constitutional monarchy, a liberal government of the bourgeoisie. Until Philippe's arrival on the scene, European states had stood for strong monarchies, and kings were near absolute. France now acquired a broad constitution which greatly limited kingly power, and before long, popular agitation for similar reform began to be felt in Italy, Belgium and finally Poland.

On 28 November, a group of Polish nationalists broke into the Belvedere Palace in Warsaw and killed a Russian general whom they supposed to be Grand Duke Constantine. The next day a handful of Poles gained control of the Warsaw garrison. Within the week, however, the short-lived rebellion had collapsed and order was restored. The mutinous events of the Decembrist revolt had been indelibly impressed on the tsar's mind, and now, with the Warsaw events, the worst of Nicholas' suspicions were confirmed: liberalism and constitutional experiment were insidious and intolerable. A period of harsh repression followed in Poland and an intensive programme of Russification was inaugurated.

As the revolutionary movements of Europe gained momentum in the years following 1830, Nicholas increasingly became the embodiment of autocracy and orthodoxy. 'His system was inflexibly logical, his convictions unshakeable,' wrote Baron Jomini, a Swiss in the Russian service and an advisor to the tsar. His mandate was not by vote; it was God-given. 'Right or revolution: such were the two extreme terms between which he allowed no compromise.' Austria especially looked to the tsar for moral and material support in the events of crises. Austrian Chancellor Metternich and Nicholas found much to admire in one another.

At home Nicholas continued with reform programmes, and by these the vast majority of the population – the peasants – reaped benefits. The minority, however – intellectuals and the rising middle class – fared considerably less well, as a plethora of laws were promulgated effectively suppressing creative thought. Foreign travel was prohibited and censorship laws were extended and ruthlessly enforced. The word '*demos*' was expurgated from textbooks on Greek history, and it was forbidden to write of Caesar's death as an assassination – he 'perished'. From one scientific work the expression 'forces of nature' was removed by diligent censors. Newspapers published heavily censored news and offered little or no editorial comment. Anatomy texts were to exclude anything which might 'offend the instinct of decency'. Writers were muzzled and scores of offending authors found themselves in Siberia, including such notables as Dostoyevsky. 'Russian literature was compared to a plant trying to grow on the edge of a crater,' commented one historian. The individual thinker was stifled; responsibility and initiative perished. Whereas Europe was ablaze with revolutionary fire, Russia barely knew the smoke.

And what was this country that was ruled by the Emperor of All the Russias? It was then, as it is today, the world's largest country – at the time covering one seventh of the earth's habitable surface. For over four centuries, Russia had grown at a rate of nearly 70 square miles [180 square kilometres] a day. By 1852, some 67 million subjects lived within that territory, a land that encompassed some 160 distinct races, nationalities or tribes, speaking 110 languages and dialects, and adhering to 35 religions. The greatest ethnic division was the Slavs, who numbered approximately three-quarters of the whole. For this group especially, the idea of absolute power was, for the most part, unshakeable. 'God is Master of the Word,' wrote the eighteenth-century historian Ivan Pososh-kov. 'The tsar is master in his country. In the domain assigned to him, he can create, like God, everything he wants.' The emperor was the alpha and the omega of the nation's well-being.

Some thirty years preceding Nicholas' visit to England, the red coats of the Cossacks of the Guard, riding fifteen abreast, appeared at the Pantin Gates of Paris. Behind them, mounted on a dark Arab mare – ironically a gift from Napoleon, rode Tsar Alexander I. At his right, representing the emperor of Austria, was Prince Schwarzenberg and on his left, Frederick William, King of Prussia. Napoleon's grand army had been decisively routed by the allies at Leipzig and the French emperor was on the run. On the brilliant morning of 31 March 1814, the victorious allies paraded the length of Champs Elysées; the might and grandeur of Russia was on full display before the joyful Parisians. The spectacle of the day was not forgotten in the West. What was to prevent Russia from 'liberating' Europe once more sometime in the future? In 1820, Napoleon solemnly warned from his exile on St Helena, 'The barbarians of the North are already too powerful, and probably in the course of time will overwhelm all Europe, as now I think they will.' The tsar who was welcomed so enthusiastically at Woolwich in 1844, was the ruler of a seemingly boundless territory of awesome might. 'The Emperor Nicholas is master of Europe,' Prince Albert gushed enthusiastically.

On the Tuesday after his arrival in Britain, a grand military review was held at Windsor Park. The emperor, the King of Saxony, Prince Albert and nearly all the gentlemen were on horseback. Nicholas wore the striking uniform of the Preobrozhenski Regiment – dark green tunic, white trousers and black helmet with white feathers. The brilliant star of the Most Noble Order of the Garter stood out conspicuously. The Duke of Argyll wrote:

Never before and never since have I felt myself in the presence of such a King of men. His whole form and aspect were those of perfect manly beauty. He must have been at least six foot four [1.93 metres] in height, with shoulders well thrown back, and a fine military carriage. And this was crowned by a head of singular beauty, manliness and power. In features it approaches very nearly the pure Greek ideal, in which the nose and the forehead are in one continuous line . . . his whole expression was that of conscious will, of energy, and of power. His eyes were splendid, vigilant and watchful, without being at all restless or unsettled.

Prince Albert, in a field marshal's uniform, wore the Russian Order of St Andrew. The King of Saxony was dressed in a uniform of dark blue and gold and he wore the insignia of the orders of the Garter and of the Golden Fleece. The queen and the ladies of the party arrived in open carriages.

The troops participating in the review came from nine different horse and artillery regiments and the whole was commanded by Viscount Cobermere. As the inspecting party approached, the band struck up the Russian national anthem. The emperor rode well at the head of the group, scrutinizing carefully the condition and bearing of the troops. The inspection was followed by a march past. A witness later remarked on the 'very fine cheer when the old Duke of Wellington passed the Queen's carriage, and the really beautiful salute of Prince Albert, who rode at the head of his regiment and of course lowered his sword in full military form to the Queen, with such a look and smile as he did it!' and declared, 'I never saw so many pretty feelings expressed in a minute.' Following the march past, Victoria departed from the park to loud applause and cries of 'God, Save the Queen!' For the next hour, the troops executed various drills and a series of intricate evolutions. On returning to the castle, the emperor expressed to the queen his deep admiration of the condition of her troops. He especially praised the speed and precision of the artillery drill.

The army which Nicholas admired with such delight was the same which within eight brief years would invade the southern reaches of his empire. When the invasion finally came, the effects of forty years of British military inactivity showed conspicuously. Not since Waterloo had the soldiers of the queen seen battle. Military reviews, drills, and endless 'square bashing' do not make for an efficient fighting force. Midway through the war, de Tocqueville wrote, 'The heroic courage of [British] soldiers was everywhere and unreservedly praised, but I found also a general belief greatly exaggerated, that [Britain] is utterly devoid of military talent, which is shown as much in administration as in fighting, and that even in the most pressing circumstances, she cannot raise a large Army.'[2]

The magnificent charge of the Light Brigade, the war's most celebrated event, was of no strategic importance whatsoever, other than serving as a symbol of the epic courage of the individual soldier. The great battles of Crimea were won by the hardened, coarse, illiterate common soldier, who, at the same time, was long-suffering, shrewd and stolid. To him can the honours be laid – not to the army's high command, not to the civilian heads of the auxiliary services, and certainly not to the cabinet or parliament. It was this same courage and deeply ingrained sense of duty which permitted the British army to face impossible odds and, in the end, usually overcome.

In 1815, Napoleon was safely tucked away on St Helena and, among the great powers, the harmony wrought by the Concert of Europe brought four decades of peace. By mid-century the British military had fallen into scandalous neglect. Parliament had other priorities on which to spend money. J.W.

Foresque, the chronicler of the British army, illustrates with an example:

> The meanness and improvidence of the Commons were incredible. They would not supply money enough for good-conduct medals to permit a medal to be given to every man who had earned it. They allowed men who had earned good-conduct badges to pay three shillings a piece for them: so that, practically, the better a man behaved the more heavily he was fined. Moreover, they withdrew good-conduct pay from private soldiers upon their promotion to be sergeants.

As late as 1856, parliament was informed that it cost more per year to keep a convict in prison than to maintain a soldier in the army. A convict in cells, it was noted, was allocated on an average 1,000 cubic feet (28 cubic metres) of air space, whereas the soldier in most barracks was allowed 400 cubic feet (11 cubic metres), and in many military garrisons and hospitals the figure fell as low as 300 cubic feet (8.5 cubic metres). The death rate of military-age civilians was 8 per 1,000; in the infantry, the non-combat rate was 20.4 per 1,000. Tuberculosis was the great killer; for every civilian who died, five soldiers succumbed. The Commons steadfastly refused to build fresh barracks to replace the unventilated and thoroughly unhealthy, antiquated structures.

Uniform worn by the troops was picturesque but too tight – oppressive in the summer, and insufficiently warm in winter. In the extreme temperatures of Canada, for example, the trooper was issued his uniform and nothing else – no greatcoat or woollen muffler. If he possessed the means, he was permitted to purchase gloves. Daily food rations were a pound of bread and three-quarters of a pound of beef. Vegetables, pork and other foodstuffs were acquired on the soldier's own initiative and often illegally. Professor Woodward gives us some details:

> The only cooking utensils were two coppers, one for meat, the other for potatoes. The meat was always boiled beef; there were two meals a day – breakfast at 7:30, dinner at 12:30. A third meal was provided only a few years before the Crimean War, and at the men's expense. The pay of a private of the line was nominally seven shillings a week but half of this sum was taken for messing, and one shilling 10 pence for general maintenance and washing . . . No amusements were provided for him, and the state made a profit of £50,000 a year out of canteens where contractors sold bad drinks at high prices. The men were never in proper health, and the bad conditions led to bickering and quarrels, and, above all, to drink and venereal disease. Discipline under these conditions was maintained by severe and brutal punishments.[3]

Sixty per cent of the infantry was illiterate and it was deemed desirable to keep it that way. Outside the army, reforms in education were rapidly taking place; inside the army matters related to education continued the preserve of chaplains. Educational reforms, it was feared, would bring revolutionary propaganda. 'If ever there is a mutiny in the army,' cautioned the Duke of Wellington, 'and in all probability we shall have one – you'll see that these new-fangled schoolmasters will be at the bottom of it.'

Such was the condition of the common soldier, of the trooper who paraded on that warm June day at the Windsor Park review, who cheered the Emperor of All the Russias and who lustily shouted, 'God, Save the Queen!' And what of the officers and administrators who stood above this solider?

In the British army of the time, there were two classes of

officers: cavalry and infantry officers – these were gentlemen, and artillery and engineering officers – these were not gentlemen. The gentlemen most commonly purchased their commissions; the others did not. The purchase system was a hallowed tradition of the military establishment, supported strongly by the likes of Wellington and Palmerston. According to Woodhan-Smith, it was reported of Palmerston, 'He thought it was very desirable to connect the higher classes of Society with the Army; and he did not know any more effective method of connecting them than by seniority . . . if the connection between the Army and the higher classes of society were dissolved, then the Army would present a dangerous and unconstitutional appearance. It was only when the Army was unconnected with those whose property gave them an interest in the country, and was commanded by unprincipled military adventurers and it even became formidable to the liberties of the nation.'

The purchase system eventually became so complicated that the war office was compelled to issue an official scale of tariffs which detailed the exact amounts to be paid for various commissions. Prices were high. In 1836, the old Earl of Cardigan purchased the position of lieutenant-colonel of the 11th Light Dragoons for his young son, who eventually brought glory to the family name by leading his troop in the celebrated charge at Balaklava. The price paid was £40,000, a sum equivalent to the entire annual income from the earl's stables, or over £600,000 in modern times (somewhat in excess of the £5,176 provided for in the tariff scale). It goes without saying that the practice of commission purchase not only excluded qualified candidates of slender means but also quashed advancement opportunities for many.

And over the vast structure of the purely military, there spread an incredible hierarchy of cumbersome civilian bureaucracy. Prior to 1854, the responsibility for the army was in the hands of the Secretary of State for War and the Colonies – the assumption was that these were joint and complementary interests. Under him was the Secretary at War. The former decided the important questions of military policy whereas the latter was responsible for the finance, and frequently the two did not see eye to eye. It was the Secretary at War who transmitted the government's wishes to the Commander-in-Chief of the Army. This gentleman was a general headquartered at the Horse Guards, and his principle duties were to oversee discipline, promotion and appointment throughout the Army. The Master General of Ordnance, yet a separate appointment, was responsible for the artillery, engineers and production of military equipment. The Home Office bore responsibility for matters related to militia, yeomanry and volunteers. The Treasury, still another authority, had under it the commissariat which oversaw transport, victualling and supply of troops stationed abroad. The Master General of Ordnance, on the other hand, tended to these same responsibilities for troops at home. Other civilian organizations included: the Army Medical Board, the Audit Office, a Paymaster-General's Department and a Board of General Affairs, which oversaw matters related to clothing. Each entity assiduously guarded its autonomy and territory, with jealousy and intrigue permeating all. Clashes of interests were the order of the day. Such was the structure of the British army before Crimea – a setting truly worthy of Gilbert and Sullivan.

On the evening of the grand review, Nicholas attended another splendid banquet in the Waterloo Gallery, in the same glittering ambiance as on the previous evening. After dinner, the tsar retired with Aberdeen to a private room where the two continued the discussions of the previous night. Motioning the foreign secretary to a comfortable armchair, the tsar began, frankly and openly: 'Let us sit down. I will forget that I am emperor. You forget that you are minister of England. Let us be I, Nicholas, and you, Aberdeen.'

The emperor began by expressing candidly his opposition to France and in particular its king. 'Louis Philippe has meant well of Europe; this I frankly admit. I myself can never be his friend . . . in order to give himself position and to strengthen himself in it, he has attempted to undermine and to ruin my position as Russian emperor. This I will never forgive him.'

Nicholas then outlined the dangers France presented in the eastern Mediterranean, particularly in Turkey. He connected Britain with Russia as facing these threats in common. 'Turkey is a dying man,' the tsar argued. 'We may endeavour to keep him alive, but we shall not succeed. He will, he must die. That will be a critical moment. I foresee that I shall have to put my armies into movement and Austria must do the same. I fear nobody in the matter but France.'

When Turkey collapses, Nicholas went on to state, the problem of succession will be real. 'What will France require?' he asked. 'I fear much . . . in Africa, in the Mediterranean, in the East itself.' A strong central government in Egypt, dominated by France, might easily close to Britain the important commercial routes to the Orient. 'In such a case must not England be on the spot with the whole of her maritime forces?'

The few areas of disagreement between Britain and Russia, his majesty went on to explain, were small and relatively unimportant. Russia, to Britain's annoyance, steadily refused to recognize the newly-established Kingdom of Belgium. British and Russian commercial rivalry in Persia was growing. Minor border clashes between the forces of the two countries periodically sparked on the frontier of Afghanistan. All these problems the tsar agreed to resolve in common. What was important, he insisted, was an Anglo-Russian accord on Turkey, for here, potentially, was the most likely point of future conflict. 'By land Russia exercises over Turkey a preponderant influence; by sea, England occupies the same position. Isolated, the action of these two powers might do great harm; combined, it might do much good.' Nicholas desired to provide against 'events which, in the absence of concert, might compel him to act in a manner opposed to the views of the British government'.

'I know I am taken for an actor,' the tsar concluded, 'but indeed I am not. I am thoroughly straightforward. I say what I mean, and what I promise, I fulfil.' During the four-day visit to Windsor, the tsar took every opportunity to impress on members of the government the necessity of coming to agreement on the Turkish question.

On the afternoon following the discussions with Aberdeen, the emperor met with the prime minister. 'Years ago,' he began 'Lord Durham was sent to me, a man full of prejudices against me. By merely coming to close quarters with me, all his prejudices were driven clear of him. This is what I hope by coming here to bring about with you, and with England generally. By personal intercourse I trust to annihilate these prejudices.'

The tsar then came quickly to the point: 'Turkey must fall to pieces,' he said to Peel. 'Nesselrode denies that but I for my part am convinced of it. The sultan is no genius, but he is at least a man. Let some misfortune happen to him, what then? I do not claim one inch of Turkish soil, but neither will I allow that any other shall have an inch of it.'

The emperor spoke so loudly and heatedly that Sir Robert delicately suggested that his majesty move away from the open window, lest persons outside might overhear what was being said. Nicholas took a few paces towards the centre of the room and continued in a softer tone.

'I do not want Constantinople,' he said, 'but if the Ottoman throne falls by its own fault, if it succumbs as a result of its lack of vitality, in a word, if the empire is dissolved, never shall I permit Constantinople to fall into the hands of England, or France . . . if the English or French or any others take Constantinople, I will expel them; and I do not think expulsion would be a hazard, for I would be on the ground before either of these forces. Once in Constantinople, I shall never leave.'

Peel raised the objection that perhaps the time was not yet ripe to determine the disposition of the Ottoman empire. Turkey, after all, was not yet dead.

The tsar agreed. 'We cannot now stipulate,' he replied, 'as to what shall be done with Turkey when she is dead. Such stipulations would only hasten her death. I shall, therefore, do all in my power to maintain the status quo. But nevertheless we should keep the possible and eventual case of her collapse honestly and reasonably before our eyes. We ought to come to a straightforward and honest understanding on the subject. It is necessary to found some just foundations which might serve as basis for an honest agreement – similar to that already existing between Russia and Austria.'

On Friday, the queen, her distinguished guest and the court returned to London, arriving at Buckingham Palace about noon. That evening her majesty tendered a state dinner at the palace, attended by 260 guests. The dinner was followed by an evening party at which members of the diplomatic corps were presented to the emperor. The queen herself introduced the ladies, while Prince Albert presented the gentlemen. An awkward protocol problem developed. What was to be done with the representatives of those countries which Russia did not recognize or with which the tsar had broken relations – Belgium, Portugal and Spain, for example? The emperor resolved the embarrassing issue by agreeing to receive these diplomats, with each of whom he subsequently chatted most amicably. In conversation with the French ambassador, however, Nicholas pointedly avoided reference to Louis Philippe.

On the following morning, the emperor visited the United Service Club and toured the new parliament buildings at Westminster. He inspected the houses minutely and with evident interest, but offered no comments on the new home of the 'mother of parliaments'. While driving through streets of London, the tsar's carriage crossed Trafalgar Square, where his majesty observed and commented upon the unfinished statue of Nelson's Column. On being told that the funds allocated for its construction had been depleted, the emperor ordered that £500 be immediately subscribed from the Russian treasury. An equal sum was given for the monument being prepared for the Duke of Wellington. The press was infuriated. 'Trophies to British valour ought to be erected by British generosity,' cried the *Illustrated London News*. 'The Emperor flings out his dole to the poor, distressed nation, as if saying what you cannot finish at your expense, complete at mine! . . . the Government is supine – as it is in all matters that do not fill the Exchequer – and the people are indifferent but neither are so poor as to be compelled to take the gifts.'

Shortly after one o'clock, the emperor left Buckingham Palace in an open carriage to attend luncheon given by the Duke of Devonshire at his estate in Chiswick. Accompanying the tsar were Prince Albert, the King of Saxony and five carriages with members of the suites, servants, outriders and military escorts.

'The weather was glorious,' wrote the Duke of Argyll. 'All the approaches to the beautiful gardens were festooned with lilac and laburnum. The magnificent cedars which overshadowed the porch and eastern façade of the Palladian villa spread their delicate tracery overhead against a sky of intense blue, flecked with a few creamy and peaceful clouds.' The carriages travelled slowly along the main drive of the estate, in order to permit the 700 luncheon guests a close look at the imperial party. The duke received his visitors at the grand entrance and, as they alighted, the massed bands of the Coldstream Guards and of the Royal Horse Guards struck up the Russian national anthem, while the imperial standard was hoisted on the summit of the mansion.

In one of the apartments, hung with paintings by Titian, Raphael, del Sarto and others, Nicholas received the most distinguished of the invited guests. A brief concert was then presented in the music saloon by the duke's orchestra, following which lunch was served. The imperial party was escorted into the rather intimate 'summer parlour', lavishly transformed for the occasion into a medieval military pavilion. On the background of the Russian colours – white, blue and red, the arms of the emperor and of the queen were emblazoned. Crowned decorative shields, alternating the initials 'N' and 'V' were embroidered into the silk canopy of the room. The tables were set for sixteen and, 'the repast being properly a *déjeuner*', silver plate was used instead of gold. Flowers and colourful clusters of exotic rich fruit in rich bowls decorated the centres of the tables.

After the meal, the imperial party went outdoors where they were joined by other guests who had eaten in adjoining rooms. Coffee was served under the spreading branches of a magnificent cedar tree, and there the emperor held court. With presentations concluded, the company dispersed in groups about the grounds. Some went to dance the polka in the 'music saloon'; some strolled across the wide lawn to attend a band concert; others inspected the conservatory. The King of Saxony, accompanied by a small suite, was rowed across the placid lake by the duke's yellow-liveried water-men. There, on the lawns, the king examined the giraffes, which had been especially imported for the occasion. The emperor, after planting a tree in the gardens to commemorate the occasion, left to return to London.

Eight days had elapsed since the state visit began, and all was warmth and cordiality. Nicholas and Victoria found much to admire in one another; the ministers and the tsar were getting along famously; the British press and public responded enthusiastically to the Russian emperor. Everyone basked in the glow of mutual respect and apparent affection. The British were reassured by the presence of the *gendarme de l'Europe*, the preserver of the concert of Europe, the one strong ally they had to help keep the French from once again throwing the delicate balance of power out of kilter. In those balmy days of June 1844, a situation such as the Crimean War seemed an incredibly absurd possibility. Yet, before eight years had passed, Russian guns were to fire at an Anglo-French fleet standing off Sevastopol, and a formidable army bearing the colours of Britain and France was to invade the shores of the Russian empire.

3

THE CRIMEAN WAR
– WHAT WAS IT?

The allied landing in Crimea took place in September 1854. From the declaration of war to the signing the peace, twenty-eight months passed. And as noted, during that period over half a million men died. In all theatres, it is estimated that the allies lost 252,000 men, and the Russians 246,000. They died on the battlefields, in hospitals, at sea and on the steppes. They died by bullet and shrapnel, of cholera and disease, of starvation and by freezing. In Sevastopol alone over 102,000 defenders were killed, wounded or reported missing. Such was the Crimean tragedy and such was the toll for 'the only perfectly useless modern war that has been waged'.

What was the Crimean War?

Few wars in history reveal greater confusion of purpose or richer unintended consequences than the Crimean War. The war is remembered for the legendary charge of the Light

Brigade, vividly immortalized by Tennyson.[4] It also conjures up pictures of the 'Lady with the Lamp', Florence Nightingale, wending her way among the hospitalized at Scutari. And, in more than one city of the world, streets bear such familiar Crimean names as Alma, Balaklava, Inkerman and Malakoff.

The war was not localized to a remote peninsula jutting out into the Black Sea. Battles were fought in what is today Romania and Bulgaria, in Asiatic Turkey and on the frontiers of Persia. Major campaigns took place in the Caucasus. In the middle of Armenia, the siege of Kars, for example, with massed attacks of 30,000 troops, surely deserves the same sort of recognition as accorded the battles that took place in Crimea itself.

Nor was the war limited to the region of the Black Sea. Some 1,500 miles (2,400 kilometres) north of Crimea, gunfire was exchanged on the White Sea and Archangel was blockaded. On the Arctic Ocean, some twelve miles (twenty kilometres) from the Norwegian frontier, Russian batteries fired on British ships. The town of Kola was attacked, the guns silenced, and the settlement of 1,000 inhabitants was put to the torch by British marines.

For two summers, Anglo-French fleets brought war to the Baltic. At one time there were fifty-eight allied ships sailing the waters, bearing as many as 3,400 guns and 33,000 men. Russian military authority was imposed on Estonia, Latvia and Poland, and her garrisons at Helsingfors (Helsinki), Sveaborg, Revel and Kronstadt were strongly reinforced. Some 12,000 French troops participated in the siege of Bomarsund, an island garrison lying between Sweden and Finland.

In the Pacific, fever was also strongly felt. Australians expressed major concern at the defenceless state of Sydney and Melbourne – it was known that Russian frigates were cruising the South Pacific. The shipping interests in Calcutta submitted a petition to the government pleading for naval protection along the sea routes to China. In Hong Kong the military authorities strengthened defences, while in Hawaii Kamehameha IV, King of the Sandwich Islands, prudently declared his neutrality. In August 1854, a British squadron of five ships, commanded by Rear-Admiral David Price, attacked Petropavlovsk on the Kamchatka Peninsula, northwest of Japan. The shore batteries together with the fifty-six guns of the Russian vessels *Aurora* and *Dvina* repulsed the invaders. Price committed suicide and the attack was suspended.

On the eastern shores of the Pacific, it was business as usual for the British-owned Hudson's Bay Company and the Russian-owned Russian-American Company. Each was sympathetic to the other's problems and priorities, so they carried on trade amicably with one another throughout the war. The naval base at Esquimalt in British Columbia was reinforced, giving much comfort to the concerned citizens of Victoria. In Canada, monies were raised for the Patriotic Fund: when the £20,000 donation was sent, half went to the British and half to the French. Napoleon, in acknowledging this gift, spoke warmly of bygone days when Canadians were French colonists. The Earl of Elgin, as Governor General of Canada, transmitted to Britain 'loyal addresses' from the legislative assembly, the municipal councils of some of the towns, the ministers and elders of the Presbyterian community and the chiefs of six Indian nations. Similar addresses and donations to the Patriotic Fund flowed to London from New Brunswick, Newfoundland, Barbados, Grenada, Gibraltar, New South Wales, South Australia and New Zealand.

Americans were unabashed Russophiles. One observer of the contemporary Washington scene wrote, 'The Russian diplomats have generally been on the most friendly terms with

Congressmen and citizens generally, while the Prussians and the Frenchmen have been having several little difficulties with the Department of State and with the residents of Washington.' In St Petersburg, a United States attaché remarked, 'Relations with the leading Russians, from the Emperor down, are all that could be desired.' The United States Ambassador in Russia, Neil Brown, found Nicholas 'perfectly irresistible', and called his handshake 'a good Republican grasp'. He reported to Secretary Marcy, 'His Majesty has as kind feelings towards the United States as he can have towards a country whose institutions are free.'

Little wonder that President Pierce declared, 'We desire most sincerely to remain neutral but God alone knows whether it is possible.' The Anglo-French alliance, which was forged to fight 'the barbarian of the North', had as its other declared purpose 'to act in entire harmony . . . [with respect to] policy affecting all other parts of the World, including the Western Hemisphere'. Under such threatening circumstances, the maintenance of strict neutrality was difficult, and before long American partiality to Russia became evident. 'The American people knew little of either the causes of this conflict or the issues at stake, but they sided almost instinctively with Russia,' Foster R. Dulles tells us. One source of pro-Russian sentiment, or rather anti-British feeling, was the large number of politically-oriented Irish immigrants. Typical of the Irish response to Crimea was the large public rally held in New York in 1854 to welcome the prominent rebel William Smith O'Brien, who had been imprisoned by the British. Anti-British speeches were the order of the day, and it is recorded, 'Three rousing cheers were given for the tsar.'

In Kentucky a troop was raised to travel to Crimea in aid of the tsar. Webb and Company of New York executed their commission for a steamship ordered by the tsar and – contrary to established rules of neutrality – it was delivered to Russia.[5] The ministers of Britain and France called on Secretary of State Marcy to protest the alleged fitting out of Russian privateers in the United States. Colonel Samuel Colt of Hartford, the famous arms manufacturer, supplied the Russians with materials and technical skills. Fifteen American mechanics went to Russia to help build railways, and thirty American physicians and surgeons served with the Russian forces in Crimea, most of them medical students from Paris. But in Illinois a discordant note was struck: the state legislature passed a resolution condemning the 'aggressive policy of the Emperor of Russia', and requiring the governor 'to forward to the aforesaid Tsar a copy of the above resolution'. The occasion of battle was seized upon by the eminently practical Secretary of War, Jefferson Davis, who dispatched a three-man commission to the continent 'to survey the art of war in Europe', and in particular 'to report on clothing, transport, weapons, ordnance, fortifications and bridges'. The commission had instructions, among other things, to ascertain 'the use of camels for transportation and their adoption to cold and mountainous countries'.

As the bloody struggle progressed in Crimea, one major power after another broke its neutrality and sided with the allies. The United States, however, remained firm in its skewed neutrality, and more than once Nicholas – and later Alexander II – sent notes of thanks to Pierce and Marcy for 'encouraging words and kindly deeds'. Midway through the war, the United States offered to mediate the conflict, a reciprocation of the Russian offer to help end the War of 1812. By the time the conflict ended, it has been noted, 'The United States was the only nation in the World that was neither ashamed nor afraid to acknowledge her friendship for Russia.'

To the military scientist, the Crimean War was one of

notable firsts and lasts. It was one of the last times that the
massed formations of cavalry and infantry were employed –
'the thin red line' was to disappear forever. Henceforward,
armies would rely on open, flexible formations and on trench
warfare. For the British in particular, it was the end of an era:
never again would their soldiers fight in full-dress uniform.
Never again would colours be carried into the fray, and the
infantry would no longer march into battle to the stirring tunes
of regimental bands.

The Crimean War ushered in the age of the percussion-cap
rifle. The new Minié rifle was the decisive weapon, replacing
the clumsy smooth-bore musket. The weapon fired a cartridge,
not a ball, with accuracy far superior to the old firelocks. The
British army took the French firearm, modified it to its
requirements, and set up a factory at Enfield to manufacture
the 'Enfield Rifle', which was soon to become standard issue
for all the queen's troops.

Military operations found use for the new electric telegraph,
and the word 'telegram' came into being. Now politicians back
home would be able to exercise greater control over the
generals in the field. The light military railway was first put
to use, and its operation between Balaklava and the front
proved invaluable to the allies. Photography came into its
own, the special results of which delighted military and naval
intelligence. The *Journal of the Society of Arts* announced,
'Headlands, lines of coast, forts, fortresses, dispositions of
fleets, armies, face of country and military positions, may be
instantaneously taken, and, if stereoscopically, with a model-
like accuracy which it would defy a verbal description to
emulate.' Roger Fenton accompanied the armies and effectively became the first war photographer.

Working in the field with him was W.H. Russell, the first
professional war correspondent, sent by *The Times*. So accu-

rately did Russell report the details of battles, of allied strengths and weaknesses, casualties and state of morale, that one Russian observed, 'We have no need of spies, we have *The Times.*'

And, as already noted, from Crimea emerged the founder and originator of modern nursing, 'one of the most remarkable human beings than can ever have lived', Florence Nightingale. Not only did she establish an ordered system of hygienic hospital care, but she revolutionized the treatment of the common soldier. This daughter of wealthy, cultured and socially minded parents forsook the brilliant marriage which was intended for her and found instead a vocation in ministering to the sick. Nursing at the time was the concern of the most disreputable stratum of the lowest class, often the domain of inebriated prostitutes. Nightingale's obstinate determination, highly developed administrative skills and extraordinary powers of persuasion made her a legend in her own time. In October 1854, she sailed for Crimea in company with thirty-eight nurses and within a month she had 5,000 wounded in her care. Six months after her arrival, the hospital death rate fell from 44 per cent to 2.2 per cent. In unspeakable conditions of filth, squalor and shortages, she toiled ceaselessly, often twenty hours at a stretch, to ease the plight of the private soldier. The suffering and appalling agony of the wounded and the superhuman effort of this petite heroine are vividly portrayed in Woodham-Smith's monumental biography of Nightingale.

Nightingale's long shadow eclipses a lesser-known personality, one which cannot be permitted to pass without mention. Mary Seacole did not spring from a cultured, upper-class British family. Quite the opposite: this adventuresome Jamaican came from a modest West Indian home, the daughter of a Scottish soldier and a free black woman.

As an herbalist, Seacole became expert in dealing with cholera and yellow fever, and, when the Crimean War broke out, she volunteered her services to attend the warfront sick and injured. Because of her ethnicity, in London she was refused even a preliminary interview by the female authorities in charge of nurse recruitment. 'Doubts and suspicions rose in my heart for the first and last time, thank Heaven,' she wrote. 'Was it possible that American prejudices against colour had some root here? Did the ladies shrink from accepting my aid because my blood flowed beneath a somewhat duskier skin then theirs?'

Undaunted, Mary set off on her own to Turkey and eventually found herself in Balaklava running the so-called 'British Hotel' – a convalescent home, really, for the sick and wounded. In the evenings, she oversaw the operation of the hostel, but during the day she was at the battlefront, tending to the fallen. She rapidly became a familiar figure to the fighting men, easily identifiable by her outrageously colourful garb and by the mule she led, laden with provisions, bandages and an array of 'medical equipment'. When Sevastopol fell in September 1855, she was the first woman to enter the city, where she passed out refreshments and tended the wounded. Although she became a popular figure with the British public, the government was long in recognizing her heroism – the Crimean Medal was awarded her with little fanfare only years after the war. A black heroine from the Caribbean.

Cure of sickness and its prevention is greatly dependent on diet. The allied armies in Crimea, and those which came after, owe much to a Frenchman who for twenty years was the chief chef of London's prestigious Reform Club. Early in 1855, the unpredictable Monsieur Alexis Soyer dismayed England's clubmen by simultaneously announcing his resignation from the Reform Club and his intention to travel to the east to take charge of the kitchens. Soyer had no lack of confidence in his skills and in the role he envisioned for himself. ('I knew that Miss Nightingale would be of great assistance to me in the hospitals in the Crimea.') Once out at the seat of war, the resourceful Frenchman energetically set about to design kitchens of every sort – for hospitals, for ships and for the field. He invented new stoves, ovens and cooking appliances. He produced new types of breads and sauces, and he trained scores of soldiers in the art of cooking. A plethora of simple and tasty recipes came from his pen, and these were eagerly adopted by the fighting men.[6]

Just as the Minié rifle and explosive shells changed the face of the army, so the iron-clad, screw-propelled warships affected the fleet. 'We must not blind ourselves,' cautioned *Bentley's Magazine*, 'that our "screws" are, up to this time, not a novelty in war, but an experiment.' The experiment was a decisive success and ushered in an end to the age of sail. The tsar's fleet was on the defensive, and its naval engineers used every conceivable ingenuity in developing new weapons. The *boulet asphyxiant* was invented in 1839 by a Frenchman. Monsieur Fortier offered it to his government but the minister of marine refused it; instead, the Russians accepted it. 'The programme of Fortier's invention describes it as a liquid fire burning under water, and destroying life by suffocation in all who happen to be within a certain distance of its explosion.' A technical report on the weapon concluded, 'If the Emperor of Russia is really interested in possession of this deadly element of destruction, the combined navies of the whole Universe will be powerless against him.'

Submarine navigation was developed. 'A startling experiment had already been made at Marseilles where Doctor Payerne, in company with three sailors, went to the bottom in the presence of hundreds of spectators, and rose a considerable distance and climbed the portholes of a man-of-war without being perceived by the crew.'

In England, a device known as 'MacIntosh's Portable Bouyant Wave-Repressor' was publicized. The invention was a machine 'based on the cause of the generation of sea waves and the correct theory of their repression'. It 'subdued' storm waves and permitted the making of harbours 'at places now inaccessible during storms'.

The Crimean War as a Russo–Turkish conflict was one in a series which seemed to resurface every generation: 1768–72, 1787–92, 1806–12 and 1828–29, continuing on to 1875–78 and 1914–18. As a war involving Western powers, it was the first time that Russia fought a European coalition, and it was the first occasion in modern history that Britain and France found themselves fighting on the same side. As an invasion of Russia, it was also one in a series: Napoleon in 1812, the Germans in 1916–18, the Western allies in 1919–20 and the Germans again in 1941–44. Geography, weather and Russian obstinacy combined to defeat each of these invasions. On reflection, it was providential that the Crimean allies, having landed in Crimea, did not press on into Russia's interior.

In the forty years preceding Crimea none of the great European powers had fought each other, but in less than twenty-five years following that struggle Europe suffered five great wars: Franco-Austrian (1859), Danish-Austro/Prussian (1864), Austro-Prussian (1866), Franco-Prussian (1870) and Russo-Turkish (1878). The lineage of each of these conflicts can be directly traced to the Crimea outcome.

One result of the war was that it helped to bring about the International Red Cross, which was established in 1864 by the Geneva Convention. The dispatches of newspaper correspondents from the front vividly described the death and misery associated with the campaign. Exposure to the elements,

pneumonia, typhus, gangrene, cholera and the shameful in-
adequacy of medical services aroused European concern. A
more developed sense of the value of human life was engen-
dered, and greater respect began to be accorded to the rights of
the individual soldier.

Perhaps the most significant outcome of the Crimean War
was that it removed the fearsome shadow of Russian might
from European affairs. In 1815, after the tsar had led the
coalition which vanquished Napoleon, Russia had appeared
the most powerful state in Europe. Following the revolutions
of 1848, it became not a matter of mere supremacy, but one of
domination – Russia was the superpower of the time. This was
when Nicholas came to be called the '*gendarme de l'Europe*'.
The disastrous outcome of the Crimean War saw Russia
tumbled from its lofty pedestal; the gendarme had become
effectively emasculated. In the two decades that followed the
war, Russia found itself just one among equals, and no longer
the superpower. Then, with the spectacular development of the
German empire after 1870, the tsar's one-time supremacy was
ceded to the kaiser.

After the humiliating defeats suffered in the war, Russia
realized it could not compete with Western Europe, whose
economic and social order was being transformed by the
industrial revolution. The tsar's government had been grie-
vously discredited by the exposure of corruption within the
country's political and economic structures. Despite the country's spectacular material advances in the preceding decades,
its technological backwardness – particularly its gross inade-
quacy in terms of transport infrastructure – was vividly
demonstrated. It was, as one historian put it, 'the swan song
of the old order in Russia . . . for Russian history the end of the
middle ages and the beginning of modern history.' With the
signing of the Treaty of Paris in 1856, the mammoth task of

reconstruction was launched, bringing with it a hectic period of reform, one that centred on emancipation of the serfs, and modernization of laws. It was only later when Alexander II and his successors ceased reforming from above that the revolution grew from below. Can it not therefore be said that the seeds of the Bolshevik revolution of 1917 germinated in the fertile soil of the Crimean War's aftermath?

During the war Russia found itself isolated, an isolation that continued after the signing of the peace treaty. Even Austria – its single, true friend – had forsaken Russia early on. At the start of the conflict, Emperor Francis Joseph I declared neutrality, but then he vacillated and abandoned his alliance with Nicholas I. Ultimately, he threatened to join the allies, and this helped to persuade Nicholas to come to the peace table. Even Palmerston deemed the betrayal 'a shabby game'. The altered state of Russo-Austrian relations helped to sound the death knell of the Concert of Europe.[7]

If Russia stood alone at the end of the war, so did Austria. Francis Joseph had lost Russian friendship, and he had failed to gain that of Britain or France. Both these powers found the Austrians too temporizing, too cautious and unreliable. And throughout it all, as the conflict developed, Count Camillo Cavour, the Sardinian prime minister, a 'stout, spectacled, whiskered figure, affable and fluent of speech, and full primed with technicalities of every sort', stood at the sidelines, observing the unfolding events. In the twelfth hour of the war, 'This far-reaching statesman, gambling as the greatest statesmen must often do for the highest stakes, persuaded the Turin Parliament to send a Sardinian contingent to the Crimea.'

In April 1855, King Victor Emmanuel waved farewell to 15,000 of his troops as they set sail for Balaklava. By the time the contingent returned home, twenty-eight had been killed at the Battle of Tchernaya and a thousand had succumbed to cholera. Losses surely, but infinitesimal compared to those of other nations. Fortune, however, favours the brave. When the peace conference assembled in Paris, there he was – Count Cavour, seated as an equal among the statesmen of the great European powers. Soon the 'Italian question' was pushed to the table – Austrian presence in the Italian peninsula had to cease.

Austria's arrogant domination of Italy, Cavour argued, was a permanent danger to peace and a threat to the balance of power; the continued presence of her troops on Italian soil was contrary to the provisions of the Treaty of Vienna. Lord Clarendon, who had been carefully primed by the Sardinian, went on to condemn the mediocre governments of Naples and the Papal States, and the issue of Italian unification came into debate. The assembly listened to the opening arguments, but it very soon became evident that there was little stomach in pursuing further the matter of Italian unification or, for that matter, of pressing for an Austrian withdrawal from the peninsula. Cavour, however, was not totally disappointed – he had secured for his little country an equal place among the great powers. Napoleon III indicated sympathy for his aims, and nobody had rushed strongly to support Austria – least of all, Russia. Within three years of the Paris conference, Sardinian and French troops were fighting side by side against the isolated Austria, from whom independence was eventually wrestled. The unification of Italy followed.

In Britain the cessation of hostilities also precipitated reform – a reform of the army. The Crimean War was the first conflict in which the public at home fully appreciated the privations and sufferings, the courage and the stubborn endurance displayed by the private soldier. The submarine cable, telegraph and photography permitted news reports to be filed as stories developed.

The new accounts gave full and instant publicity to mis-management. Early in the war they told of glaring food shortages, inadequate shelter and transport, inefficient leader-ship and conspicuous lack of medical provisions. Public out-rage at the bungling was enormous, and reforms were not long in coming. The new regulations affected every facet of army organization – terms of service, officer commissions, medical and hospital techniques, barrack construction, auxiliary ser-vices, training programmes, and so forth. Army procedures made obsolete by forty years of military inactivity were rapidly transformed. The war checked the decay which might have been the ruin of the British army and made it unfit for the more vital tasks it faced in the future.

The monetary cost of the war for the British was relatively small. Throughout the struggle business was active, capital remained available for investment and employment was full. Much of the cost of the war was met by borrowing, but over half the £70 million expended on the war was covered by sharply increased income taxes.

Turkey met the cost of the war by raising loans which were guaranteed by Britain and France, and 'the sick man of Europe' now found himself obligated to the West twice over. The English and French bond holders became a new influence in the internal affairs of the Porte. As part of the peace settlement, the allies were successful in persuading the sultan to declare Christians and Moslems equal before the eyes of the law. Religious discrimination was ended, and the right of public office confirmed, as was the right to maintain churches and sectarian school. Turkey now moved closer to developing into a Western country and to entering the family of European powers with its integrity and independence guaranteed. The Crimean War had postponed the collapse and partition of the Turkish empire.

So the war, and so the rich unintended results, immediate and long-term. Who a decade earlier might have deemed such an upheaval possible, particularly among those who conferred with Nicholas during his 1844 visit to Britain?

On returning to London from Windsor, the tsar was surprised to find that an imperial physician, Dr Maudt, had arrived from St Petersburg. News of the ailing Adina was not good: she was suffering from advanced tuberculosis. One lung was already totally destroyed and there was no hope for the girl's recovery. The distressed emperor resolved to return home immediately, and ordered that arrangements be made for his departure on the next day.

Nicholas was to leave England as rapidly and as short of notice as was his arrival. During the nine days of his visit, the emperor did not fail to impress the British, and had certainly won the hearts of the ladies. 'It is not the monarch who was so magnificent a person, but the man who was so truly imperial,' gushed a female admirer. Most important, however, were the results of his discussions with Sir Robert Peel, Aberdeen and other members of the cabinet. Nicholas had achieved his purpose – the two countries had reached an accord. It was agreed by Russia and Britain that in the interests of peace, the independence of Turkey had to be assured, and that everything would be done to maintain Turkey in its existing weak state. Weak, but not too weak – the sultan had to be strong enough not only to withstand French domination but to bring about much needed internal reform.

It was further agreed that 'if anything unforeseen should occur in Turkey' – that is, should the sultan's government fall of its own accord or should a foreign power threaten the existence of Turkey, Britain and Russia would act in concert. The tsar gave his solemn promise not to do anything without consulting Britain. Peel and Aberdeen did likewise, promising that Britain would not act unilaterally. In addition, it was agreed that if in the future it became evident that the sultan could no longer be maintained, the two countries would come to an understanding on the details of an Ottoman partition, to be arranged between themselves and Austria – irrespective of any French claim or objection.

There would now be full cooperation between Britain and Russia on the question of Turkey. The '1844 Accord' was a secret arrangement between Britain and Russia, but, unlike München-grätz, it was not a signed document. The agreement was an oral one with both parties acknowledging it as being binding – sealed by a handshake and the *parole de gentleman*. 'It is extremely fortunate that Nicholas . . . should also be a man upon whose honour and veracity strong reliance may be safely and securely placed,' wrote Lord Melbourne, the leader of the opposition. After the emperor's return to St Petersburg, Nesselrode composed a memorandum in which the principal sections of the pact were summarized in written form. By an exchange of ministerial letters the British government formally accepted the memorandum. Future peace in the Eastern Mediterranean and in the Straits was assured. What with Münchengrätz and now the London accord, Russia, Britain and Austria were bound to act in common on the matter of Turkey, 'in the interest of all'.

What Nicholas failed to perceive at the time, however, was the one great weakness of the pact. Although it was agreed to complete arrangements for the succession to the Ottoman domains 'in advance to dissolution', the process of determining such time was not stipulated. Either party, in disagreement with the other, could view an Ottoman collapse as being either imminent or remote. In the crisis of 1853, as will be seen, this became a matter of heated argument, and failure to agree on the issue was a critical cause of the war.

On the Sunday of his departure, accompanied by Baron Brunov and members of the suite, Nicholas, in full dress uniform, attended church at the Russian chapel. After the service, the emperor paid farewell visits to Sir Robert Peel and to Baroness Brunov. The tsar then had a late lunch with the queen and Prince Albert at Buckingham Palace. At five o'clock, her majesty, together with the Princess Royal and the Prince of Wales, escorted the tsar to the grand entrance hall. There Nicholas saluted Victoria and warmly shook hands with all the ladies and gentlemen of the court, and officers of the household. He climbed into the carriage where Prince Albert waited, and, with a final wave, took leave of the queen.

The line of six carriages proceeded rapidly to Woolwich, where the royal salute was fired. While the luggage was shipped aboard the steamer and final preparations made, the tsar toured the dockyards. He viewed with particular interest the 120-gun *Prince Albert*, then under construction. Nicholas finally bade farewell to Prince Albert, shook the hands of those who came to see him off, and boarded the *Black Eagle*. As the anchor was being weighed, a small boat was observed being energetically rowed by a frantic seaman. From the tiny craft a large bundle of fresh straw was hoisted on board for the emperor's sleeping sack. Even in the most luxurious quarters of imperial palaces or of foreign courts Nicholas adhered to his Spartan habit of childhood and slept on the stuffed leather sack of army issue.

Before quitting England, Nicholas distributed a profusion of jewels, snuff boxes and money. To the domestic staff of Buckingham Palace he left £3,000; to the captain of the *Black Eagle* and to the executive officer and chief engineer he gave diamond rings, and to the crew he awarded £400. The poor of St George's Parish, Westminster, received a large sum, as did the German Hospital and the household of the Russian Embassy. And jewellery was showered on the many others who had attended him.

The *Black Eagle* made way, and from the deck his majesty saluted his final farewells. The steamer passed rapidly down the Thames and out of sight to the East.

4

'SOME FATAL INFLUENCE AT WORK'

It was called 'the world's most curious and unnecessary struggle'. And a strange war it was – but stranger still, the reasons for it. Thiers, one-time President of France, spoke of it as 'a war to give a few monks the key of a grotto'. A simple view perhaps, but one not without basis. 'The Crimean war,' argues Professor Henderson, 'was the result of diplomatic drift and ministerial incompetence,' – which is undeniable. 'The War and its causes,' observes Engels drily, 'was a single colossal comedy of errors in which at every moment the question was asked: "Who's being swindled here?"' A swindle it was. And who were the culpable?

There are five *dramatis personae* upon whose shoulders the blame for the Crimean tragedy may be squarely brought to rest. Napoleon III, who sought to emulate his illustrious uncle, but who was 'too small for the great things he set out to do'. The ambitious Nicholas I, who in the 1,000 year tradition of his antecedents, focused a covetous eye on Constantinople, the pearl of the crumbling Ottoman empire. (Both emperors, it might be noted, were intransigent and between them, there was bitter personal animosity, bordering on hate.) The bombastic and imperious bully, Prince Menshikov, special envoy of the tsar, sent to deal with 'the wretched Turks', arrived at the Porte on the eve of the war breathing arrogance and insult. (Some years earlier, the prince had been emasculated by a shot from a Turkish gun.) Stratford Canning, Her Britannic Majesty's iron-willed ambassador to Constantinople, who was accustomed to wielding his power and influence without question – even that of the foreign office. And the bellicose Lord Palmerston, a powerful man in a weak coalition cabinet, who had little faith in Russia and who sought above all to maintain Turkish strength.

The war arose seemingly haphazardly from a series of trivial and unrelated events by which the great powers inexorably drifted into collision. 'Some fatal influence seems to have been at work,' Aberdeen lamented. First, in France, Louis Napoleon acceded to the throne, with a pressing need to consolidate his tenuous position. 'Napoleon,' remarked Bismarck, 'was vaguely aware that he needed a war,' for only war would bring glory to the new empire and satisfy national vanity. (It would also clean the stain of his uncle's inglorious retreat from Russia in 1812.) Then, in Britain, during the climactic year of the nation's drift into the war, the fractious coalition government became robbed of strength. In Austria, Emperor Francis Joseph – Nicholas' 'cousin, son and intimate friend' – engaged in vacillation, so deceiving the Russians that the tsar raced blindly along the path leading to the conflict.

In 1848, the Magyars rose in bitter revolt against Hapsburg rule. The revolution was ruthlessly quashed – largely through the strong military support given Austria by Nicholas I – and thousands of Hungarians fled to Turkey. And, as will be seen, this development wrought a shattering blow to the tsar's valued London accord.

The flight of Hungarian refugees and the giving over to 'a few monks the key of a grotto' were two defining issues in the build up to the war. But at the root of it all were the divergent interests and ambitions of intransigent rulers – Napoleon III and Nicholas I in particular – coupled with diplomacy gone askew. Into the fabric of the build-up, however, were woven other threads – those of commerce and economic interests.

In the decades preceding the tsar's visit to England, and in the period immediately following, industrialization came to Russia, and the empire made such spectacular strides that serious economic rivalry developed with Britain. In the twenty year period of 1825–45, for example, the import of heavy machinery into Russia increased nearly thirty-fold; in the same time the number of factory workers more than doubled, as did the number of manufacturing firms. As the spinning jenny gained acceptance, a large number of textile factories opened, and imports of raw cotton increased 280 per cent. Steamship navigation, railways and improved roads linked developing industrial centres. Banks and insurance companies were chartered and the finance minister was successful in stabilizing the rouble. Trade with the Caucasus flourished, and the empire's Asiatic expansion brought commercial relations with China. By 1840, a favourable balance of trade with that country had at last been achieved; seven years later, the ratio of Russian exports to imports in relation to China was 12:7.

Agriculture also saw spectacular advancement in productivity as new techniques and equipment were introduced on the estates. In 1825, for example, there were 7 sugar-beet factories; in 1853, there were 380. Within a twenty-year period wine production tripled, and in a ten-year period potato harvests quadrupled. But it was the production and export of grain which made the most notable gains at this time. In the years 1832–40, Russian grain commerce increased at a rate of 56 per cent per annum. The 'great bread basket' of southern Russia exported vast quantities of wheat from the port cities of the Black Sea. In 1845, 2,222 ships departed from these ports; within two years the numbers grew to 4,231 departures. The maritime flags of Turkey, France, Britain, Austria, Tuscany and Sardinia were an altogether common sight in the imperial harbours of the south. And, it should be noted, these ships sailed out into the world through the Bosphorus, past Constantinople and the Dardanelles.

The trans-Caucasian provinces were serviced by land and by sea. Overland routes were opened into Turkey, Poland, Finland, Moldavia, Persia, Siberia and China. The Baltic and White Sea ports, although closed by ice during the long winter months, together accounted annually for more shipping than did the Black Sea.

In the first decades of the nineteenth century, Britain was Russia's strongest trading partner. In 1832, for example, Russia sent Britain 73 per cent of its total export, and in return received 41 per cent of all British foreign sales. Heavy machinery and manufactured goods from Britain were exchanged for tar, hemp, iron, copper, flax and grain – especially wheat.

As Russia's manufacture output advanced in the 1840s and 50s, and as commercial relations with neighbours strengthened, the enormous volume of trade with Britain began to diminish. Raw materials were now required for industry at home and tariffs 'peculiarly unfavourable to British trade' were raised to foster its growth. After 1840, the Russian textile industry was in direct competition with British textiles; not only were Russians buying Russian, but they were now selling in other foreign markets. As early as 1841, the British envoy at St Petersburg, Lord Bloomfield, warned London: 'The great object of the prohibitive system in Russia, and in the protection shown the home manufacturer, is to undersell British produce in the East. Hitherto they may have failed . . . but Russians are persevering people and as the Empire advances in civilization and as the means of transport improve, the proximity of Russia to these countries may have a pernicious effect on British trade.' Russia's developing commerce was already menacing; the day might come that the tsar's empire would prove itself an outright threat to Britain in India and the East.

Russia's remarkable economic growth during the period was paralleled to a less spectacular degree by Turkey. Manufacturing plants within the Ottoman empire produced increasing quantities of finished goods, and agriculture flourished especially in the Turkish European provinces. The potential of Turkey as a trading partner was not lost to Britain. As early as 1833, Palmerston sent a special envoy, David Urquhart, on a secret mission to Constantinople to report on the extent of the country's economic development and, particularly, to assess trade possibilities.

Urquhart reported back enthusiastically on the 'infinite riches of this inexhaustible Empire,' and of the exciting opportunities for trade. The Turks, he reasoned, could not rely on France in view of their recent conflicts with that country in Egypt. As for Russia, historically it was no friend to the sultan, and he had every cause to be alarmed over the tsar's encroaching influence at the Porte. Britain, however, was not only above any suspicion but possessed a powerful navy, which in the event of conflict with Russia could be advantageously offered the sultan. Urquhart concluded that it would be in her majesty's best interest to cultivate strong economic and political relations with the sultan.

The envoy went on to argue that virtually anything imported from Russia could be gotten in Turkey. Furthermore, by extending British influence in the Ottoman empire, Russian designs on Turkey, Persia, India and the East would be more easily checked. Urquhart's recommendations were accepted, and for the next twenty years they formed the basis of British policy towards the Porte.

In 1838, an Anglo-Turkish commercial treaty was signed by which Britain received distinctly more advantageous tariff terms than did other powers, and trade between the two countries grew phenomenally. In exchange for machinery and manufactured goods, Turkey exported grain to Britain. In 1838, scarcely any grain was exported; in 1842, 988,000 bushels were sold; in 1852, the quantity shot up to 15 million bushels. Colonel Rose, a British agent in Constantinople, cautioned Lord Clarendon that the dissolution of Turkey would be 'the signal for the ruin of British trade and interests'.

So, at the time that Britain's commercial relations with Russia were coming under strain, relations with Turkey were becoming more intimate. By 1849, Ambassador Stratford Canning felt the time ripe to propose a treaty of alliance with the Turks. The country must make 'a more determined and systematic support of the Ottoman Empire', or otherwise 'turn Turkey over to Russia', urged the persuasive envoy. Initiatives and decisions regarding Eastern affairs now seemed to emanate from Stratford's desk in Constantinople, at first imperceptibly but then with gaining momentum. His influence on Downing Street was intense. On the eve of war's declaration, Clarendon appeared to echo Stratford's sentiments: the purpose of this 'battle of civilization against barbarism', he first announced was 'to maintain our honour and self respect'. He then went on to declare self-righteously, 'We want nothing for our trade, and we fear nothing for our Indian possessions.' An embroidered bending of truth.

From Nicholas' viewpoint, his state visit to Britain in 1844 had been a brilliant success; he had charmed and persuaded the British into an accord over Turkey. London, too, had been pleased – peace in the Straits now seemed assured. Aberdeen was especially satisfied with the outcome of discussions. As late as 1854, three days after the formal declaration of war on Russia, he told the House of Lords, 'I see nothing to find fault with [the accord] . . . I should be perfectly ready again to subscribe to the opinions which it embodies.'

The agreement reached during the tsar's 1844 visit was a secret understanding between two countries – rather than between an autocratic sovereign and a constitutional government. Nicholas viewed the accord as something binding, but successive British cabinets looked upon it merely as a moral obligation on individual ministers. Since no document was drawn up and deposited at the foreign office, Brunov had to acquaint each successive change of government with the agreement's details.

Despite growing commercial rivalry, the Anglo-Russian alliance remained reasonably intact through nearly a decade of imperialistic rivalry and international tension. That the accord collapsed so suddenly, and that Britain invaded Russia, is principally explained by two apparently unrelated developments that took place far from the theatre of concern. In Eastern Europe, the Hungarians rose up in revolt and in Western Europe the French toppled their king.

The year was 1848, and it was not a good one. Throughout most of Europe people suffered under adverse economic conditions. The boom years of the early 1840s were followed by a depressive slump. Capital became scarce, bankruptcies were declared and general unemployment ensued. Food prices rose to unprecedented levels. The grain harvests of 1845 and 1846 were exceptionally poor. The potato blight which so tragically affected Ireland spread across the continent and ruined crops as far east as Bohemia. Food riots broke out in Belgium, France, Germany and Italy. As if by the design of some dark force, an epidemic of typhus developed, followed by cholera. Ships packed with desperate refugees sailed to America, perilously loaded to capacity.

Within this want and unrest, revolutionary movements grew. Socialists and anarchists called for the toppling of monarchies and changes in the established order. The ideas of Mazzini, Bakunin, Bentham, St Simon, Blanc and others took hold. In January 1848, Marx brought out his Manifesto of the Communist Party. 'The workers have nothing to lose but their chains. They have a world to win. Workers of the world, unite!'

The economic crisis of this violent annus mirabilis hit France with particular severity. The railway construction boom collapsed, and 600,000 workers were laid off. Coal mines shut down and iron works closed. The embittered unemployed joined bankrupt businessmen in expressing dissatisfaction with the government of Louis Philippe. Reforms to address corrupt electoral procedure were demanded. The king refused any such consideration and forbade political meetings of any nature. The citizens then found other means to gather. Large dinners were organized, ostensibly to consider matters of the palate, but discussion at the outset focused on the more urgent considerations of the political situation. On 22 February, word leaked out that an exceptionally large banquet was planned in Paris. Despite the government's refusal to grant a permit, a crowd gathered. The Marseillaise was sung and the excited cry rang out, 'Down with Louis Philippe!' During the night, the number of angry protestors swelled and large demonstrations were held in the streets – by morning barricades had sprung up. On the evening of the 23rd, a march was organized on the foreign office at the Quai d'Orsay. The king's troops stood in readiness to receive the demonstrators. When the crowd appeared, tempers flared, guns fired and sixteen 'martyrs' fell. By early morning, the city found itself in the throes of revolution. The king was unable to cope and shortly after noon of that same day Louis Philippe abdicated, and hurriedly departed for England, where he landed at Dover, bearing the name, 'Mr Smith'. The tricolour was hoisted atop the city hall and the republic was declared re-established.

By March, the sunny days of the established order had darkened, as the storm clouds of the French revolution drifted across the face of the continent. In Sicily, angry crowds took over the Palermo garrison and drove out the Neapolitan King Ferdinand II. In Belgium, radicals unsuccessfully attempted to overthrow the established government. German princes acquiesced to liberal pressure and granted reforms. King William II of Holland hastily granted parliamentary reforms in a bid to placate the dissatisfied middle-class. Even the Papacy found itself forced to divest some temporal powers – Pius IX granted a constitution to the Papal States.

The thunder of nationalism and constitutionalism echoed particularly loudly in Italy. Here the Congress of Vienna had established eight separate states, each under a separate ruler, with Austria the dominating influence. 'Italy is but a geographic expression,' Metternich commented drily. Now, thirty-three years later, the peninsula seethed with the great nationalistic passion known as the Risorgimento. In 1831, Mazzini, an exile in Marseilles, launched his new society, 'Young Italy'. Each member swore to dedicate himself 'wholly and forever to the endeavour . . . to constitute Italy one, free, independent, republican nation'. Thousands throughout 'the geographic expression' flocked to the revolutionary banner and sought the re-establishment of 'the greatness that was Rome'.

The first blow against the Austrians was struck by the Milanese – the citizens forsook cigars. The lucrative tobacco monopoly was at the time the preserve of Hapsburg authorities: the decision to boycott smoking not only affected considerable revenues, but it was recognized as being a blatant anti-Austrian statement. On 3 January, the Austrian commissariat issued a supply of cigars to all soldiers of the Milan barracks with orders that they be smoked in the streets. The Milanese reacted with predictable anger, and throughout the day collisions took place between the citizenry and the military. To protect themselves and their cigars, the troops drew swords, resulting in many citizens being killed or hospitalized. Tensions built up, and before long all of Lombardy was affected; the slightest spark threatened to blow the whole into insurrection. In the weeks that followed, demands were made of the Austrians – liberate political prisoners, lift censorship, establish a national assembly, do away with the old police force and establish a new corps, one under the orders of the municipalities. Nothing happened.

The sensational news of the successful overthrow of Louis-Philippe spread quickly in Italy, and on 17 March an agitated crowd assembled before government house in Milan. Tempers grew and an ugly restlessness developed, causing the duty guardsmen to fire a blank volley. At this, a sixteen-year old youngster drew a pistol, and shouting '*Viva l'Italia*!' he fired at the troops. The mob pushed forward and in a short time overpowered the guard, imprisoned the vice-governor and hoisted the white, red and green flag of the republic. By sunset, barricades were thrown up throughout the city and the greatly outnumbered Austrian garrison found itself fighting for its very existence. Within five days, the Austrian commander General Radetzky ordered a retreat. Shortly afterwards, the new Venetian Republic was declared.

At the time that these events unfolded, the revolutionary storm had already broken out in other parts of the Hapsburg empire. In Hungary, in Bohemia and finally in Vienna itself, the revolt spread. 'We seek to surround the imperial throne with constitutional organization,' declared Louis Kossuth to the Hungarian diet, 'and to obtain the grant of a constitution to all countries within the Austrian Empire.' He denounced Vienna as a 'charnel house' from which 'a pestilential air blows towards us'. The diet received this daring speech with enthusiasm and voted an address to the emperor, demanding a constitutional government for Hungary.

Inspired by Kossuth's urgings, the Viennese began massive demonstrations, and on 13 March a procession of students and workers swarmed into the Ballhausplatz, where the chancellery stood. 'Down with Metternich!' echoed from Vienna's walls. The crowd swelled into a mob and marched on to the Hofburg, the imperial residence. There the predictable happened – the troops opened fire. The people became spurred into greater fury and fighting broke out, which quickly spread to other quarters of the city. The chancellor counselled the agitated emperor to stand firm and to send in the troops, while courtiers urged the emperor to dismiss the chancellor.

By eight o'clock that evening, the situation had become unbearable, but at long last Ferdinand made up his mind. Prince Metternich was summoned to the imperial study and was dismissed from the office which he had held for thirty-nine years. The banner which 'one part of the century followed while another stood up against it' had fallen; an era had closed.

'Tell the people,' muttered Ferdinand, '. . . tell them that I agree to everything.' On the following day, Metternich slipped quietly through the garden gate of his residence and made his way into exile.

As with the fall of the Bastille in 1789, so with Metternich: an epoch had come to an end. Hardly had the chancellor departed Vienna than the subjected peoples in various parts of the empire militantly agitated for reform. In Hungary, the diet successfully forced the emperor to accept its demands for the abolition of feudalism, an end to press censorship and the establishment of its own responsible ministry. Count Batthyány became prime minister, and Louis Kossuth minister of finance.

In Vienna, a reactionary ministry was set up under Prince Felix von Schwarzenberg who took on the dual titles of President-Minister and Foreign Minister. Within nine days of assuming office, the prince successfully persuaded Ferdinand to abdicate on grounds of ill health. To take his place, the eighteen-year old Francis Joseph came to the throne, a new emperor advised by a reactionary government and one who was unhampered by commitments made to Hungarians. A fresh constitution was promulgated which was designed more to give unity to the empire than to give liberty to its subjects. All was now set for the imperial government to take action against the rebellious Maygars.

The Hungarians refused to recognize Francis Joseph and reaffirmed their allegiance to their 'legitimate king', Ferdinand. On 13 April, the Hungarian diet, goaded into resistance by the new constitution, issued a unilateral declaration of independence. The Hungarian Republic was proclaimed and on the following day, Kossuth was elected 'responsible governor-president' and a virtual dictator. Hungary suddenly found itself an independent republic, one which was viewed by

Europe as a champion of revolution. All too soon, however, the newly declared republic was invaded by an Austrian army determined to reverse the tide of events.

The new republic desperately sought to consolidate its position by seeking international recognition. Urgent messages were sent to London and Paris. In a pathetic appeal to President Taylor in Washington, Kossuth declared, 'I myself and the entire Hungarian nation . . . desire peace and friendship with all the states, but especially with the United States of America . . . and promise to maintain peace in the world, and to serve humanity and civilization which the American nation was the first to represent so gloriously.' Taylor responded by sending a special envoy, Dudley Mann, to Vienna in order to confer with the American chargé d'affaires. Mann was to size up the Hungarian situation, ascertain 'the probable issue of the present revolutionary events', and assess the chances of forming 'commercial arrangements with that power favourable to the United States'. Little encouragement from America, and silence from Britain and France.

Francis Joseph found himself in the distressing position that military strategists so dread: an army divided on two fronts. In Italy, close to 160,000 troops were required to maintain the *pax Hapsburgensis*. This left a mere 20,000 men with which to keep the peace at home and to deal with the rebellious Magyars. The young emperor appealed to the tsar:

> From my childhood, I have been accustomed to see in Your Majesty the firmest supporter of the monarchical principle and the sincerest, most faithful friend of my family. It is enough for me to be convinced that Your Majesty, with the great wisdom that distinguishes him, has realized the true character of the struggle, of which Hungary is the blood-stained arena, to be sure of the help of his powerful arm.

The *gendarme de l'Europe* responded promptly:

> The Emperor of Austria has requested Our cooperation against
> Our common enemy. We shall not refuse him. We have ordered
> Our various armies to advance in order to quell the revolt and
> to annihilate the audacious criminals who are attempting to
> destroy Our peace and Our lands.

The common campaign against Hungary, it was agreed,
would be a family matter between the two reigning houses.
Nicholas was the fatherly friend to his youthful cousin. The
tsar expected little in return, save the satisfaction of serving
Austria, from which no doubt undeniable gratitude would
flow. By forcefully responding to Austria's appeal, however,
the tsar was also sending a message of warning to the Poles –
dream not of revolution in Russian Poland

The tsar dispatched Field Marshal Paskevich to Hungary
with a force of 100,000 troops – the fate of the Hungarians
was sealed. Outnumbered, surrounded on all sides and torn by
internal strife, there was little to be done. On 10 August, after
suffering a resounding defeat at Temesvar, General Görgei
surrendered to the Russians and his army of 30,000 men.
'Hungary lies at the feet of Your Majesty,' Marshal Paskevich
telegraphed the tsar.

The revolutionary crises in the Hapsburg empire had
passed. Kossuth, members of this cabinet, and nearly 5,000
Hungarians and Poles fled across the Danube and sought
sanctuary in Turkish territory. The Turks, to whom hospitality
was a sacred duty, readily accepted these refugees. And out of
this arose a new crisis, international in scope, one which nearly
brought the great powers of Europe to war. Within two
months of Görgei's surrender, the spirit of the Anglo-Russian
accord of 1844 was dealt a shattering blow; mutual confidence

between the two nations would never be the same. The threat of war stepped closer to reality.

The Russian armies had crushed the Hungarians, and Francis Joseph resumed his authority over the Magyars. To the Austrian, however, the Hungarians were rebels and rebels were to be punished. Count Batthyány was sentenced to the ignominious death by hanging. In attempting suicide to avoid the infamy of death by the rope, the former president of the Hungarian Republic inflicted such grotesque wounds on the neck that the hangman refused to proceed with the execution. Instead, the count was shot by three marksmen. Over a hundred other Hungarian leaders were executed, including thirteen generals and some Catholic priests. Hundreds were imprisoned by order of General Haynau; countless were fined. The best of Hungarian society was pressed into the Austrian army for service at the meanest tasks. Nobles found themselves as drivers of artillery, under the orders of common corporals. From the Jewish community of Pest, General Haynau demanded payment of £18,000, the sum to be raised within twenty-four hours. In town squares, crowds gathered to watch noble ladies being stripped to the waist and flogged on their bare backs. The world's free press howled in indignation. England's passionate denunciation of foreign inhumanity resounded alike in the great halls of Westminster and in the shopkeepers' cottages of Morton-on-the-Marsh. Angry petitions flooded the foreign office censuring the monstrous behaviour of the Austrian authorities.

The more fortunate leaders of the unsuccessful revolution were safe in exile. Among the refugees welcomed by Sultan Abdul Mejid were the principal leaders of the shattered Hungarian army, including such notables as Generals Joseph Ben and Branislaw Dembinski. Not for a moment, however, could it have been supposed that the imperial hunt would allow such quarry to escape. The Austrians were determined to have Kossuth, 'the man who was the Hungarian Revolution'. The Russian emperor was no less resolute that his Polish subjects who sided with the Hungarians should not escape and become free again to sow seeds of revolt elsewhere in Europe. Russia and Austria lodged joint demands of Abdul Mejid – surrender the fugitives without delay.

On receiving the extradition demands, the sultan wasted little time in summoning the British ambassador to the palace. Should a confrontation arise with the Russians, Abdul Mejid desired to know of Stratford Canning, what support might Turkey expect from Britain? The reply he would be giving the two emperors would substantially depend on the envoy's response.

Stratford Canning paused in thought. Not only did the personal welfare of the refugees lie in the balance, but, more importantly, so did Russia's apparently hostile intentions on Turkey. Time was of the essence and communication with Downing Street was painfully slow. The ambassador was not long in hesitating. In the event of an armed confrontation, he assured the sultan, Britain would render Turkey all possible assistance. The agitated sultan was delighted. No further doubt remained as to the answer he would give Nicholas and Francis Joseph: under no circumstances would the refugees be surrendered. A die had thus been cast.

5

STRATFORD AND
THE HUNGARIANS

In the annals of diplomacy, it would be difficult to find a parallel example of a diplomat's exercise of personal initiative entailing so grave a commitment entered into so freely. In these same annals, it would be equally challenging to name a personality less controversial or more fascinating than that of the ambassador in question, Stratford Canning, Viscount Stratford de Redcliffe. One historian charges, 'The principle responsibility for the actual outbreak of the Crimean War should be assessed to Stratford Canning.' Although this indictment may not be a hundred per cent accurate, there is no doubt that Stratford played a leading and critical role in its inception.

For sixteen years, with a few brief periods of interruption, Stratford held sway in the Turkish capital. His unparalleled influence was exercised throughout the Ottoman empire with an almost despotic authority. Sultan and humble subject alike referred to him as the Great *Elchi*, or 'great envoy'. Jews, Nestorians, Arabians, Druses and all others suffering from persecution, discrimination, or any wrongdoing looked to the Englishman to right a wrong or for assistance. Lord Raglan, the supreme commander-in-chief of the British expeditionary forces to Crimea, once remarked to a junior officer, 'Lord Stratford wishes this; and I would have you remember that Lord Stratford's wishes are a law to me.'

It would be a mistake to look upon Stratford as a common ambassador, executing the wishes of his government. In his day foreign representatives were considerably more independent of home authorities than they are today. 'When he began his diplomatic career,' explains Lane-Poole, Stratford's nineteenth-century biographer, 'communications with the Foreign Office in London were slow and occasional. To receive an answer to a request for instructions involved a delay of up to four months, and by the time the instructions came the crisis for which they were required would in all probability be past. The Minister was thus compelled to act on his own responsibility, and partly in consequence of his distance from home, partly because the Foreign Office chose to leave him unnoticed for nearly the whole of his earliest mission when he was but a boy-minister, he acquired the habit of action on his own responsibility to a degree which no modern ambassador can realize.' To be hampered by instructions from home was intolerable to one who had for so long successfully exercised personal initiative.

Stratford Canning was the first cousin of George Canning, the prime minister. At a young age, Stratford went to Eton, where he confessed to having been 'somewhat of a prig'. An excellent student, his sole athletic distinction was achieved by his participation in the college's first cricket match against

Harrow, which team, incidentally, included the young poet Byron. Stratford then entered King's College, Cambridge where, he noted, the scholars enjoyed 'the questionable privilege of drifting in their degrees without examinations'. Canning's university studies were interrupted by his appointment as second secretary of the British embassy in Copenhagen. In 1808, Stratford was sent on his first mission to Constantinople, where a year later at the tender age of twenty-four, he was appointed minister plenipotentiary. Within months of his arrival at the Porte, the young diplomat had sized up the prevailing situation of the Ottoman empire. He reported to his illustrious cousin, then the foreign minister: 'Destruction will not come upon this Empire either from the north or from the south; it is rotten at the heart; the seat of corruption is in the Government itself.'

In 1820, Stratford was appointed minister to the United States and spent four miserably unhappy years in Washington. He complained of everything: the society, the heat, the lack of diversion, the provincialism and the streets. The sole redeeming feature of the capital city, he claimed, was the clean air.[8]

The strength of his character and, equally, the negative attitude he held towards his posting became quickly evident to President John Q. Adams. He wrote of Stratford, 'He is a proud, high-tempered Englishman . . . with a disposition to be overbearing, which I have been often compelled to check it its own way. He is, of all foreign ministers with whom I have had the occasion to treat, the man who has most tried my temper . . . He has great respect for his word, and there is nothing false about him . . . Mr Canning is a man of forms, studious of our society and tenacious of private morals. As a diplomatic man his great want is suppleness, and his great virtue is sincerity.'

For nineteen years after quitting Washington, until 1853,

Canning served in a number of European capitals, including four appointments in Constantinople. Twice he interrupted his diplomatic career to stand for parliament. He was elected on both occasions and served briefly, the first time representing Old Sarum – 'the rottenest borough on the list' – with a mere eleven constituents. Twice he was offered the governor-generalship of Canada and twice he refused it – he had once travelled from Niagara Falls to Quebec City and had seen all he cared to of that vast land. Now, in 1853, he was back again in Constantinople.

What sort of person was Stratford? How did he gain such influence over the Ottomans? The diplomat, notes Lane-Poole, believed firmly, 'Nothing is unimportant which concerns the honour of England.' The biographer goes on:

The thought of the Sovereignty which he had to impress on an ignorant nation inspired him to an almost heroic ideal of conduct . . . his own responsibility for the worthy maintenance of English honour, led him to a line of action which served almost to embody a doctrine of the divine right of ambassadors.

Perhaps he carried this high view of the dignity of an ambassador too far. He certainly earned the reputation of arrogance and even of vanity by such pretensions. His stately manner and proud look were pointed to as proof of personal conceit. But it may well be doubted whether he could ever have acquired that transcendent authority over the Turks which is inseparably associated with his memory if he had been less majestic, less tenacious of his dignity. The Oriental takes you as you would be taken, and to acquire his respect you must impose yourself upon him. And it is impossible . . . to compel the Turkish mind to action without the aid of such outward machinery.

President Adams spoke of Stratford as being 'over-bearing'; in fact, he was simply quick-tempered. His attachés in particular were awed by their terrifying master: it was said that none would converse with the ambassador without keeping a firm grasp on the door handle, ready for instant retreat. A.W. Kinglake, the war's nine-volume chronicler, observes,'His fierce temper, being always under control when purposes of state so required, was far from being an infirmity, and was rather a weapon of exceeding sharpness, for it was so wielded by him as to have more tendency to cause dread and surrender than to generate resistance.' The Turkish ministers lived in terror of a personal visit from the ambassador. 'When the set face of the *elchi* himself penetrated the Sublime Porte, panic seized every official, and the Grand Vizier, himself, would condescend to hasten in a tremor of anxiety to meet his inexorable visitor and learn his behests.'

The Turks were especially impressed by the *elchi*'s seemingly inexhaustible resources: they could never tell what powerful weapon he held in reserve. 'High words he spoke and there was always something behind to be used in the last extremity; and above all other qualities, it was this suspicion of latent power that impressed the Turkish imagination.'

During his years in Constantinople, Stratford's influence and power was felt in every corner of the Ottoman empire. The question of apostasy was perhaps the first notable instance of the *elchi*'s sway over the Porte. Islamic law of the time required that any Christian who embraced Islam and then recanted was to be executed. In 1843, a young Armenian was arrested for apostasy, tried, condemned and executed. Strong notes of protest were submitted by the European embassies and Stratford was 'authorized to require the Porte' that all such executions cease. The grand vizier expressed deepest regrets but insisted that the Koran was distinct and final on the matter –

apostasy was punishable by death. 'A law prescribed by God Himself was not to be set aside by any human power,' he argued.

Undaunted, Stratford went to the Koran, and after patient study came to the conclusion that 'Mohammed in condemning renegades to punishment had in view their sufferings in a future date and not their decapitation here.' The ambassador further concluded that the Prophet never actually prescribed execution for apostasy and that this custom was simply a tradition founded on uncertain grounds. The authorities were thus advised and crisis immediately ensued. Consultations were had with the mullahs and one learned council after another debated the matter with no consensus being reached. The government, however, fully appreciated its quandary, finding itself truly between a rock and a hard place. As one Turkish minister wrote, 'If we refuse, we lose the friendship of Europe; if we consent, we hazard the peace of the Empire.' Rifaat Pasha begged Canning to settle the dispute 'amicably and confidentially', but Stratford gave no ground – the law required changing. The sultan continued for a time to refuse Stratford's demand but eventually his determination petered out, and finally after vainly pleading for a British change of heart, he conceded. The law was changed in accordance to Stratford's dictates; the great *elchi* had prevailed.

Following his victory with the apostasy issue, Stratford went on successfully to pressure the sultan to issue a decree abolishing torture within the empire. Next, he secured official recognition of the Protestant Church in Jerusalem, something long-sought by the King of Prussia. Frederick William IV sent Stratford his profuse thanks. The envoy then took up the cause of Protestant Armenians and secured for them certain rights and recognition. He forced the removal of the Pasha of Salonika, whose actions toward the Christian community were deemed inhuman. A Greek monk was saved from false accusation 'by the mere presence of a British Vice-Consul, who had no claim to interfere, but who threatened to send a report to the Embassy'. Such was the *elchi*'s influence with the sultan and his ministers.

Before long, Stratford found himself involved in virtually every aspect of Turkish government. He counselled on the reorganization of the army, suggested reforms in education, proposed new roads and transport facilities. Ministers who opposed his designs were unmade; those who supported him flourished. 'It was hard to resist the imperious Ambassador to his face,' writes Kinglake. 'If what he directed was inconsistent with the nature of things, then possibly the nature of things would be changed by a decree of Heaven, for there was no hope that the Great Elchi would relax his will.'

Between the British ambassador and the Russian emperor, little love was lost. In 1832, Stratford had been nominated envoy to St Petersburg, but for reasons of his own, Nicholas took the sensational step of refusing to accept him. Following this humiliating rebuff, Stratford resisted and thwarted the Russian government at every opportunity. It was he who in 1844 warned his government of Russia's growing preponderance in Turkey. It was he who five years earlier urged an Anglo-Turkish alliance against Russia. It was he who opposed the extension of Russian influence in the Danubian Principalities. And it was Stratford, newly returned to Constantinople, who now offered full sympathy and support to the Turks on the matter of the Hungarian refugees.

'The question of extradition has been raised for a sinister purpose,' Stratford warned Palmerston. 'Her Majesty's Government will sympathize with the Sultan and be earnestly disposed to rescue him,' he urged.

In the meantime, the tsar's personal emissary, Prince Radizvill, had arrived at Constantinople with an ultimatum to the Turks: surrender the refugees forthwith. The prince went on to hint that 50,000 Russian troops stood ready to march into Turkey. The sultan however was unimpressed – he had, after all, the friendly assurances of the formidable British ambassador. Politely, but firmly, he rejected the Russian demand. On 17 September 1849, with nothing further to be done, Prince Radizvill quietly left Constantinople. On that same day, Russia and Austria severed diplomatic relations with the Porte, and the flags of the two countries were hauled down at the embassies.

Even before Radizvill's ship weighed anchor, Stratford had dispatched a message to Vice-Admiral Sir William Parker, Commander of the Mediterranean Fleet. He informed the admiral of the situation at Constantinople and requested that 'a part at least of Her Majesty's Mediterranean squadron might be available for any purposes of demonstration'. The envoy had full confidence that Palmerston would approve this startling initiative, and there now remained only to await the word from the prime minister confirming the commitment he had made to the Turks.

News of the turbulent events in Constantinople reached London before the end of the month. 'It will be necessary to give the Sultan the cordial and firm support of England and France,' Palmerston wrote to Stratford two days prior to the receipt of his envoy's dispatch, 'and to let the two governments of Russia and Austria see that the Turk has friends who will back him and defend him in time of need.' On the very day that Stratford's dispatch was received, the sultan's minister to the Court of St James, Mehemed Pasha, presented Turkey's formal request for British moral and material support. Two weeks had now passed since the flags of Russia and Austria had been hauled at the Porte. The threatening situation was unfolding with alarming speed.

In Westminster, parliament was in recess. The balmy weather of early autumn had drawn most of the ministers to their country estates and it would take days to gather the cabinet together. But Palmerston held no doubts what the ultimate decision would be. Immediately upon receipt of Stratford's dispatch, he sent off the private letter he had written earlier. Britain not only will lend Turkey full moral and material support, but she will induce France to cooperate jointly in whatever action may be necessary. Tell the Turks 'to keep up their spirits and courage' – all this will soon be made official. The cabinet was summoned and it eventually assembled to approve Palmerston's initiative. On 8 October, orders were issued by the admiralty, officially dispatching Parker's fleet to Basika Bay, just outside the Dardanelles.

In Paris, the French cabinet was 'divided and perplexed'. Foreign Minister de Tocqueville wrote to Drouyn de Lhuys, French ambassador in London: find out exactly how far the British intend to go. 'If they want us to assist them, they must dot their i's.' Louis Napoleon, however, who had recently come to the presidency, was ardently for the adventure, regardless of dotted or undotted i's. The president prevailed and on the 10th, the French Mediterranean fleet was ordered east to join Admiral Parker.

In London, Ambassador Brunov solemnly warned Palmerston that a penetration of the Dardanelles by any warship would be a contravention of the 1841 Straits Convention, and might lead to a confrontation.[9] 'But, my dear Baron,' Palmerston assured the distraught Russian, 'as long as Turkey remains at peace we fully intend to maintain and respect the reciprocal engagement between us. A use of naval forces in the neighbourhood of our Empire should not be regarded in your eyes as a demonstration against you.'

Dispatching the fleet to the Dardanelles, Brunov countered, would give the Turks a semblance of security, complicating further negotiation with the Porte on the refugee question. The ambassador was especially upset that Stratford had such wide-ranging authority. At any given moment, he could order the fleet into the Straits. The Russian complained that Stratford had the power of war or peace. Palmerston assured Brunov that the envoy's powers 'sufficiently were limited by his instructions'. He had full confidence in the British ambassador's discretion. The fleet would not enter the Dardanelles.

Those early days in October grew increasingly perilous. The Radizvill mission had failed, and the tsar's envoy was on his way home. Parker's fleet was already in the Ionian Sea and the French fleet was on the move. And at Whitehall, Brunov made little impression on the British government. Four empires now tottered perilously on the brink of war.

While war fever gripped Constantinople, Paris and London, matters in St Petersburg were taking a more favourable turn. On the 5th, Faud Effendi, the sultan's personal emissary, had arrived in secret at the Russian capital and negotiations on the refugee question had got under way. Faud was told by Chancellor Nesselrode that an amicable settlement might be possible, but all depended on the tsar's personal decision. However, he cautioned, 'If powers pretended to interfere in the question at issue, His Imperial Majesty would not listen to any terms of accommodation whatever.'

Before news of the Anglo-French fleet movements had reached St Petersburg, Faud was granted an audience with the emperor on 16 October, and the two held a lengthy meeting. That evening Nicholas informed a surprised and much relieved Nesselrode that the Hungarian refugee issue had been settled – Russia is forsaking all claims, and normal relations with the Porte were to resume at once. Three days later the *Official Gazette* announced that the tsar had heeded 'this direct appeal on the part of an intimate ally'.

When news of the tsar's unilateral action reached Vienna, Austria voiced strenuous objection, but Nicholas paid little heed to the remonstrance. He had done enough for Austria in quelling the rebellious Hungarians. Insofar as St Petersburg was concerned, the refugee question was now settled and continuing peace assured. Ultimately, after the details of repatriation had been fully worked out, over 3,000 refugees were returned to Austria with full amnesty. Louis Kossuth was invited by the United States to emigrate to America, and a frigate was sent to collect him.[10] Bem and others embraced Islam and entered the service of the Turks.

News of the day, however, travelled lamentably slowly, and tidings of the St Petersburg settlement simply reached London and Constantinople too late. On the 19th, Ambassador Brunov again called on the foreign secretary. 'While the Porte remains at peace,' Palmerston reassured the Russian, 'the principle of closure in the Straits stands.' As for Stratford, Whitehall's confidence in the British ambassador had not diminished.

At the very moment this interview was taking place, Stratford was completing a design of his own. A formal treaty of alliance between Britain and Turkey, he decided, had to be induced. Such an agreement would have the highest economic and political significance for Britain. And to achieve this end, the sultan must be so firmly persuaded of threatening catastrophe that he would readily agree to British assistance in the defence of Constantinople. If no actual agreement took place, the Turks would nevertheless be sufficiently impressed by the excitement to be convinced that Britannia had saved the day. An alliance could be wrought.

Parker's fleet was expected any moment at Basika Bay. To avert a possible attack on it by Russia, it was deemed essential to secure permission to anchor it in the immediate vicinity of Constantinople, despite the 1841 Straits Convention. In the final days of October, a flurry of dispatches were exchanged between the British consul at the Dardanelles and the Turkish military governor. A fresh study of the convention's provisions resulted in an ingenious interpretation. The Turks and British agreed that the convention did permit warships to enter the Dardanelles, but only up to the Narrows – the point where in Classical times Leander entered the water to meet Hero.

The urgency of the looming threat was impressed upon the Porte, and the excited sultan granted the British fleet carte blanche to sail wherever it may be required. Any objections to the penetration of the Dardanelles, Stratford reasoned, would outweigh 'the advantages, essential as they are, of a sheltered anchorage and an easy approach to Constantinople'. On 2 November, the fleet sailed through the Straits. By serendipity, on that very same day Austria satisfactorily concluded negotiations with the Porte on the question of the Hungarian refugees and the issue appeared settled.

When news of Britain's scandalous violation of the Straits reached St Petersburg, the outraged tsar ordered a vigorous protest. Bloomfield was summoned to the foreign ministry and an explanation was demanded. The entry of Parker's fleet so deep in the Dardanelles, the ambassador explained smoothly, was entirely due to inclement weather, which threatened the safety of the ships. In London, Palmerston hastily assured the Russian envoy that despite earlier promises, the fleet's entry into the Straits had been 'an exceptional measure'. Prime Minister Russell acknowledged to Brunov that Stratford was 'a man who quarrelled with his own bread and butter'. Brunov nevertheless insisted that, unless her majesty's government immediately ordered a withdrawal of the offending fleet, he would recommend to St Petersburg that Admiral Lazarev's Black Sea squadron be sent into the Bosphorus. Two more days of talks were held between the two at the foreign secretary's palatial country home, 'Broadlands', in Hampshire. Palmerston was conciliatory and agreed to a prompt recall of the fleet. He refused, however, to accede to Russia's request of a reprimand for Parker.

As these exchanges were taking place, Stratford decided that the maintenance of the fleet at its existing anchorage was both futile and dangerous. The Hungarian refugee question, after all, had been settled by both Russia and Austria, and cause for armed demonstration had dissipated. Little further might be gained. He wrote to Parker, 'Under present circumstances, I think it of real importance that you should take the squadron outside . . . I am sorry for the change.' On 13 November, the fleet sailed out through the Straits back into the Mediterranean – before the receipt of any such order by London.

Soon after the fleet's withdrawal, a formal note of apology was delivered by Bloomfield to the Russian government, in which Palmerston denounced Stratford's interpretation of the Straits Convention. The two countries agreed that the rule respecting closure of the Straits to foreign warships would henceforth be rigidly enforced. If ever a British agent broke the rule, the Russian government would be justified in counter-action.

Nicholas was placated by the British apology, and the matter was brought to a close. The turbulent events generated by the Hungarian revolution had brought Britain and Russia to the brink of war. Yet, through negotiation and diplomatic exchange, peace prevailed, and the 1844 accord stood intact – at least for the time being. Its foundation, however, had sustained irreparable damage.

The Straits Convention had been violated by Britain with impunity and with virtual disregard to the sultan's authority. The Turks, however, had gained a significant diplomatic victory over Russia. And throughout the crisis, Stratford had openly displayed his personal antagonism toward the tsar, yet somehow managing to maintain London's continued support. As long as Palmerston continued in the foreign office and Stratford in Constantinople, reasoned Nicholas, Britain could no longer be relied upon to help keep the peace in the region. It was also a concern that Stratford Canning had been given personal control of the Mediterranean squadron – a dangerous precedent had thus been created.

Peace had been narrowly preserved in those autumn months of 1849. Within four years, however, virtually the entire scenario would be repeated. Palmerston would still be in the foreign office, and Stratford in Constantinople. Another squadron of British ships would once more sail through the Straits, and as before it would be summoned by Stratford and under his control. Turkey would score a further diplomatic victory over Russia, and that success once more would come through third-power intervention. But this time it would be through the efforts not of Britain, but of France. A France ruled by a restless Louis Napoleon, no longer president but king.

6

NAPOLEON III AND JERUSALEM

The Orleans monarchy had fallen in France on 24 February 1848. With the departure of Louis Philippe for England, control of the government was given over by the chamber of deputies to a group of republican and socialist leaders. For the first few days of the Second Republic, it was uncertain which flag would fly from the windows: the tricolour or the red flag. The leader of the republicans, the poet and historian Lamartine, in an impassioned speech persuaded the provisional government to adopt the tricolour. The left was successful, however, in insisting that a red rosette be attached to the staff.

By early March, the stifling restrictions on the press had been lifted and in the ensuing four months over two hundred new periodicals and papers entered publication. On 5 March, notice was given of a general election in April. The suffrage was extended to all males over twenty-one years of age – the electoral list was thus increased from 240,000 to 8,000,000. On 23 April, over 80 per cent of the enlarged electorate went to the polls and voted in favour of a constituent assembly, one that was distinctly moderate in temper. Of the 840 constituencies, the socialists, labourites and communists carried less than a quarter. Beaten at the polls and deprived of authority, the radicals again took to the streets. A futile insurrection was attempted in June, abruptly ended with the arrest of some 15,000 insurrectionists, many of whom were imprisoned, deported or executed. The left was effectively suppressed, but in the process, the government of the Second Republic lost much of the people's confidence.

By November, the new constitution had been completed, providing for a separation of powers. Legislative power was vested in a chamber of deputies, elected by universal male suffrage. Executive power was given to a president, also to be elected by the people, who was to hold office for four years and be ineligible to stand for re-election.

A plebiscite for the presidential election was called for 10 December. As election day drew closer, it became obvious that France had become weary of the established political leaders. The socialists had already fallen and the republicans, after the June uprising, had resorted to military rule. Since the downfall of Louis Philippe ten months earlier, no one person had successfully captured popular imagination. What was required was a fresh face. The country cried for a man disassociated with the events of the previous months, one who could guarantee orderly government.

Such a man the French found in Prince Louis Napoleon, nephew of the great emperor, recently returned to France from exile in England. As head of the Napoleonic clan, Prince Louis succeeded to his uncle's prestige: to the peasant his very name personified law and order. The leaderless workers were delighted with his pamphlet *L'Extinction du pauperisme*. For the patriots and militarists Louis embodied *la gloire*. On election day it was a landslide victory for Napoleon – nearly 75 per cent of the vote went to him – and on 20 December, Prince Louis Napoleon took the oath as President of the French Republic.

Napoleon was elected to power on the platform of prosperity and lasting peace. Prosperity he gave; peace, he did not – within six years, he went to war against Russia. 'He says he has been forced into a war,' wrote a contemporary. 'We believe him. We thought that he was a victim of the ambition of Russia, or of [the English] desire to destroy Cronstadt and Sebastopol . . . now we find that he has been the great promoter of war . . . that every decisive move has been prompted by him.'

Louis Napoleon did not exactly cut a presidential figure. His short legs and long torso gave him am awkward appearance. He looked taller on horseback. Particularly striking was Louis' moustache – long, black, and waxed. The gaze of the first Napoleon was penetrating; the gaze of his nephew was lacklustre. Louis had been likened to 'a weaver oppressed by long hours of monotonous indoors work, which makes the body stoop and keeps the eyes downcast.'

There was, however, much that was attractive in Louis' personality. He was friendly and good-natured. The more people got to know him, the more they liked him. They were charmed by his courtesy and gentleness, by his gravity and the occasional flashes of wit. All too easily he won over children, scholars, ministers and women. In England, he especially endeared himself to the country gentlemen by rapidly mastering the skills of riding to the hounds. (Louis' horsemanship might have attracted the admiration of his artillery-minded uncle, whose skills in the equestrian arts left much to be desired.)

People considered Louis dull. In conversation his ideas flowed sluggishly. His face did not exude brilliance. He toiled slavishly, however, over his studies, and scores of tracts, letters and pamphlets flowed from his pen. He wrote on social questions, on constitutional matters, on Swiss politics, on the sugar question. He brought out a *Manuel d'artillerie, des idées napoléoniennes*. He theorized on the building of a canal through Nicaragua, and on recruiting for the army. He corresponded with republicans and with socialists. During his years in exile in England, he was accepted not so much as a serious pretender to the throne, but rather as an original.

Louis was the son of Bonaparte's younger brother, Louis, King of Holland. His mother was Hortense de Beauharnais, daughter of Bonaparte's first wife, Joséphine.

The young Prince was brought up by his mother in Germany, Italy and Switzerland. It was at the gymnasium at Augsburg that Napoleon acquired his German accent. As a young man, Louis espoused the cause of liberalism, which to him was synonymous with Bonapartism. In 1830, he joined the Carbonari and fought for the liberal revolution in Italy. Narrowly escaping arrest by the Austrian authorities – largely through the good offices of Hortense, he escaped to France. There he plotted with the republicans and was promptly expelled to England.

In 1832, Bonaparte's son and legitimate heir, the Duke of Reichstadt, died. Louis' father, living comfortably in Florence, showed no desire to lay claim to the Bonaparte inheritance. Neither did Uncle Joseph, the former King of Naples and Spain. Louis Napoleon grasped the opportunity and proclaimed himself the true heir to the Bonaparte legacy. Thereafter, all his studies, toils and efforts were devoted to regaining his rightful position from the hateful Bourbons.

For hours, he sat studying and planning. The strength of his imagination helped him to plot elaborate enterprises and schemes. Yes it was too weak to give a foretaste of his reaction to a crisis situation. Recklessly he ploughed into action, but when he came face to face with danger he got frightened and withdrew.

The view of the imperial throne was never lost to Louis. He longed to stand on a height from which he might see the world gazing up at him. Coupled to this grandiose ambition was a passionate fondness for the melodramatic, for the scenic effect, for the heroic surprise. Had Louis been a simple man, history doubtlessly would have passed this eccentric without notice. But the accident of his birth made Louis a pretender to the throne of France.

Louis staged his first great spectacular at the age of twenty-eight. With the aid of a handful of romantic-minded friends, the young prince instigated a revolt of the Strasburg garrison. His chief accomplice was old Colonel Vaudry, a veteran of the imperial army and commanding officer of the 4th Artillery Regiment. On the morning of 30 October 1836, Vaudry announced to his men that a revolution in Paris had deposed the king. He persuaded the troops to recognize Louis as Napoleon II, and then ordered them to arrest the prefect and the commanding officer of the garrison. Platoons of gunners marched to the houses of the two men and, without incident, placed both under house arrest. The remainder of the garrison was oblivious to these events.

Dressed in the historic uniform of his uncle, meticulous to the detail, Louis set off to interview the captive general, confident in his powers to persuade the old soldier to join his ranks. General Voiral was un-amused, unimpressed and uncooperative. Louis then went to the barracks of the 46th Regiment, accompanied by a suite of 'imperial staff'.

The men of the 46th were taken aback at now being introduced to their new sovereign, Napoleon II. In their perplexity, the assembly was held in a respectful but suspicious silence. At this point, Lieutenant Colonel Talancher, Colonel of the Regiment, having been apprised of earlier events, burst in on the assembly. He ordered all the gates closed and angrily marched up to the self-styled emperor. The gentleman of letters, dressed in the unreal costume of the great conqueror, stood awkwardly on the unfamiliar parade square. Facing him was a very real colonel whose barracks had been invaded and who now sputtered furious and indignant anger. It was a dreadful situation – not entirely unexpected – but dreadful nevertheless. The colonel demanded that the charade close forthwith. Louis hesitated, flushed and succumbed. The short-lived conspiracy was at an end. Stripped of swords and decorations, Louis and the unfortunate Vaudry were ingloriously locked up with the remainder of the 'imperial staff'.

The king's ministers urged imprisonment for the young pretender. Louis Philippe, however, was unwilling to make a martyr for the Bonaparte cause. The unfortunate Prince was conveyed to Lorient, where he was put on board a ship bound for America. In his pocket he carried £600, which the King had generously awarded the exile. A year later, having secured a Swiss passport in New York, Prince Louis was back in Europe, hatching new plots to regain his rightful throne.

Such was the man who in 1848 came to the Presidency in France – all quite legitimately.

At the time that the Russians were helping to suppress the Hungarians and that Louis Napoleon was mounting the heights of power, events of an entirely different nature were unfolding far from the imposing palaces and elegant cabinet rooms of Paris, London and St Petersburg. In the torpid hills of Palestine, a seemingly 'insignificant quarrel between ignorant monks' was assuming international importance. It was this quarrel over 'keys, stars, doorkeepers, gardens, domes and outbuildings' which ultimately involved the most powerful armies of Europe in battle. What Palmerston once termed 'a matter in itself so unimportant' may be regarded as the immediate cause of the Crimean War.

From the earliest centuries of Christianity, the venturesome, moved by faith and by the desire to touch and kiss the spots 'where Christ's holy feet have trod', made their way to Jerusalem. In the middle ages, the desire was so strong that it compelled countless thousands to undertake crusades of conquest of the barren and distant land. By the nineteenth century the fervour of these *pélerins* or pilgrims had not diminished – they continued to arrive in droves in the Holy Land. Everywhere, religious communities had sprung up. Greeks, Georgians, Armenians and even American Congregationalists founded hospices which offered shelter to the pilgrims.

Over the centuries, the alluring mystery of the shrines had been cleverly exploited by the enterprising local clergy. The holy places were big business, and the pursuit of money fostered an incessant rivalry between churches. Moslem governors were constantly required to arbitrate claims of jurisdiction, and frequently Turkish soldiers had to be stationed with fixed bayonets at the most sacred places in order to prevent Christians from shedding one another's blood.

Acts of violence, sanguinary quarrels and extreme jealousies characterized the Christian brotherhood in Jerusalem. In 1842, for example, the Greeks at great expense restored the badly decayed basilica at Bethlehem. They adhered meticu-

lously to the original design: among other areas, they reno-
vated the north transept and the steps leading from the main
altar to the Grotto of the Nativity. Both these areas were under
the jurisdiction of the Armenians, whose counsel, the Greeks
had lamentably neglected to solicit beforehand. The Armenians were infuriated and promptly obtained a *firman* from the
governor, by which all the work completed by the Greeks was
ordered undone. The Armenian jurisdiction was successfully
asserted, and they now had 'the miserable satisfaction of seeing
their sacred building fast falling to decay'.

The rivalry for control of the shrines was especially strong
between the Eastern Orthodox and the Roman Catholics –
Greeks and Latins. In AD 636, Khaliph Omar signed a *firman*
by which the Greeks were confirmed in possession of the
Christian holy places. Over the following eleven centuries,
the Latins disputed the Greek privileges, and, depending from
which quarter greater pressure was brought to bear on the
Muslim rulers – from Rome or from Constantinople, possession of the sanctuaries alternated between the rival factions. In
1740, a treaty was concluded between France and the Porte by
which the Latins received full rights in the Holy Land. The
Greeks, naturally, found this unacceptable, and the traditional
dispute continued. In 1757, an ordinance by the sultan settled
a particularly violent quarrel – entirely to the satisfaction of
the Greeks. The Latins were ordered expelled from the Church
of the Tomb of the Virgin and from the Holy Sepulchre. Other
important sanctuaries were also placed under the guardianship
of the Orthodox.

In 1808, a fire destroyed the Church of the Holy Sepulchre,
and the Greeks received permission from the Turks to rebuild
the edifice. Subscriptions poured in from the Orthodox
throughout the world and before long the work was completed. In the course of this noble undertaking, the Latin tombs

of Godfrey de Bouillon and of Baldwin inexplicably disappeared without a trace. Even more mysteriously, on the dome of the church, the statues of the four Evangelists shed their Roman robes for Greek vestments. Orthodoxy was visibly on the ascendancy.

Additional rights and prerogatives were claimed by the Greeks, leading to fresh dissension. In 1819, an unusually sanguinary dispute between Greek and Latin monks prompted the governments of Russia and France to interfere. The King of France claimed to act as 'hereditary protector of the Catholics in the East', and the Emperor of Russia as 'sovereign of the greater number of the followers of the Greek Church'. As a preliminary step, it was agreed that each of the countries should send an envoy to the Holy Land in order to obtain accurate information on the points of the dispute. Monsieur Marcellus and Ambassador Dashkoff worked in close cooperation and there was every promise of a speedy and satisfactory settlement to the problem. The Greek Revolution of 1821, however, brought the negotiations to a temporary end.

The stream of pilgrims continued to flow into the Holy Land. Especially from Russia, where the rite of pilgrimage was held sacred. During Christmas 1831, it was estimated that of four thousand pilgrims, all but four were Orthodox. From all over the tsar's vast empire the Russians came. 'From Lake Baikal, from Archangel, from the Carpathians, from the Caucasus came ragged peasants in procession, chanting their hymns, confessing their sins, trusting in the simple precepts of the gospel . . . at Christmas and at Easter fifty millions of Russians turned their eyes and prayers toward Jerusalem, where pilgrims of their race were kneeling before the shrine of the Redeemer.'

In nineteenth-century France, however, religious zeal had been all but extinguished by 'enlightened' revolutionary thought. Pilgrimages and interest in the Holy Land dissipated. 'The closest likeness of a pilgrim which the Latin Church could supply was often a mere French tourist, with a journal and a theory, and a plan of writing a book.' The French foreign office, from time to time, made token protests in support of its traditional position as protector of the Latin Church, but that was it. Professor Temperley cites one reference, dated 1850:

> the Latins are dissatisfied with the inefficiency of French protection for a long time past . . . but especially within the last few years. They complain that the French have suffered the Greek ecclesiastics to usurp, by gradual encroachments, most of the sacred localities in Jerusalem and Bethlehem . . . complaints of French inefficient protection are not novel.

It was at this point that Louis Napoleon made his entrance on the European stage. Within two years of his election, he had successfully consolidated control over government administration. The next step was to gain the attachment of the country at large, and to achieve this, he concluded, the Church had to be won over. From the beginning of his rise to power, the clergy and the 'Christian community' favoured him; indeed, he secured office largely through Roman Catholic assistance. An intimacy with the Church would not only lead to the desired approbation of the Catholic citizenry, but also assure Louis a powerful, socially conservative ally, since 'the men in black' were the strongest barrier against revolution.

Napoleon Bonaparte was called 'the restorer of altars', and now his nephew determined to follow suit. Government grants flowed to the churches and to religious charitable organizations. The laws governing monastic communities were simplified. Religious instruction was made compulsory in secondary schools, and the Church was permitted an increasingly freer hand in all aspects of education. Little wonder that the clergy considered Louis' government 'a heaven-sent blessing'.

With many old claims revived and ancient privileges restored, the elated Clerical Party now looked to the East. France had sacred obligations in the Holy Land. The question of the Latin claims to Jerusalem shrines, they urged, was a matter of national honour and Catholic priority. Napoleon agreed.

So it was that, on 26 May 1850, General Auplick, the French ambassador in Constantinople, received a dispatch from Paris. The envoy was to call on the Turkish authorities and to make a formal demand that the sultan recognize the rights of France in the Holy Land, as stipulated by the Treaty of 1740. *Firmans* issued since then, giving Greeks virtual control of the holy places, must be revoked. Auplick was to announce that unilateral abrogation of bilateral treaties could not be recognized by France, however old they were.

From Constantinople, Stratford Canning apprised Palmerston of the situation: 'General Auplick has assured me the matter in dispute is a mere question of property and of express treaty stipulation. But it is difficult to separate such questions from political considerations: and a struggle of general influence, especially if Russia, as may be expected, should interfere on behalf of the Greek Church, will probably grow out of the impending discussion.' To resurrect claims which had been dormant for nearly a century was a dangerous diplomatic practice. The tsar could hardly be expected to agree to the expulsion of Greek monks from the shrines which they had lovingly tended for decades. It was certain that he would not tolerate the virtual disintegration of the Orthodox Church in Jerusalem, which any such action would bring. Russian Ambassador Titov delivered a vigorous protest of the French claims. The shrines, he argued, were Orthodox by virtue of the Treaty of Khaliph Omar, signed in AD 636.

What were the precise issues of the French claims, which ultimately led to the allied invasion of Crimea? The first and most sensitive question was that of the key to the principal door of the Basilica of Bethlehem – should the Catholic monks not have possession of such a key in order to pass through the building into the Grotto of the Nativity? The Orthodox balked at the suggestion, but finally allowed that their co-religionists might be issued with a key to the sanctuary's lesser door. But such compromise was unacceptable to the claimants. In the initial diplomatic exchanges that took place on the matter, Chancellor Nesselrode queried whether the key was 'an instrument for opening a door, only to be employed in closing that door against Christians of other sects, or . . . simply a key – an emblem'. Assurance was given that the demanded key was indeed real, one for unlocking doors: 'Its evil quality was not that it kept Greeks out, but that it let Latins come in.'

In addition to the burning issue of the sanctuary's key, the Latins also demanded not only a key to each of the two doors leading to the Holy Manger but the privilege of a cupboard and a lamp at the Tomb of the Virgin. Two further demands were included: the right to worship once a year at the Shrine of the Blessed Virgin in the Church of Gethsemane, and the privilege of placing in the Sanctuary of the Nativity a silver star emblazoned with the arms of France. As for the Stone of Anointing and the Seven Arches of the Virgin at the Church of the Holy Sepulchre – these were claimed as the outright property of the Latin monks.

With Auplick and Titov each aggressively pressing the case of their respective governments, Sultan Abdul Mejid found himself between a rock and a hard place. The Russian army was stationed in the Principalities and could march on Constantinople with virtual impunity. On the other hand, the French freely fleet sailed the Mediterranean and could easily threaten his possessions of Tripoli and Tunis. An additional consideration: Russia had recently menaced Turkey over the Hungarian refugee question, and France had volunteered to aid the sultan. Mejid appointed a commission to examine the matter of the holy places. After prolonged deliberations, it concluded that the AD 636 *firman* by which the Greeks were granted rights had to be rejected. The century-old treaty with Catholic France, the commission ruled, superseded the twelve-hundred-year agreement with the Orthodox.

The argument between the two powers, however, was anything but decided. On 13 September 1851, the tsar wrote to the sultan, 'The Emperor of Russia was persuaded that no changes would be allowed to take place as to the possession of those sanctuaries.' If any change took place in the status quo, his ambassador would immediately quit Constantinople. At this stage, Auplick was recalled by Paris and Monsieur de Lavalette was appointed to succeed him at the Porte. The new envoy quickly sized up the situation. 'If it depended on me,' he wrote, 'I would not hesitate to make use of the great naval force possessed by France in the Mediterranean, and by blocking the Dardanelles bring the question in debate forthwith to a satisfactory issue.'

The matter of the holy places now assumed alarming proportions. Two great powers were deadlocked in a bitter argument that threatened to resolve itself only in war. Two powers championing the cause of two rival churches. Yet curious to note, neither of the churches displayed the least interest in the quarrel. The Metropolitan of Moscow, Philaret Drasdov, decidedly refused to become involved in the dispute and Pius IX showed equally little disposition to interfere. En route to his new post in Constantinople, Ambassador de Lavalette stopped in Rome and was received by the Pope. '*A ma grande surprise*,' the envoy wrote later, 'the Holy Father showed little inclination to pursue Jerusalem's copulas and Bethlehem's keys.'

As these developments were unfolding, France found itself in a constitutional crisis. The constitution of the Second French Republic precluded the president from standing for election to a second, consecutive term. All of Louis Napoleon's efforts to persuade the national assembly to pass an amendment came to naught. He had quarrelled with the assembly, and the obstinate legislators were in no mood to appease him. On 2 December 1851 – the anniversary of the date of Napoleon Bonaparte's coronation and of the Battle of Austerlitz, his greatest victory – Louis sprung a coup d'état. Leading opposition deputies and unfriendly journalists were arrested; an uprising in Faubourg Saint-Antoine was crushed with some bloodshed; martial law was proclaimed in the provinces. The champion of law and order had prevailed against a largely imaginary socialist plot, and France was again declared safe from rabid radicals.

Within three weeks of the coup, Louis had sufficiently consolidated his position to call for a plebiscite. Some eight million Frenchmen went to the polls; 7,481,000 voted in his favour. This approved his actions and gave him the right to draw up a new constitution. The fresh document named Louis Napoleon as president for ten years and gave him virtually dictatorial powers.

In the months which followed, Louis Napoleon did everything to fill France with imperial ideas. He undertook an extensive tour of the country, and everywhere was greeted by enthusiastic, cheering crowds. His advance agents prepared the ground, and, spontaneous or not, the acclamations and adulation seemed to invite the president to assume the imperial title. Louis himself said nothing – he wished to appear in the eyes of Europe as having his hand forced by the popular will of his people. It seemed that the citizens of France, to ensure a stable government, desired the restoration of an imperial crown.

In St Petersburg, news of Louis' coup was received with mixed reactions. On the one hand the tsar's court joined 'men of order' throughout Europe in applause – French radicals and liberals had been subdued. 'The threatened interests of society are now assured protection,' proclaimed the *Universe*. On the other hand, however, there was now a very real concern that Louis might grab for an imperial crown. He had, after all, successfully taken steps in direct imitation of his august uncle of some four decades earlier. Would Louis Napoleon dare to challenge the Treaty of Vienna and stand up to Europe?

Article II of the treaty emphasized that Napoleon Bonaparte and his entire family were 'forever excluded from Supreme Power in France'. The great powers further agreed 'to concert themselves . . . for the general tranquillity of Europe', should someone make a future attempt at a 'criminal usurpation' of the throne. In 1815, Great Britain, Austria, Prussia and Russia were firmly unanimous in their determination. How resolutely would Europe now stand?

Within days of the coup, the Russian ambassador to Vienna, Baron Meyendorff, met with the Austrian chancellor, Prince von Schwarzenberg. What would Austria's position be if Louis Napoleon assumed the imperial title? Schwarzenberg responded that 'for the general tranquillity of Europe' his title would have to be recognized by all great powers, especially if the prince-president promised a peaceful foreign policy. Austria was anxious not to endanger European status quo.

By early autumn, it was clear that Britain, Prussia and Russia shared Austria's unwillingness to go to war merely to prevent the establishment of a second empire in France.

Nicholas made it clear, however, that an assumption of the imperial crown by Louis Napoleon would be tantamount to usurpation. 'An emperor without divine right is not an emperor. He will be an emperor in fact, but never an emperor by right.'

In November 1852, Louis once more called for a referendum, but this time on the question of transforming the republic into a hereditary empire. The people responded overwhelmingly, and voted 7,824.000 to 253,000 in favour of re-establishing the imperial crown. Accordingly, on 2 December, the coronation took place and President Louis Napoleon became Napoleon III, Emperor of the French.

'For us there can be no question of NIII,' declared the Russian tsar. 'The cipher is absurd. I am of the opinion that he must be called "Louis Napoleon, Emperor of the French", and that's all. If he becomes angry, all the worse for him. If he becomes rude Kisselev [the Russian ambassador] will quit France.' Nicholas informed Nesselrode that any autographed correspondence with the upstart should not bear the salutation customary of monarchs, *'Monsieur, mon frère'*. 'My friend' would suffice. To recognize the numeral 'III' implied recognition of the long-rejected numeral 'II', as well as of future ciphers. The impossible man was seeking acknowledgement of the continuation of a dynasty founded in 1804, in addition to which he was providing for its future.

Within a week of Napoleon's coronation, Britain formally recognized his title and Victoria dispatched a letter to 'my brother'.[11] Soon thereafter recognition came from Francis Joseph in Vienna, Frederick William IV in Berlin, Bismarck in Frankfurt and other European governments. But from St Petersburg only an icy silence flowed – the tsar stubbornly persisted in his refusal to recognize the self-styled emperor. The emotional and sensitive Napoleon continued in his bitterness with Russia; he was unforgiving. He not only considered this an intolerable personal slight, but it was an insult to the nation. Echoing his illustrious uncle, Louis declared, 'Everything for the French people.' And the French people were being grossly mistreated.

In the twelve month period that Napoleon spent in his climb to the throne, distant matters such as the holy places were put aside. With pressures from Paris relaxed, and those from St Petersburg growing, the sultan appointed a fresh commission to review the delicate situation of the sanctuaries. But this time it was a new group and less pro-French. Among the delicate questions posed anew: should the Catholics be allowed to replace a silver star which the Greeks had filched from the Sacred Manger? Might they have a key to the great door of the Church at Bethlehem, and, if it were given, would they be justified in placing it in the lock? And then, if they did place it in the lock, might they turn it and open the door? Trivial and academic as these matters appear, they were the burning concerns of the time, issues critical enough to bring about war.

By early February, the commission submitted its findings to the sultan. Two separate, contradictory documents were drawn up, a note addressed to the French and a *firman* given to the Russians. In the note, the Catholic claims were acknowledged and new privileges given, while the *firman* awarded the Orthodox the maintenance of all existing rights and an unaltered status quo. Abdul Mejid was well pleased with the work of his latest commission and with the judgement – an equitable decision that should please everyone. The French received their note with delight and the Russians were overjoyed with their *firman*. From the sultan's point of view, the tiresome business was satisfactorily brought to a close.

It did not take long, however, for these peculiar arrangements to be exposed, and the impact of Turkish casuistry was quickly understood in St Petersburg and in Paris. It was bitterly felt; the dispute was far from settled. Further discussions and negotiations over the holy places could hardly have been expected to progress amicably, considering the lamentable state of relations between Nicholas and Napoleon. Each ruler was determined to be the dominant force in matters related to the Ottoman empire and each held antipathy and grievance against the other.

'Certain persons declare that the empire means war,' Napoleon had announced early in his reign with typical Gallic aplomb. 'But I say – the empire means peace . . . it means peace because France desires it, and when France is satisfied, the world is tranquil.' Peace, however, brings a nation neither honour nor dignity, and certainly not the fulfilment of the grandeur which the new emperor deemed essential for nation and for his dynasty. Years earlier, Napoleon in his *Les idées napoléoniennes* had committed himself to the restoration of France's natural frontiers. More impressively, he had dedicated himself to the task of bringing freedom to oppressed nations. Hardly would either noble aspiration be attained through peaceful means. A war was inevitable.

But there was more to it than simple restoration of imperial boundaries, or backing the causes of others. From the day of his accession, Napoleon III feared the possibility of a renewed alliance of the four great powers – Britain, Russia, Austria and Prussia. It was this same coalition that had defeated his distinguished uncle, the founder of the dynasty. The coalition had to be broken. 'The question of the holy places and all that relates to it is of no real importance to France,' declared French Foreign Minister Drouyn de Lhuys long after the war had started. 'This entire Eastern Question serves the imperial government as a means of destroying the continental alliance which during the course of nearly half a century has paralysed

France. At last, an opportunity has presented itself to sow
discord in the powerful coalition, and the Emperor Napoleon
has grabbed it with both hands.'

As soon as Abdul Mejid's most recent move was fully
digested by Paris, Napoleon ordered his ambassador to the
Porte, Marquis de Lavalette, to return to his post and demand
satisfaction. And to convey his envoy to the Porte, Napoleon
ordered that his envoy was to sail up the Dardanelles to
Constantinople on board the three-decker, 90-gun *Charlemagne*.

As stipulated by the Straits Convention, by no stretch of the
imagination could this capital ship meet the definition of 'light
vessel'. As we have seen, the Russians had once protested
vehemently this same sort of violation of the 1841 treaty. The
Turks, however, were quick to explain that the *Charlemagne*
was expressly invited by the sultan for the sole purpose of
serving as a model for his shipyards. Invited or not, the
appearance of the mighty frigate, 'conveying successfully
her mass artillery and men against the most rapid of currents
of the Bosphorus, by the sole power of the screw,' as Professor
Temperley puts it, made a great impression. Could the French
win a naval victory over the Russians? Yes, concluded the
Turks for it was obvious that Napoleon's screw-propelled
battleships were significantly more effective than anything
the tsar possessed. Under these new, sensational circumstances, they decided to carry out yet a third review of the
situation as it related to shrines of the Holy Land. 'Thus a little
instrument, a screw, affects and will probably still more affect,
great political events,' wrote Colonel Rose, the British chargé
d'affaires. 'In fact,' adds Temperley, 'the French screw was
beginning to turn.'

From Munich, Thouvenel, Napoleon's ambassador to Ba-
varia, sent home a dire warning: 'What is the meaning of this

dispute which we've begun in Constantinople on the question of the holy places? . . . I know the East and I can assure you that Russia will not acquiesce. For her the entire question is one of life or death, and it is essential that this be realized in Paris, if it is intended to see the matter through to the end.' Whether Napoleon understood or could even guess that for Nicholas the matter was one of 'life or death' appears irrelevant. He was determined to see the matter through 'to the end', and he continued to apply pressure with increasing force. So successful he appeared to be that he felt confident enough to order a new silver star to be made, in readiness for replacement at the Holy Manger. The handsome piece bore an inscription in Latin and carried the date 1740.

At a special council assembled by the sultan, Faud Effendi, the Porte's newly appointed foreign minister, eloquently argued for concessions to France. He spoke with enthusiasm of the rising position of the resurrected French empire. He praised the resolute character of Emperor Napoleon III and warned of the warlike spirit of the French nation. An alliance with France, he pointed out, would better allow Turkey to resolve pending matters in the Principalities and in Montenegro. And he reminded the council of the *Charlemagne* – it would be dangerous to provoke Napoleon in view of the power of the French fleet which now so freely sailed the coasts of Turkey's Mediterranean possessions.

Faud's sombre words produced the desired effect. 'In the month of December,' Kinglake writes, 'the star was brought with much pomp from the coast. Some of the Moslem Effendis went down to Jaffa to escort it, and others rode out a good way on the road that they might bring it to Jerusalem with triumph. On Wednesday, the 22nd of the same month, the Latin Patriarch, with joy and with a great ceremony, replaced the glittering star in the sanctuary of Bethlehem, and, at the same time, the key of the great door of the Church, together with the keys of the Sacred Manger, was handed over to the Latins.'

7

THE SICK MAN OF EUROPE

At the start of 1853, Turkey's overall condition was far from healthy, and to European statesmen the Ottoman empire appeared to be in an advanced state of decay. It would seem that Sultan Abdul Mejid himself recognized this. Early on in his reign, rather than face grim realities, he assumed an ostrich-like posture by physically withdrawing himself from the geographic centre of government. Nearly two miles away from the great public buildings of Constantinople, across the Bosphorus, he erected for himself the fabulous rococo Palace of Dolmabache, an elaborate refuge of some three hundred rooms, not counting the Spartan cells of a multiplicity of concubines. The world's largest ballroom was illuminated by a four-ton chandelier; the throne room was over a 150 feet (45 metres) long. Fourteen tons of gold leaf went into the building's decoration; the sultan's bed was of solid silver.

His was a life of receptions, banquets, balls and other

entertainments. The palace theatre featured plays and panto-mimes, in which pretty page boys assumed the roles of leading ladies and, much to the audience's delight, fell in love with equally handsome boys. It was to this hedonistic hideaway that Mejid escaped the tiresome concerns of state, delegating to the grand vizier the true burdens of state. From time to time, he permitted himself to receive high personages or to sign one document or another.

Abdul's mother was a simple bath attendant. So convinced was she that the death of her husband, Sultan Mahmud II, was due to over-indulgence in drink that she did everything in her power to deny the temptation to her sixteen-year-old sultan son. First she destroyed the remains of Mahmud's vast cellar by smashing 50,000 bottles of the finest champagne, brandy and wine against the harbour walls of the Bosphorus. Then, she deliberately set about to cultivate her 'frail, narrow-chested, dull-eyed, sickly-looking, mild and gentle' son with the pleasures of the harem. Abdul responded with delight and became 'enfeebled early in his reign by excessive indulgence'. Sadly for the mother, these diversions proved insufficient, for the young man 'when he became impotent at an early age . . . took to the bottle'.

While Abdul Mejid revelled in the extravagant life of Dolmabache, his empire was rapidly slipping into financial bankruptcy and moral decay. The Moslem population was in decline, principally through the widespread practice of abor-tion. Nationalistic aspirations permeated all corners of his domains and local revolts, demonstrations and massacres frequently went unsuppressed. In the Asian provinces, law-lessness was rampant and, in the Balkans, Christians were becoming increasingly restless. Towards the end of 1852, open rebellion broke out in Montenegro and the sultan dispatched 'the flower of the Ottoman forces' to deal with the rebels.

There, Omar Pasha became locked in battle, much to the alarm of neighbouring Austria. Before long, emotionally charged petitions began to arrive at St Petersburg – Orthodox brethren in Montenegro clamoured for deliverance from the infidel. Let the Protector of the Church, their mighty northern brother, save the besieged Montenegrins.

To Tsar Nicholas, this was the final straw – time was at hand, once and for all, to settle the 'Eastern question'. The 'insolent Turk' had to be taught not to make light of Orthodoxy. The 'wretched people' must be compelled to meet all Russian demands in the Holy Land and to understand that they were not to molest Orthodox Christians. Sir Hamilton Seymour, the newly appointed British ambassador to St Petersburg, was summoned to the chancellery by Chancellor Nesselrode and informed that a 'demonstration of force' was about to take place, but that Britain need not be alarmed. Orders were then issued for 144,000 soldiers to advance to the frontiers of the Danubian provinces.

The tsar realized of course that such a show of strength was a direct challenge to Napoleon III. He feared little of the French, however, so long as the British remained neutral. And not only was Nicholas entirely confident of that neutrality, but he was certain it would be benign. In the first place he reasoned, Great Britain had become a pacific nation whose energies seemed to have shifted from militancy to commerce. Secondly, his own, personal relations with Victoria, her court and her ministers was exceptionally cordial. But most importantly, Nicholas continued in his firm faith in the strength of the 1844 agreement. During the state visit which led to the accord, he had had frank and open conversations with Aberdeen, then the foreign minister, and now this same friend was the prime minister. Nesselrode's memorandum in 1844, embodying the substance of the discussions, had been received by the foreign minister without protest. Nicholas knew, further-more, that, as much as Aberdeen was well disposed towards himself, he disliked Napoleon III.

That Britain would remain neutral was one thing. Also important at this juncture, however, was to bring that state into immediate accord on the partition of the Ottoman empire whose collapse was conspicuously imminent.

On 9 January, Grand Duchess Elena, the tsar's sister senior by twelve years, held a soirée at her elegant palace on the banks of the Neva. The emperor attended, as did Sir Hamilton Seymour, the British ambassador. Nicholas quickly spotted the envoy and engaged him in brief conversation, quite naturally focusing on the 'Eastern question'. This was to be the first of four encounters between the two, which eventually proved significant for the start of war – the so-called 'Seymour conversations'.

'You know my feelings with regard to England,' the emper-or began. 'It is essential that the two governments, that is the English Government and I, and I and the English Government, should be on the best terms. The necessity was never greater than at present. I beg you to convey these words to Lord John Russell. When we are agreed, I am quite without anxiety as to the rest of Europe; it is quite immaterial what the other countries may think or do.'

The tsar paused and then added, as though an after thought, 'As to Turkey, that is another question. That country is in a critical state, and may give us all a great deal of trouble.' Nicholas then offered a gloved hand to Sir Hamilton and intending to withdraw, he concluded, 'Now I will take my leave of you.'

The full significance of the tsar's last statement was not lost on the Englishman. Un-awed by the august presence of his majesty, Seymour persisted. 'Sir,' he entreated, before Nicholas had an opportunity to withdraw, 'with your gracious permission, I would desire to take a liberty.'

'Certainly,' replied Nicholas. 'What is it?'

'Her Majesty's Government are anxious over the affairs of Turkey. Perhaps you would be pleased to charge me with some additional assurances which may calm this anxiety.'

The emperor at first hesitated but then he spoke quite openly. 'The affairs of Turkey are disorganized. The country seems to be falling to pieces. The fall will be a great misfortune, and it is very important that England and Russia should come to a perfectly good understanding on these affairs, and that neither should take any decisive step without apprising the other.'

Sir Hamilton indicated that this precisely was his own view of the matter. The tsar continued, 'We have on our hands a sick man – a very sick man. It will be a great misfortune if one of these days he should slip away from us, especially before all necessary arrangements were made. However, this is not the time to speak to you on this matter.' Nicholas took his leave of Seymour and the envoy soon returned to the palace of the British embassy, there to make a report on the frank exchange.

A fortnight later, Sir Hamilton was summoned to the imperial palace. Nicholas wished to continue the conversation the two had begun at his sister's reception. 'I found His Majesty alone,' wrote Seymour. 'He received me with great. kindness.'

'You know the dreams and plans in which the Empress Catherine indulged,' began the emperor. 'These were handed down to our time. While I inherited immense territorial possessions, I did not inherit these visions – those intentions, if you would like to call them. On the contrary, my country is so vast, so happily circumstanced in every way that it would be unreasonable to desire more territory or more power than I possess. On the contrary, I am the first to tell you that our great, perhaps our only danger is that which would arise from an extension of an empire already too large.'

The tsar went on to explain that in Turkey there were several million Eastern Orthodox, 'whose interests I am called to watch over'. The 1774 Treaty of Kutchuk-Kainardji specifically allowed the Russian tsar special rights over these Christians and Nicholas fervently considered himself the sole protector of the Orthodox Church, if not of all Christian faiths in Turkey.[12]

'Things have come to such a pass,' the emperor continued, 'and Turkey has by degrees fallen into such a state of decrepitude that, as I told you the other night, eager as we are for the prolonged existence of the man, he may suddenly die upon our hands. We cannot resuscitate what is dead.' And once more Nicholas urged that the two countries draw up contingency plans in the event that Turkey crash. Such planning was essential, he argued, to avoid incurring 'the chaos, confusion and the certainty of a European war, all of which must attend the catastrophe if it should occur unexpectedly'.

'Your Majesty no doubt realizes,' replied Seymour, 'that my government is habitually disinclined to taking engagements upon possible eventualities. I would imagine this especially to be applicable to the idea of disposing by anticipation, so to speak, of an old friend and ally.'

The dialogue continued, the tsar all the while arguing for a bilateral agreement on the Ottoman empire. Finally, growing impatient, he declared: 'Now, I desire to speak to you as a friend and as a gentleman. I tell you plainly that if England thinks of establishing herself one of these days in Constantinople, I will not allow it.' For his part, Nicholas undertook likewise not to establish himself there, 'as proprietor, this is'. Then he added, 'As occupier I do not say. It might happen that circumstances, if no previous provision were made, if everything else should be left to chance, might place me in a position of occupying Constantinople.'

Seymour dispatched to London a full report of this latest conversation, which Lord Russell studied and then promptly wrote back: 'In the first place, no actual crisis has occurred which renders necessary a solution of this vast European question.' Furthermore, the dissolution of Turkey, over which the tsar shows such concern, 'is not definitely fixed in a point of time . . . [it] may happen twenty, fifty or a hundred years hence.'

'Under the circumstances,' Russell concluded, 'and especially in view of the friendly feelings toward Abdul Mejid, which both Nicholas and Victoria share, it would hardly be consistent at this moment to chart a disposition of the Sultan's dominions. It might further be noted that an agreement made in such a case tends very surely to hasten the contingency for which it is intended to provide.' The British government categorically renounced any intention of taking Constantinople and reiterated full assurance that should Turkey fall nothing would be done without communicating with the emperor. Russell urged that 'the utmost forbearance should be manifest towards Turkey' and that 'military and naval demonstrations to coerce the Sultan should, as much as possible, be avoided'.

In his letter, the foreign minister also warned that the sultan should be advised to treat his Christian subjects according to the principles of religious freedom 'which prevail generally among the enlightened nations of Europe'. The more impartiality and equality the sultan shows to the Orthodox minority 'the less will the Emperor of Russia find it necessary to apply that exceptional protection which His Imperial Majesty has found so burdensome and inconvenient, though, no doubt, prescribed by duty and sanctioned by treaty'.

'Prescribed by duty and sanctioned by treaty.' What a singularly unfortunate admission that was. Eventually 40,000 Englishmen would lay down their lives fighting for the strenuous denial of the tsar's right upon the protection to which Lord Russell here candidly agreed.

On 20 February, the Grand Duchess Hereditary held a soirée. The emperor was there and so was the British ambassador and predictably, they once more engaged in conversation. 'Well,' said the tsar to Seymour, 'so you have got your answer and are to bring it to me tomorrow?'

'I am to have that honour, sir,' answered the envoy, 'but your Majesty is aware that the nature of the reply is very exactly what I had led you to expect.'

'If your government has been led to believe that Turkey retains any elements of existence, your government must have received incorrect information.' Nicholas insisted. 'I repeat to you, that the sick man is dying and we cannot allow such an event to take us by surprise.'

The emperor paused in reflection and then announced pathetically, 'If I could hold but ten minutes conversation with your ministers – with Lord Aberdeen, for instance, who knows me so well, who has full confidence in me, as I have in him . . . I do not ask for a treaty or a protocol . . . a general understanding is all I require – that between gentlemen is sufficient . . .' The brief exchange was ended with the tsar announcing, 'No more for the present . . . you will come to me tomorrow.'

On the following day, Sir Hamilton did call at the Winter Palace where he met with the emperor in his study. He read Russell's dispatch to the tsar, following which the most significant of the 'Seymour conversations' took place. Nicholas emphasized that what he desired most was Britain's 'declaration or opinion as to what ought to be permitted in the event of the sudden downfall of Turkey'.

'Perhaps Your Majesty would be good enough,' countered Seymour, 'to explain your own ideas upon this negative policy.'

'Well, there are several things which I never will tolerate: I will not tolerate the permanent occupation of Constantinople by the Russians . . . [or] by the English, or French, or any other great nation. Again, I never will permit an attempt at the reconstruction of a Byzantine Empire . . . still less will I permit the breaking up of Turkey into little republics, asylums for the Kossuths and Mazzinis and other revolutionaries of Europe. Rather than to submit to these arrangements I would go to war, and as long as I have a man and a musket left I would carry it on. These are at once some ideas. Now give me some in return.'

'Well, sir, how would it be if, in the event of any catastrophe occurring in Turkey, Russia and England were to declare that no power should be allowed to take possession of its provinces. That the property should remain, as it were, under seals, until amicable arrangements could be made as to its adjudication?'

Nicholas disallowed such a proposal, arguing that in the absence of provincial governments within the Ottoman territories, Turkey would become plunged into internal strife, lawlessness and 'in short, chaos and anarchy'. The subject then turned to the other powers, France foremost. What the French thought, declared Nicholas did not matter in the least so long as Britain and Russia were in accord. And Austria?

'Oh!' replied the emperor much to Seymour's surprise, 'but you must understand that when I speak of Russia, I speak of Austria as well. What suits one, suits the other. Our interests as regards Turkey are perfectly identical.'

The tsar went on to emphasize that his policy towards the Turks was one of moderation. The military demonstration he had ordered was simply 'a show of force to prove I have no intention of being trifled with.' And then, Nicholas quite openly outlined his proposal for the disposition of Turkish territories whenever the Ottoman empire was dissolved.

'The Principalities[13] are, in fact, an independent state under my protection – this might so continue. Serbia might receive the same form of government. So again with Bulgaria: there seems to be no reason why this province should not form an independent state. As to Egypt, I quite understand the importance to England of that territory. I can only say that if, in the event of a distribution of the Ottoman succession upon the fall of the empire, you should take possession of Egypt, I shall have no objection to offer. I would say the same thing to Candia [Crete]: that island might suit you, and I do not know why it should not become an English possession.'

In conclusion, the tsar informed Seymour that he was satisfied with Russell's memorandum, but that he hoped it might be 'amplified'. 'Induce your government to write again upon these subjects – to write more fully and to do so without hesitation. I have every confidence in the English Government.'

This brought to an end the four remarkable conversations the tsar had with her majesty's representative in St Petersburg. Seymour now became more convinced than ever that Nicholas was 'an intriguing hypocrite', whose primary ambitions were to precipitate the collapse of Turkey and to drive a wedge between England and France. In his dispatches to London, Seymour accused Nicholas of being 'intentionally inexplicit' as to the possibility of 'a temporary occupation' of Constantinople.

Downing Street, however, was considerably less suspicious of the emperor's overtures. In a formal letter to the tsar, the government accepted the emperor's assurances that he would not take possession of Turkish territories. In turn, it was promised that Britain would likewise desist from any such move. The note reiterated that the Ottomans were not so moribund as to require Britain to enter any sort of secret agreement with Russia. Russell clearly and definitively rejected any further discussion concerning the demise of Turkey.

At the time of this diplomatic exchange Lord John Russell was the foreign minister, an office he held with little enthusiasm. As leader of the house, Lord John was primarily interested with parliamentary reform. Energy-consuming concerns such as those of Constantinople were not of immediate concern to the septuagenarian. His relations with Aberdeen, furthermore, were strained and he longed to regain the premier's office. It is more than probable that Seymour's dispatches from St Petersburg did not receive the close consideration they deserved. It was said, 'A golden opportunity of settling the Eastern question by arrangement with Russia was thus lost at the beginning of 1853; that however unacceptable the specific propositions of the tsar might have been, on no account should the chance of our understanding with Russia have been allowed to slip away.'

In understanding the actions of the cabinet, it is important to note that, during the period in question, Britain suffered from a series of fractious governments. Whigs versus Tories; ministers' jealousies, distrust and resentments of one another; lobbying for positions – all this was the prevailing order of the day. During the twenty-year period, 1834–54, there were seven changes of government, with eight changes of prime minister. Three of them also at one time or another served as foreign secretary, Russell and Clarendon, twice. Had there been in the chair one determined prime minister with a strong, cohesive cabinet the events leading to the war might well have been otherwise.

While Russia and Britain exchanged views, the Turks and

the Montenegrins exchanged gunfire. The calls from the rebellious Montenegrins for Russian assistance went unheeded. The Turks nevertheless were having little success in subduing these rebels. At last Austria, whose armies were massed on the Ottoman frontiers, determined to bring the matter to an end. Francis Joseph dispatched Count Leiningen to the Porte with instructions to demand the immediate withdrawal of the sultan's troops from the beleaguered territory. If within ten days the ultimatum was not accepted, Austria would summarily mobilize for war.

The Turkish ministers were well aware of Russia's pledge to support any Austrian action. Without further deliberation they hastily acceded to Leiningen's demands and a withdrawal from Montenegro was ordered. Austria prevailed and Francis Joseph expressed 'his deep gratitude' to the tsar for the good offer of assistance he had given. As in 1848, Austria and Russia again acted in concert. Nicholas was so well pleased that he conferred on the Austrian foreign minister the insignia in diamonds of the Order of St Alexander.

No doubt about it: Austria had sent a powerful spokesman to Constantinople and he had succeeded in his mission. Nicholas determined to follow suit, for more than ever now he 'felt the necessity of speaking to these wretched Turks with firmness'. He too would gain his way by sending an extraordinary mission to the Porte. 'The emperor,' wrote Nesselrode, 'is very irritated with the sultan and thinks it necessary to intimidate him to avoid being obliged later to come seriously and actually to war, which according to him must at all cost be avoided.' And to head this important assignment, the emperor appointed Prince Alexandre Sergeyevich Menshikov.

The envoy's instructions were straightforward: he was to regain for Orthodoxy the position it held in the Holy Land before February 1852, including repossession of the lost shrines. Full privileges, furthermore, were to be accorded to Orthodox Christians throughout the Ottoman empire. Most importantly, Russia's right to protect these Christians must receive the sultan's confirmation by the signing of a *sened*, or convention. Lastly, should France in any way interfere with these arrangements, a secret defensive agreement was to be signed between St Petersburg and the Porte.

If within three days demands were not met, the prince was to leave Constantinople. He was ordered, furthermore, 'not to deny but to confirm [rumours] of military preparations'. The 'wretched Turks' would indeed be spoken to with firmness.

The tsar's choice of Menshikov to head this delicate mission was singularly unfortunate, perhaps fatal. Through ineptitude and outright bungling, the prince helped Europe in taking a giant step closer to the catastrophe of Crimea. What prompted the emperor to select this man for such a crucial assignment, when so many thoroughly capable and knowledgeable diplomats were available, is a puzzle which has long disturbed historians.

'The man who shone so brilliantly in the drawing rooms of St Petersburg possessed neither the frankness nor the liberality . . . nor even the knowledge required to carry weighty diplomatic negotiations through to a successful issue,' observes Professor Grünwald. As Head of the Admiralty, Menshikov for twenty years annoyed seamen with his total ignorance of naval matters. Concurrently, as governor-general of Finland, he displayed a complete lack of interest in Finnish affairs, 'even in the capacity of a tourist'. He was 'very gentlemanlike and agreeable, but of trenchant wit and liking to make jokes *et donner le change* upon serious matters,' wrote Clarendon to Stratford. 'That is the wittiest man in Russia,' Meyendroff comments, 'great talent for witty remarks, but a negligible mind and dubious character.'

'It was understood that he held the Turks in contempt,' writes Kinglake, 'and it was also said that he entertained a strong contempt for the English. He had not been schooled in diplomacy, but he was to be entrusted with the power of using a threatening tone, and was to be supported by a fleet held in readiness, and by bodies of troops impending upon the Turkish frontiers. The Emperor Nicholas seems to have thought that harsh words and a display of force might be made to supply want of skill.' All said, the prince was nevertheless a favourite of the tsar.

The broad instructions which the newly appointed envoy carried away from St Petersburg were drawn up personally by Nicholas. Chancellor Nesselrode was not consulted, and Menshikov did not bother to call on him before quitting the capital. 'Menshikov understood that the emperor planned on war with Turkey alone, and not with Europe, and he unhesitatingly decided to bring about expeditiously the tsar's secret wish,' charges the Soviet historian, E.V. Tarlye. 'The prince had no doubt that Turkey in this duel, on a one-to-one basis with Russia, would be totally demolished. Since he was not in the least interested in the diplomatic exchanges which had taken place to date, he did not concern himself with them. Prior to his departure he merely acquainted himself with the names of the Turkish ministers who backed France, with the view of securing their immediate dismissal. With Sultan Abdul Mejid the prince determined not to stand on ceremony.'

On 28 February, the sixty-gun corvette, appropriately named *Thunderer*, sailed into the Bosphorus bearing the Prince Governor of Finland, aide-de-camp to the Emperor of All the Russias, together with his suite. Nearly a week had passed since the tsar's last interview with Seymour. Menshikov came ashore in grand style and was escorted to the palace of the Russian Embassy by a crowd of enthusiastic, cheering Greek Christians. It was obvious that the Russian agents, sent out earlier for the purpose, had prepared the ground well.

On the following day a glittering array of Russian officers arrived on another special steamer, among whom was Vice-Admiral Kornilov, Commander-in-Chief of the Black Sea Fleet. News spread through the city that the Russian cavalry was close to the Moldavian frontier and that the Sevastopol squadron was preparing to sail at short notice. Menshikov sent his credentials and haughtily requested that the grand vizier welcome him at the gate of the Porte. This unprecedented demand was indignantly refused.

On 2 March, accompanied by his entire suite, Menshikov entered the Porte to pay a ceremonial visit to Grand Vizier Mehemed Ali, the sultan's brother-in-law. Strict rules of protocol called for the ambassador first to present himself to the foreign minister, Faud Effendi, who would then escort the emissary to the grand vizier. Although Faud was one of the ablest members of the government, in Russian eyes he was 'guilty of perfidy', directly responsible for the Orthodox losses in the Holy Land. Menshikov would have nothing to do with the foreign minister. He arrogantly strode past the open doors of Faud's office and made his own way to the grand vizier. The high insult was intolerable and by the end of the day Faud had tendered his resignation.

The doors of the grand vizier's chambers were thrown open and the prince marched in with his entourage. An audible gasp of astonishment issued from the vizier's court – the Russian envoy had neglected to dress in the customary regalia of an ambassador's uniform, instead of which he wore a plain civilian frock coat and carried a top hat. An affront of this magnitude was palpable, but Mehemed Ali contained his anger admirably for the duration of what must have been a taxing ceremonial visit.

News of the day's events was quick to circulate. The Greek community was elated, the Turks were terrified, and the foreign embassies were alarmed. At the British and French embassies, both ambassadors were away on leave and not due to return until early April. Alarmed by Menshikov's actions and attitude, the chargés d'affaires, Colonel Hugh Rose and Viscount Benedetti came together and decided to call for the support of an Anglo-French fleet to Constantinople. Colonel Rose informed the sultan of the decision and the Turks were greatly reassured. Benedetti – who, in 1870, was to play a significant role in the events leading to the Franco-Prussian War – telegraphed Paris, while Rose sent a message to Malta ordering Admiral Dundas to dispatch a squadron to the Bosphorus. Dundas hesitated and referred the request to London. Downing Street refused compliance and rescinded Rose's order. The French government, however, acted with alacrity and a squadron of the Mediterranean fleet was ordered to Salamis.

When news of the French fleet movement reached London, Clarendon, newly replacing Russell as foreign secretary, urged France immediately to recall the ships. 'A policy of suspicion was neither wise nor safe,' he informed Walewski, Napoleon's ambassador to the Court of St James. He went on to explain that the British government fully trusted the tsar from whom it 'often had received the most solemn assurances that it was both his interest and his intention to uphold the Turkish Empire and that if any change in policy was contemplated by Nicholas, the intention would be communicated without hesitation or reserve'. Walewski's determined urgings that Britain join in a demonstration of strength went unheeded. A note was sent to the Russian emperor in which a full explanation of the 'Rose incident' was offered, together with expressions of regret for the misunderstanding.

The emperor was more than pleased with Aberdeen's disavowal of Rose and with Britain's refusal to support France. Nicholas expressed 'warm approbation' and official thanks were sent to London. Full assurances were reiterated that Menshikov had no secret agenda at Constantinople and that questions relating to the Orthodox Church were Russia's sole grievance with Turkey. 'We did quite right in showing confidence in the pledged word of the Emperor of Russia,' Clarendon subsequently declared.

On 16 March, Menshikov met with the newly-appointed foreign minister, Rifaat Pasha, and he submitted his proposals – more correctly, his demands. Agreement must be had over the Greek rights in the Holy Land. An 'arrangement' was to be made by which the Russian emperor would receive firm guarantee of a protectorate over all the sultan's Orthodox subjects. To this end a *sened* had to be signed to 'attest to the sincerity of the understanding,' according to a draft which he planned to submit.

Some days later, the prince presented his proposed draft of the *sened*, which was received by the Turkish government with consternation. News by then had been received of Britain's refusal to send its fleet, thus further complicating the equation. Pasha pleaded with Menshikov to withdraw the stipulations of the proposed convention and he assured the Russian that all might be arranged amicably without a *sened*. He requested time to formulate matters more clearly. Menshikov was sufficiently impressed with the sincerity of the protests that he agreed to delay in bringing matters to a head – and this, as will be seen, was a grievous and naive error.

*   *   *

It has been said that the Crimean War has the distinction of having taken longer to be declared than any war in modern times. In the diplomatic exchanges which finally led to the declarations, none were as significant as those which took place in the final days of March, 1853.

While Menshikov carried on initial negotiations with the Turks, Stratford Canning was making his leisurely way back to Constantinople to resume his post as Her Britannic Majesty's Ambassador to the Sublime Porte. On 24 March, during a brief stop-over in Vienna, Stratford was received by the Austrian emperor. Francis Joseph assured the Englishman that Austria had no intention of compromising the sultan's territorial integrity. He went on further to emphasize that there was no understanding to the contrary with Russia; Austria had nothing but goodwill towards the Porte.

As these events were unfolding, Napoleon III was developing increasing restlessness. In the first months of 1853, France had stood alone in Europe. Austria was apparently in accord with Russia and Prussia went along with Austria. Britain not only gave every indication of benevolent toleration of the tsar's Eastern policy, but also appeared to support him. Come what may, Napoleon now determined to detach Britain from her concert with Russia. Insofar as he was concerned, if a balance of power were to be had, it could only be through a formal entente between France and Britain.

On 22 March, a declaration was issued by Quai d'Orsay, in which general notice was given that the government of France considered the question of Turkey to be a general European affair. 'In the event of a single Russian soldier crossing the Turkish frontier, France will consider herself released from any obligation imposed upon her by the treaties of 1815 [Congress of Vienna] and free in all respects to act as she thinks fit.' Any aggrandizement of Russian or Austrian Empires would be followed by an expansion of the French empire. And Napoleon made it no secret that he was looking north, at Belgium.

The Congress of Vienna had united Belgium with Holland purposely to create a strong state to guard the lower Rhine against France. In 1830, the Belgians successfully rebelled against the Dutch King William I, and established themselves as an independent state. Leopold of Saxe-Coburg-Gotha, a German prince and British subject, accepted the new throne and married the daughter of Louis Philippe. The future of the constitutional monarchy clearly depended on the attitude of France, through whose support the rebels won victory in the first place. In the two decades which followed the founding of the new kingdom, Belgian resentment against the French grew in direct proportion to the growth of French influence in the internal affairs of their tiny country.

By early 1853, Franco-Belgian relations had reached straining point. The little kingdom was now considering removing all French officers serving in its army. On 22 March, Monsieur de Bouteneval, Napoleon's minister in Brussels, called on Belgian Foreign Minister Monsieur Brouchère. The Frenchman brought with him a menacing message: an outbreak of hostilities in Turkey would signal a French invasion of Belgium.

King Leopold appealed to his niece, Queen Victoria. Initial reaction in Britain to the French threat was one of dismay and perplexity. It did not take long, however, to recover and to send the Belgians full assurance of British support in such threatened eventuality. France, however, continued to press her intentions. 'If Russia, in contempt of treaties, can violently seize Constantinople, other powers might also invade any other state which might be near him . . . the first step towards a dismemberment of Turkey inevitably would lead to the remodelling of the whole map of Europe.'

In Constantinople, Menshikov was pressing his demands on

the Turks; in Brussels, de Boutenval was rousing the Belgians; in Vienna, the Austrian emperor was reassuring Stratford Canning; and, in St Petersburg, Nicholas was growing more irritated and impatient with the British. It was so conspicuously obvious to the tsar that the demise of Turkey was at hand. So, why did not Britain respond to his proposals regarding the division of the Sultan's empire? On 22 March, Seymour, whose suspicions of Russia's Eastern intentions had been confirmed, now advised Aberdeen to oppose Nicholas.

When, finally, the tsar's proposals for the disposition of the Ottoman empire arrived in London they were received with mild surprise. While the proposition was being discussed by the cabinet, and before an answer could be made, France had declared her ominous intentions regarding Belgium.

On the day following de Boutenval's interview with Brouchère, Aberdeen enunciated Britain's policy regarding Turkey. The occupation of Constantinople by either Russia or Austria 'would be incompatible [for Britain] . . . and must be regarded as impossible.' Britain was going to stand by Turkey. The fall of the sultan was a remote contingency; Turkey was not about to crumble. Britain wished full cooperation with Russia in maintaining the Ottoman empire and, above all, it desired peace. Her majesty's government would 'uphold the Turkish Empire, from their conviction that no question can be agitated in the East without becoming a source of discord in the West'. Belgium must not be permitted to fall; Victoria's cousin would remain on the throne. 'The Belgian question' was the catalyst that changed the British attitude towards the 'Eastern question'.

Napoleon had played his hand masterfully – Britain's disengagement from Russia had been secured; the secret accord of 1844 was crumbling, and crumbling fast. 'In these uncertain times,' lamented Nesselrode, 'it is difficult to say what quarter at the end of a few days a government must look for its allies.' For Russia, the entire outlook had become completely changed within a matter of ten short days. Austria had apparently forsaken Münchengrätz and Britain had virtually broken her understanding with the tsar. Furthermore, Napoleon had scored a brilliant diplomatic victory by successfully drawing closer to Britain. All this was grave enough, but what St Petersburg was yet in no position to appreciate, was that Stratford Canning was speedily making his way back to Constantinople to resume his post – the situation would now become even more perilous.

On the morning of 5 April, HMS *Fury* dropped anchor in the Bosphorus. 'Long before noon the voyage and the turmoil of the reception were over, and, except that a corvette under the English flag lay at anchor in the Golden Horn, there was no seeming change in the outward world,' writes Kinglake. 'Yet all was changed. Lord Stratford de Redcliffe had entered once more the palace of the English Embassy.' The event spread a sense of safety at the Porte – and awe.

Menshikov's mission was now doomed to failure. 'He had to carry the affair by assault before Turkey's auxiliaries, France and England, could intervene with effect,' observed the neutral Dutch Ambassador, Baron Mollerus. 'He did not sufficiently perceive the opportunity offered by the absence of Lord Redcliffe [Stratford]. They ought to have told him that the Turks, feeble and timorous after Menshikov's arrival, would have granted an even more extensive demand than the *sened*. But, once aided by the advice of Lord Redcliffe, they would follow no impulse but his.'

Stratford brought with him clearly defined instructions from the cabinet. He was to warn Turkey that its government was 'in a position of peculiar danger'. The stability of the Ottoman empire was severely menaced – all through grossly inefficient internal administration and the accumulated grievances of her allies. Stratford was to convince the Turks 'that the crisis is one which requires the utmost prudence on their part, and confidence in the sincerity and soundness of the advice they will receive from you, to resolve it favourably for their future peace and independence'.

The instructions further provided, in the event of danger to the Turkish government, 'Your Excellency will in such case dispatch a messenger to Malta, requesting the admiral to hold himself in readiness, but you will not direct him to approach the Dardanelles without positive instructions from Her Majesty's Government.' In framing these orders, Prime Minister Derby obviously heeded Aberdeen's advice: 'Be very careful in preparing instructions for Canning.'

Stratford's specific order was intended to avoid a repetition of Parker's 1849 entry into the Straits. 'Lord Stratford was licensed to do no more than send a message to an admiral, advising him to be ready to go to sea; and, slight as this power was, he never exhausted it; yet, it will be seen, he so wielded the instructions which entrusted it to him as to be able to establish a great calm in the Divan at a moment when Prince Menshikov was violently pressuring upon its fears, with a fleet awaiting his orders, and an army of 140,000 men.'

Upon his arrival, Stratford was apprised of the Russian demands. As he saw it, there were two distinctly separate areas of conflict. The first problem was the ongoing tiresome issues concerning the holy places. Would the Greeks or the Latins have precedence at the Shrine of the Blessed Virgin? Of what nationality should the doorkeeper be at that Shrine? To whom would belong the privilege of repairing the cupola of the Church of the Holy Sepulchre?

The second and more critical problem was that of guarantees for the future. Would Russia be given exclusive protectorate over the sultan's Orthodox Christians? Should she have the right to make demands in matters concerning the Orthodox Church? 'The Treaty of Kutchuk-Kainardji,' noted Nesselrode, 'implicates for us sufficiently a right of surveillance and remonstrance. This right is again established, and more clearly specified in the [1829] Treaty of Adrianople . . . we have, therefore, in fact, and for nearly eighty years, the very rights conceded to us which are now contested.' This was the very 'exceptional protection' which Lord Russell had earlier allowed to Nicholas – Russia had legitimate rights as 'prescribed by duty and sanctioned by treaty'. For the Turks to acquiesce on this second matter, however, meant that the future loyalty of some 12 million of the sultan's Orthodox subjects might be seriously questioned.

Stratford counselled the Turkish foreign minister 'to open the door for negotiation' on the lesser issues and to withstand all pressures for a decision on the second, larger question. To delay on the question of protectorate and, if pressed, refuse it categorically. In such eventuality, asked Rifaat Pasha, would Britain give armed assistance to the Porte if so required? For the moment, Stratford maintained a silence.

With this, the grand *elchi* offered his services as mediator between Menshikov and the French ambassador de la Cour – surely the sensitive questions related to the holy places might be settled amicably, in a gentlemanly fashion? The three of them met and much to their own surprise and that of others, they unexpectedly reached quick agreement on questions related to the shrines. The Turks were apprised of this favourable outcome, and on 3 May a *firman* was signed by which the dispute was formally settled. Russia had quite suddenly regained its claimed Holy Land privileges and Menshikov warmly thanked Lord Stratford for his good services.

The Prince Governor of Finland, pleased as he was with the

outcome of the holy places negotiations, however, was not finished. Within two days, he made his final demands – guarantees for the future must be had. In the past *firmans* were signed and readily broken. Menshikov now wanted a *sened*, or convention, by which, 'The *firman* respecting the holy places shall have the force of a formal agreement made with the Imperial Government.' The Greek Church must receive unconditional guarantee of full rights and immunities throughout the Ottoman empire. And Russia's right to protect the Orthodox subjects must be firmly recognized by the sultan, once and for all.

Rifaat received these latest demands with some trepidation and he lost little time in apprising Stratford of the situation. On the following day, the grand *elchi* sought an audience with the sultan to discuss the situation. Abdul Mejid's ministers, it seemed, were inclined to follow Stratford's earlier advice and it only remained for a firm decision to be taken as to whether to refuse the Russians categorically or not. 'My own impression is that, if Your Majesty should sanction that decision,' Stratford argued, 'Menshikov will probably break off his relations with the Porte and go away, together perhaps with the whole embassy. Nor is it quite impossible even that a temporary occupation, however unjust, of the Danubian Principalities by Russia may take place. But I feel that neither a declaration of war, nor any other act of open hostility, is to be apprehended for the present.'

Then in a most impressive tone of confidentiality, Stratford gravely announced to the sultan, 'In the event of imminent danger, I was instructed to request the Commander of Her Majesty's forces in the Mediterranean to hold his squadron in readiness.'

'The order in itself was a slight thing,' comments Kinglake, 'and it conferred but a narrow and stinted authority. But imparted to the Sultan in private audience by Lord Stratford de Redcliffe, it came with more weight than the promise of armed support from the lips of a common statesman.' Abdul Mejid could not have been more pleased with the outcome of the interview.

On the following day the Turkish government formally and firmly rejected Menshikov's demands – which action provoked in him a furious rage. He refused to accept the note as an answer to his demands, and threatened that unless the conditions were met within three days, he would consider his mission ended. A satisfactory reply must reach the Russian embassy by the 14th, or he would return to St Petersburg. All responsibility for the consequence of such a departure would be thrown on the shoulders of the sultan's ministers.

On the 13th, there was another cabinet shuffle at the Porte and Reschid Pasha became foreign minister, while Rifaat was appointed president of the council. Menshikov now placed his hopes on Reschid, 'in view of his enlightened opinion and pacific leanings'. The prince, however, again misjudged – the new government was no less inclined towards favouring Russia.

On the 14th, Reschid met with Stratford and together they drafted a note to the Russian embassy requesting a few days' delay for a response. On the 15th, Stratford went to the sultan and persuaded him to authorize the uninterrupted passage of British warships through the Straits. And on the 17th, the military governor of the Dardanelles region was instructed to allow the passage of two French warships through the waterway. That same evening an extraordinary meeting of the Grand Council was convened to render an opinion on the Russian demands. This was an assembly of the empire's most distinguished statesmen that included all the cabinet ministers, former ministers, governors and jurists of the realm. It reflected perhaps as true a representation of national feeling as was possible at the time. Turkey, it was argued, had already once submitted to the humiliating demands of another power – those of Austria. Would there now be a repeat? When the vote was taken, 42 of the 45 voices sided against Russia; Turkey would stand firm this time.

On the following afternoon, Reschid called on Menshikov. In a conciliatory tone, he assured the Russian that Turkey was highly desirous of a peaceful settlement of all issues and he presented a final proposal. No changes would ever be made respecting the status of the holy places without Russia's full concurrence, he stated. A *firman* guaranteeing the right of Ottoman Orthodox Christians would be issued. Finally, Reschid offered a *sened* which would provide space in Jerusalem for the construction of a Russian church and a hospice for pilgrims. The foreign minister's desperate overtures offered Russia virtually everything the prince demanded and more – everything that is, except a confirmation of the protectorate over the Orthodox Christians. In reacting to Reschid's proposal, Menshikov replied – as he himself later reported – with 'a dry and categorical refusal, expressed in the strongest terms'. For the Prince Governor of Finland, it was all or nothing. As a last grasp at the straw, he allowed the Porte three days to reverse its decision.

While the two men conferred, Lord Stratford de Redcliffe was ensconced on his *kaika*, leisurely relaxing on the Bosphorus. He had met with Reschid earlier that day and now he awaited the Turk's return with the latest news.

An angered Menshikov returned to the palace of the embassy and ordered the removal of the Russian flag. His mission was over and he was quitting 'this wretched city'. Records and archives were crated and stowed on board the *Thunderer* and the embassy's personnel were ordered to follow – only the commercial attaché was to remain behind. On the 18th, Menshikov instructed the captain to sail out of the harbour. At its outer reaches, he had the ship drop anchor and there, in the isolation of the still waters, he waited a full three days, all the time expecting a further word from the Turks. But all was silent, and he heard nothing. And so, in the early afternoon of 21 May, the *Thunderer* weighed anchor and set sail for home. By sunset, it had lost sight of land and had become but a mere speck on the horizon.

8

WAR FEVER RISES

Menshikov departed Constantinople; Stratford remained. In a dispatch to the tsar, the Russian envoy complained vociferously of 'the causes of his discomfiture and of the evil skill of that anti-Christ, in stately English form whom heaven was permitting for a while to triumph over the tsar and his Church'.

Before Stratford's return to Constantinople, the Turks had been vacillating and filled with apprehension. Within the forty-five days that followed, they had acquired confidence and resolution – all through the efforts of the Englishman; the *elchi*'s sway over the Porte was undisputed. Stratford had successfully brought to a close the volatile issue of the holy places, and in the process he had blocked Russia's efforts to impose its influence over the Ottomans.

Earlier that year, the dissolution of the Turkish empire had been a fair subject for speculation in continental capitals. But now Europe stood in admiration of the Ottomans, particularly over the moderation and forbearance which they had shown in dealing with the Russians. Tsar Nicholas had long been looked upon with universal awe, an emperor of fabulous power, with high regard for the sovereignty of others. Now, however, 'He stood before the world shorn bare of all his moral strength.'

When news of Menshikov's failure at the Porte reached St Petersburg, the imperial rage knew no bounds. The envoy's failure in Constantinople was entirely due to the machinations of the insufferable Stratford who, it seems, was the de facto government at the Porte. 'I feel the five fingers of the sultan on my face,' cried Nicholas. Not only was his personal envoy outdone by that ignominious Stratford, but now that same scoundrel was exercising 'a protectorate of all the churches in Turkey, including the very church of him the Tsar, him the Father, him the Pontiff of Eastern Christendom'. As Kinglake writes, 'Nicholas was wrought into such a condition of mind that his fury broke away from the restraints of even the very pride which begat it.'

Ten days after Menshikov quit Constantinople, Chancellor Nesselrode wrote to Reschid Pasha, solemnly warning him that if Russia's demands were not fully met, the sultan would suffer dire consequences. If within eight days an affirmative acknowledgement from the Porte was not had, Russian forces would cross the Turkish frontier in order to obtain 'by force, but without war' what the sultan refused to surrender voluntarily.

Within weeks, the situation on the Dardanelles had changed dramatically, and the great powers had become inexorably drawn into it. In Britain, the cabinet found itself being pulled into a defensive alliance with Turkey. Prime Minister Aberdeen continued to profess peace, but he did not advocate neutrality nor renounce a defensive treaty with the sultan. Time and again, however, he approved the dispatches which

arrived almost daily from Stratford. Taken singly, the documents appeared wise, temperate and deserving of approval,
but, as Kinglake points out, 'If a statesman goes on approving
and approving one by one a long series of papers of this sort,
without rousing himself to the effort of taking a broader view
of the transactions which he has separately examined, he may
find himself entangled in a course of action which he never
intended to adopt.'

While the prime minister passively approved, the foreign
minister aggressively urged. Writing to Stratford, Clarendon
warned that it was 'indispensable to take measures for the
protection of the sultan and to aid His Highness in repelling
any attack that might be made upon his territory . . . the use of
force was to be resorted to as the last and unavoidable resource
for the protection of Turkey against an unprovoked attack,
and in defence of her independence which England . . . was
bound to maintain.'

Bound or not bound – could Britain still have averted war?
'At that time,' writes Walpole, 'there were two courses by
which peace might in all probability have been preserved. The
Ministry might have said to the Porte, "If war ensues, England
will be no party to it." Such language, used plainly and
without reservation, would probably have forced the sultan
to make terms with Russia. Or, again, it might have said to the
tsar, "If war ensues, England will at once range herself as
Turkey's ally." Such language would, in all probability, have
induced the emperor to pause.' Had Prime Minister Aberdeen
been strong enough to issue a final word, the first course
would have been taken. Had Foreign Minister Clarendon
prevailed, the second possibility would have followed. In its
lamentable division, however, the coalition government could
not agree on an action. 'While the ship of state was drifting
without clear direction,' Walpole concludes, 'the tiller was

grasped by Lord Stratford, and the vessel steered into the whirlpool of war.'

In the meantime, St Petersburg waited impatiently for the Turkish reply to Nesselrode's letter. But then, with eight days lapsed and only silence from Constantinople, the tsar's patience ran out and he determined at last to act. On 3 July, he issued a manifesto: 'By the grace of God, we, Nicholas I, Emperor and Autocrat of all the Russias, make known to our faithful and well-beloved subjects, that from time immemorial our glorious predecessors took the vow to defend the Orthodox faith . . . now, having exhausted all means of persuasion and all means in obtaining in a friendly manner the satisfaction due to our just reclamations, we have deemed it indispensable to order our troops to enter the Danube Principalities [Moldavia and Wallachia], to show the Porte how far its obstinacy may lead it . . . we do not seek conquest: Russia does not need them. We demand satisfaction for a legitimate right openly infringed.'

By pre-arrangement General Gorchakov had on the previous day marched 60,000 Russian troops across the Pruth River into the Principalities and quickly, without incident, the Russians firmly established themselves on the edge of these territories.

The political situation of the Moldavia and Wallachia were a peculiar anomaly. The provinces were under the sovereignty of the Porte, but under the protection of Russia. Each province was governed by a *hospodar* appointed by the sultan, yet the sultan was denied the right of interference with their internal affairs. Turkish soldiers were forbidden entry into the provinces, but an armed tribute was extracted from the 2,300,000 inhabitants and sent to Constantinople. In the event of internal strife that might threaten the stability of the governments, Russia was empowered to intervene with the restoration of order. (In 1848, the Russian forces did precisely that and successfully suppressed revolutions in both provinces.)

With the arrival of the Russian armies, the *hospodar*s were ordered by Gorchakov to continue their civil duties, but henceforth they would be answerable to him. The annual tribute was henceforth to be delivered to the imperial treasury in St Petersburg and matters would thus stand until 'the occupation of the land' had been terminated.

By occupying the Principalities and pledging to hold them until his demands were fully met, Nicholas imagined that he was taking a middle course. The move was designed neither to cause war nor to secure peace – eventually, he reasoned, it would bring the desired results. It is clear that fundamentally Nicholas did not wish war. 'It is easy to bring war, but how to end it? God alone knows,' he wrote after Menshikov's return to the capital. The emperor was convinced that the ever-increasing internal difficulties besetting the Ottoman empire would soon cause its demise – in implosion, as it were. His display of force in the Principalities would merely hasten the process along, and Turkey would inevitably yield to the pressure.

Contingency plans were made however – in the event that the occupation of the Principalities failed to move the Turk, Russia would enforce a blockade of the Bosphorus and re-cognize the independence of the Principalities. If the sultan persisted in his obstinacy – then a recognition of Serbia's independence. 'You will see, everything will come out all right,' Nicholas assured Castelbajac, the French minister in St Petersburg.

Meanwhile in Constantinople, the agitated Turks were soothed by Stratford. The invasion of Ottoman territory was unquestionably an act of war, he declared. However, he went on to counsel, the sultan was not obliged to consider it such and for the moment he would be wise to hold back. The Porte was ill-prepared for war and public opinion in Western Europe was not yet wholly in sympathy with the Porte. By taking the middle course, he pointed out, the tsar was enabling Turkey to select its own time for the commencement of hostilities, if such were to be had – and which now seemed inevitable to everyone but the Russian emperor.

Nicholas was convinced that neither Austria nor Britain would oppose him. The Hapsburgs owed him much for his support in dealing with the rebellious Hungarians and Montenegrins; they would stand by Münchengrätz and not impede him. There was no doubt in the tsar's mind of Francis Joseph's support, and he was certain that should the occasion arise, the Austrians would occupy the Turkish protectorates of Serbia and Herzegovinia. As for Britain, the tsar truly believed that Russia had no conflict – Britain, after all, was his partner in the 1844 accord. In Britain, furthermore, the government was the people, the people cherished prosperity, and prosperity came by avoiding wars. In addition, Aberdeen was a vocal exponent of peace, who on more than one occasion had declared that no war would be undertaken without his personal approval. Nicholas knew the prime minister in whom he held implicit trust. War with Britain would not be. Little wonder then that, when Nicholas received John Bright, the United States ambassador in St Petersburg, he confidently denied that 'the current disagreements between Russia and Turkey could possibly lead to actual hostilities'.

How could the tsar have so mistakenly assumed Britain's non-intervention – so erringly that in the first weeks of June, he was announcing, 'Everything will come out all right'? As late as mid-April, Downing Street stood in support of Russia – French overtures for joint action in pressuring Russia had been firmly rebuffed. 'Nicholas has practised no disguise whatever as to his intentions,' Clarendon declared to parliament. On 26 April, the first of Stratford's dispatches on the Russo-Turkish negotiations arrived. Thereafter, the dispatches were marked by increasing hostility and they warned of the tsar's sinister motives in demanding the protectorate over the Ottoman Orthodox. One report charged that Russia aimed at extensive and dangerous political advantages in Turkey. Another claimed that the guaranties which Menshikov sought for the future had nothing to do with religious matters.

As time passed, the British cabinet became increasingly alarmed over developments in the East. Opinions among the ministers varied as to what posture to assume. Aberdeen – 'our only friend,' wrote Brunov – desired peace at any price. As much as he admired the tsar, he looked with scorn on the sultan whom he judged incapable of reform. Recognizing the necessity, however, of ensuring Russian moderation, the prime minister proposed that the great powers exert a 'moral influence' on the Russian emperor. Palmerston took the other extreme: an occupation of the Principalities would be a *casus belli*, and he urged that the fleet be at once ordered to Constantinople and, if necessary, penetrate into the Black Sea. A 'moral influence', he countered, could be effective only with arms ready to enforce it. Clarendon took the middle position, one which was eventually adopted: encourage the great powers to act in concert in exerting diplomatic pressure on Russia – but at the same time send a squadron to the entrance of the Dardanelles.

While Stratford agitated and the cabinet debated, the press eagerly reported on the details of the unfolding situation, each morsel of which John Bull ravenously devoured. For two generations, Britain had known only peace, and news of the looming crisis in the East was sensational, in the truest sense of the word. The *Daily News* called for the immediate dispatch of the English fleet to the Dardanelles. *The Times* cried, 'To speak of maintaining Turkey's sovereignty without the risk of war was foolish ... we should either act or keep quiet.' The *Manchester Guardian* demanded firm action and spoke of the commercial significance of Turkey to British trade. All were in accord that the tsar's agitation in the East might well provide Napoleon with the pretext to invade Belgium.

Within weeks the volatile situation on the Dardanelles had changed – virtually reversed itself– with the great powers being no less affected by it. Britain and France, traditional enemies, now found themselves drawn into increasing intimacy. As of 3 June, the ambassadors of the two countries in Constantinople were receiving identical instructions. The commander of the French fleet in the Mediterranean, Admiral Hamelin, was sent orders to co-operate fully with Admiral Dundas, and subsequently the combined fleets were ordered to arrive together at Besika Bay, 'as proof of the understanding between the two governments'. In mid-June, formal announcements of mutual cooperation and support were made in the two capitals; the new alliance had become firmly cemented.The sultan's steadfastness was as much admired as the tsar's presumptuousness was decried. Eventually, Nicholas came to deride the British press: *'Les invectives des journaux anglais sont d'une insolence et d'une trivialité qui dépassent toute mesure.'* The confidence which Nicholas had at one time placed in the British government and in the English public had quite suddenly been shattered.

Three days after the Russian crossing of the Pruth, the allied fleets were ordered to Besika Bay at the mouth of the Dardanelles. The squadrons were instructed, 'Wait before entering the Dardanelles, until Russia shall have commenced hostilities ... and the Porte has declared that she considers herself in a state of war.' The object of the manoeuvre was solely to preserve the Ottoman empire.

'A formidable fleet [now] kept watch over a formidable army. Neither movement produced war, each brought it nearer. The real danger of troops or fleets taking up advanced stations is the difficulty of retiring from them with honour. Evacuation or retreat is a confession of failure,' observes Professor Temperley.

News of the allied fleet movements threw Nicholas into further anger. When further word was brought to him that the offending fleets were at Lord Stratford's disposal, the tsar, as Kinglake drily comments, was 'in the condition of the Psalmist, when he prayed to the Lord that his enemy might be confounded'.

That foreign fleets would dare anchor at the entrance to the Dardanelles and threaten to sail up the Bosphorus was a most awful threat to Russia's strategic interests and security. Any blockade of the Baltic or Black seas, observed the young journalist, Karl Marx, in a dispatch to the *New York Tribune* would be to render the empire 'a colossus without arms and without eyes'. Russia was now being threatened with a Cyclopean condition.

Nesselrode was instructed to explain to the capitals of Europe that it was precisely this intolerable act of hostility which prompted the tsar to occupy the Principalities. The Provinces were being held as a 'material guarantee' for the acceptance of the tsar's justified demands. The Russian action was one of mere coercion – it did not mean war. The assignment given the chancellor was quite impossible. How was he to explain that the Pruth was crossed three days before the allied fleet received its sailing orders?

In Constantinople, the sultan reviewed the situation with satisfaction. He had gratefully received Stratford's personal view that the invasion of the Principalities was indeed a *casus belli*. He was even more delighted to learn that Napoleon III shared the same opinion. At the entrance to the Dardanelles, there now was anchored a powerful Anglo-French fleet, and the ambassadors of the two countries were empowered to order it not only to Constantinople but even into the Black Sea itself. And further encouraging news reached the Porte – the Khedive of Egypt and the Bey of Tunis were sending support- ing armies. Future negotiations with the Russian emperor could now result only in a favourable outcome. 'It was hard to preach peace,' writes Temperley, 'when the flames of national and religious feeling turned so high, when Constan- tinople was safe and when reinforcements were coming up.'

In Paris, Napoleon took much satisfaction in the cementing of French relations with Britain, a diplomatic coup worthy of his illustrious name. He now pressed forward – war is what he wanted, for only a war could generate military glory. A success would not only brilliantly enhance his standing in European affairs, but it would impact significantly on internal policies. Victory over the Russians not only would vindicate his uncle's disastrous defeat, but would help deaden people's memories of his violation of the oath of 2 December 1851, and of the bloodshed that followed. Yes, he required a war.

In London the divided cabinet continued to debate. Coop- erate with the tsar, urged Aberdeen, and tread softly with orders to the Besika Bay fleets. 'Words may be properly answered by words,' countered Palmerston, 'but acts should be answered by acts!' Up the Bosphorus with the fleet!

Agreement was finally reached – with Palmerston dissenting – that the occupation of the Principalities did not constitute a *casus belli*. Brunov was so informed and Clarendon dispatched a letter to Nicholas, giving assurance that the allied fleet would not enter the Dardanelles so long as Constantinople was

unthreatened. In those same days, confidential information
filtered into the Russian embassy that Britain determined not
to engage in war as long as Francis Joseph remained bound to
Russia. Austria was the one power which could persuade the
tsar to quit the Principalities, and if full agreement on the
Eastern question was ever to be reached, it would likely come
by way of Vienna. 'The question of peace or war is now in her
hands,' declared Brunov.

For the moment, Austria stood on the sidelines, a silent
witness to the events unfolding perilously close to her frontier.
The potential of Francis Joseph as a mediator was not lost
upon the allies, despite the conflicting position in which the
young emperor found himself. On the one hand, the Hapsburg
emperor owed the security of his throne to Nicholas, whom he
admired openly as a bulwark of legitimism. On the other hand,
practically speaking, if Russia would become permanently
installed in the Principalities, she would gain control over
the mouth of the Danube, in which case Austrian commercial
interests with the East would be jeopardized. Additionally it
was asked, what might the future hold for the Orthodox
Christians within the Austrian empire, if the tsar successfully
gained protectorate over the Ottoman Orthodox? Might not
the tsar's influence over Austrian internal affairs become over-
powering?

Austria viewed Britain bi-focally. The bourgeois were
friendly and sympathetic towards Britain and they looked
with favour on the ever-increasing volume of trade with that
country. The influential feudal aristocracy, however, frowned
on England as the navel of liberalism and as the sanctuary of
the Kossuths of the world.

As for the French, Austria was for the moment uncertain.
Napoleon III, a vocal exponent of Italian nationalism, could
one day encourage a Sardinian move into the Hapsburg

provinces of Italy – an argument for nurturing friendly relations with France. On the other hand, in the eventuality of such an invasion, it would be distinctly advantageous to have the support of the Russian armies.

At last, all aspects of the delicate question having been minutely examined, Austria decided on her card. On 17 June, Count Meyendorff, the Russian ambassador in Vienna, was summoned to the Hofburg and informed by the country's foreign minister that Austrian policy towards the Ottoman empire was 'entirely united' with Britain. 'The maintenance of its independence and integrity [was regarded] as of the most importance to the best interests of Austria.' Count Buol, Francis Joseph's foreign minister, further informed Meyendorff that should Austria be 'called upon to carry out an armed intervention on the frontiers, it would be in support of the authority and independence of the sultan.'

And finally, Prussia. That country, 'hitherto supposed to be hardly capable of differing with the Emperor Nicholas', was dismayed by Menshikov's arrogant behaviour at the Porte and particularly by his demands. Following the announcement of the Hapsburg position on the Eastern question, the Prussian ambassador in Constantinople received instructions to 'unite cordially' with the envoys of Austria, France and Britain and to act in concert with them.

The tsar was shattered by the reaction of a now united Europe, and he was particularly upset with Austria's duplicity. He, the saviour of Francis Joseph's throne, had now been betrayed by him. With Turkish intransigence and the taking of sides by the great powers, the gathering war clouds now loomed more threatening. During his 1844 visit to England, Nicholas in looking to the future, asked Aberdeen, '. . . so many powder barrels close to the fire; how shall one prevent the sparks from catching?' Now, ten years later, the powder barrels were indeed close to the fire. If armed conflict was to be avoided, it could happen only through mediation. In his desperation, the tsar sent out signals that he was willing to consider any reasonable proposal. The allies – Britain, France, Austria and Prussia – picked up on this, and on 22 July their ambassadors in Vienna assembled to consider the apparent deadlock. It was chaired by Count Buol.

The Vienna conference faced a Herculean task – how to maintain peace and at the same time assure Turkey's independence – this, without loss of face to the tsar? The assembly deliberated for eight frenetic days and by the time it had all ended 'as much ink was spilled on the banks of the Danube as blood was later shed in Crimea'. At the end of it all, however, a vaguely worded formula was agreed upon, designed to give the Russians satisfaction in principle and seemingly without undue offence to the Turks. Basically, it consisted of a re-affirmation of the 1774 Treaty of Kuchuk-Kainardji, which had given Russia the protectorate over the Orthodox Church within the Ottoman empire. In addition, Turkey was to consult with Russia and France on any contemplated changes to the status quo of religious communities within the empire. The four powers agreed on the Vienna Note – as in fact did Nicholas with whom it had been secretly shared. The inherent flaw of the document, however, was the offence it would cause the Porte – hardly might the sultan be expected to agree to it without a loss of honour. But never mind, agreement had been reached and the tiresome issue seemed to have been put to bed.

At the same time that the four powers laboured in Vienna, the ambassadors of these same countries in Constantinople came up with their own solution to the difficulty, one that was significantly more reasonable than the eventual Vienna Note. It will be recalled that Reschid's final offer to Menshikov was that of a *firman* which would guarantee the rights of the

Ottoman Orthodox. Stratford and his colleagues now proposed that a copy of such a document be sent to the tsar 'together with a courteous note from the Porte to Count Nesselrode, assuring the chancellor that the *firman* confirmed the privileges of the Greek Church in perpetuity, and virtually, therefore, engaging that the grants should never be revoked.' The four ambassadors at the Porte would witness the signing of the document, thereby implicating the allied powers as guarantors to the pledge. Ostensibly, here was everything that the tsar desired.

Not without difficulty the ambassadors persuaded the sultan to accept the proposal, and the document – unfortunately called the 'Turkish Ultimatum' – was dispatched by courier to the Vienna conference for approval. It was delivered on the very day that the conferees had at last reached agreement and signed the Vienna Note – just a few hours too late. The fatigued and aggravated diplomats were in no mood to reopen discussions on the matter and the Constantinople solution was shelved. It is fair to say that had telegraph communication been available at the time, it is more than likely that the Vienna conferees would have endorsed the work of their Constantinople colleagues, and then the Crimean War might well have been averted.

Russia accepted the Vienna Note with alacrity, pure and simple. The *Moniteur* hastened to publish the news and in Vienna the triumphant Boul took credit for the splendid diplomatic achievement. Aberdeen, on receiving the happy tidings, wrote to Clarendon: 'The Emperor has accepted our Note, and is ready to receive the Turkish ambassador as soon as it has been accepted by the Porte. I think this settles the affair.'

Although Count Buol had achieved four-power agreement on the issue and had secretly received the tsar's approbation, he had failed to consult with the sultan. The Vienna Note reached the Turkish government on 12 August, together with news of its acceptance by Russia. London instructed Stratford to press the sultan for his assent: '[the note] fully guarded the principle which had been contended for, and might therefore with perfect safety be signed by the Porte . . . the allies of the sultan unanimously concurred in recommending for its adoption.'

Stratford did as instructed. 'I called the attention of Reschid Pasha,' the ambassador subsequently reported, 'to the strong and earnest manner which the four powers pressed for its acceptance . . . I repeatedly urged the importance of an immediate decision and the danger of declining or only accepting with amendments.'

The twelfth of August was not an auspicious day to pressure the sultan: 'On that day the Egyptian fleet arrived at Constantinople and gave an enormous assertion of strength to the war party. The white sails of Egypt's fleet crowded the Golden Hind, the green tents of her army dotted the hills of Asia. The Franco-British squadron though not within sight, was within call. Stambul [Constantinople] was safe.'

On due consideration of the note, the sultan announced that he was pleased to accept it – but on condition that three changes be made. Otherwise the proposal was unacceptable. In the global view, his requirements were minor and of little possible consequence, but they were nevertheless Turkish amendments. The changes, Clarendon later observed, 'neither are of vital importance nor give additional security'. News of the sultan's conditions electrified Vienna. So close had the statesmen come to what they perceived as a certainty of peace. Count Boul re-assembled the frustrated diplomats. 'Work began anew in the meticulous, fastidious and thankless task of comparing two nearly identical texts. Each word was scrutinized, every syllable weighed, all periods and commas discussed. Grammarians couldn't have done more. Then, when all was thoroughly sifted and microscopically examined, it was decided that the Turks possessed little political judgement, that their demands were impertinent and their corrections of text were valueless.'

Nicholas was asked to agree to the amendments, but the tsar had already come more than half way in accepting the original note, and he was in no mood to acquiesce further on anything. He indignantly and resolutely refused the new four-power request. The Vienna diplomats were stymied and their labours had come to naught. The note, it seemed, had run its course.

Why then did the sultan decline the Vienna Note? Professor Temperley reasons that for Turkey, 'The note emphasized rather obviously a sense of dependence and inferiority.' The earlier proposal which emanated from the ambassadors at the Porte, would have 'saved Turkey's face by making the Four Powers witness of her "spontaneous" promise to Russia'. Moreover, 'The secret, submission of the Vienna Note to the tsar beforehand also injured Turkish pride . . . Europe's diplomats did not understand Turkish psychology.' Perhaps, too, the sultan had simply had enough. He made his very final concession in the Ultimatum and that was that. No doubt the arrival of the Egyptian fleet to the Porte and the war fever gripping the capital also contributed to his intransigence.

'The real blame for the rejection of the Vienna Note,' claims Professor Schmitt, 'must be laid on the French ambassador. De la Cour advised the acceptance of the Note, but he helped draw up the Turkish amendments.' There is no doubt de la Cour stoked the fires, even by such seemingly innocent enquiries as to 'landing troops on the coasts of Turkey, and . . . whether the Porte considered the Dardanelles as already open to the passage of the allied squadrons'.

But to Nicholas and many in the British cabinet, it was Stratford who bore the blame for the failures of diplomatic intervention. It was known that he personally did not approve of the Note. 'The governments of all the four powers, and their representatives assembled in Vienna, fondly imagined that they could settle the dispute and restore tranquillity to Europe without consulting Lord Stratford de Redcliffe,' Kinglake comments. 'It was plain that any statesman who forgot him in their reckoning must have been imperfect in their notion of political dynamics.' Consider the following correspondence:

Sir James Graham, MP, to Clarendon (16 August)
Stratford is hardening himself to resist the proposed Note from Vienna . . . Notwithstanding the peremptory note to the contrary. He is quite capable of advising the Turks to be refractory . . .

Aberdeen to Clarendon (19 August)
I fear Stratford intends to give us some trouble . . .

Aberdeen to Clarendon (20 August)
I have prepared the Queen for the possibility of Stratford's resignation, which I agree with you in thinking is by no means improbable . . .

Clarendon to Russell (25 August)
I have felt all along that Stratford would allow of no plan of settlement that did not originate with himself . . .

Lord Cowley to Clarendon (29 August)
You must not show me up, but de la Cour says he has no doubt that Lord Stratford's strange conduct, as he calls it, has had much to do with the attitude taken by the Porte. Publicly and officially, he adds, Lord Stratford has obeyed his instructions and called upon the Ottoman government to accept the Vienna Note; but he lets it be seen at the same time that his private opinion is at variance with his official

language, and he does not bring that personal influence to bear which would have been so useful at the present moment. De la Cour asserts further that, to his intimates, Lord Stratford uses the most violent language, that he disapproves all the proceedings at Vienna, declares war preferable to such a solution, that the position of Turkey was excellent, etc.

Graham to Clarendon (3 September)

I hope you will not allow Europe to be involved in war because Canning thinks that he can write better than anybody else, and because he is resolved to embroil matters at home and abroad, in the hope of obtaining a triumph for his own morbid vanity and implacable antipathies.

Clarendon to G.C. Lewis, MP (12 September)

Stratford, moreover, the real sultan . . . although he ostensibly and officially obeys his instructions, lets his dissent from them be known, and upon that the Turks act.

Whosevers fault it was, the Vienna Note had come to naught, and for the tsar there remained one final option to avert outright war – he would meet face to face with Francis Joseph. 'I love the Emperor of Austria as if he were my own son; I know that he will be my ally in putting an end to this foul administration of the Bosphorus, and the oppression of poor Christians by the damned infidels.' Austria, with Prussia in tow, could successfully pressure the Turks.

Towards the end of September, Nicholas journeyed to Warsaw, Olmütz and Berlin. In a series of amicable talks with Francis Joseph and Frederick William IV, he successfully persuaded his fellow sovereigns of his sincerity, so much so that they agreed to reduce their standing armies. Shortly afterwards Austria and Prussia withdrew from the dispute altogether, much to the tsar's satisfaction and to their own. Matters thus stood for the moment; insofar as Nicholas was concerned there was no further question of Austro-Prussian neutrality in the dispute. Britain and France now appeared alone in their continued support of Turkey. Queen Victoria reviewed the situation as it was in early October, writing:

> As matters have now been arranged, it appears to the Queen that we have now taken on ourselves in conjunction with France all the risks of a European war, without having bound Turkey to any conditions with respect to provoking it. The hundred and twenty fanatical Turks constituting the Divan at Constantinople are left sole judges of the line of policy to be pursued, and made cognizant at the same time of the fact that England and France have bound themselves to defend the Turkish territory! This is entrusting them with a power which Parliament has been jealous to confide even to the hands of the British Crown.

Some days later, Prince Albert wrote in like manner:

> . . . it is evident that the Turks have every inducement not to let this opportunity slip of going to war with Russia, as they probably will never find so advantageous a one again, as the whole of Christendom has declared them in the right, and they would fight with England and France actively on their side.

In Constantinople, the grand council again met with Sultan Abdul Mejid, and a reply to the tsar was agreed upon. If within fifteen days, the Russians did not withdraw their armies from the Principalities, Turkey would consider itself at war with that country. Gorchakov received the memorandum and summarily rejected it. On 4 October, Turkey passed into a state of war with Russia: 'The armies of the Crescent marched north to engage the forces of the Cross.'

A month earlier, the Anglo-French fleet found itself still at its station in Besika Bay. Concern had mounted for its safety, for in these parts winter breaks violently and severe storms could be expected by the end of October. Turkish rejection of the Vienna Note gave promise of prolonged further negotiations. Before Nicholas had rendered a decision on the amendments, the French were already urging Britain to send its fleet into the Dardanelles. Such a course would not only provide for the fleet's physical safety, but might effectively encourage the tsar to accept the amendments more speedily. Despite these arguments, Clarendon and his colleagues agreed that the French proposal was in direct contradiction of the Straits Convention. It was decided not to issue any such sailing orders, and to wait – the weather had not yet turned. But with the Turkish declaration of war, all had changed – the cabinet reversed itself and agreed to the French urgings; the fleet was ordered to join the French squadrons and to sail to Constantinople.[14]

Nicholas stood in isolation. Despite the amicable Austro-Prussian reception, the chancelleries of Europe seemed firmly united against him, and continental public opinion was becoming increasingly hostile. The sentiments of the times were best expressed in the words exchanged by Napoleon III with a Russian diplomat, as recorded by Count de Reiset, an intimate of the French emperor:

> I am resolved . . . to put forth every effort to fight against your influence and to thrust you back into Asia from whence you came. You are not a European Power, you should not be one and will not be one if France remembers the part she should play in Europe . . . Let the ties attaching you to Europe be loosened, and of your own accord you will flow towards the East and become once more an Asiatic Power. It would not be difficult to take Finland from you, the Baltic Provinces, Poland

and the Crimea. It will be a great fall for you, but you brought it on yourselves.

Nesselrode despaired of Nicholas and lamented, 'For thirty years I have imposed Russia on Europe and he is going to throw it away!' But the venerable chancellor himself was not above the tsar's suspicion. From the moment that the issue of the holy places came to the fore, the prudent statesman had been passed by. 'This son of a Catholic and a Protestant, himself an Anglican and probably the grandson of a Jewess, was not considered worthy to raise his voice in something where the interests of the Holy Orthodox Church were implicated.' Nicholas had deprived himself of this voice of wise moderation.

At this point, the tsar's temper got the better of him and his actions took on a certain quality of contradiction or even of incoherence. 'The contradiction between his words and his tortuous diplomatic transactions gave his enemies still more proofs of what seemed his duplicity,' writes Professor Grünwald. 'His language reached heights of extreme violence: he spoke of "those Turkish dogs", of that "adventurer" Napoleon III, of that "cad" Palmerston, and accused the other French and English Ministers of being "cowards" and "scoundrels". At the same time he expressed to General Goyon, his wish to receive a visit from the French emperor "as a brother", to "show the world", he said, "how much I appreciate him, how much homage I pay to his fine qualities and his character". He begged the King of Belgium – a man he had offended – to put the advantages of peace with Russia to Queen Victoria and the merchants in the City.'

To the Queen herself, Nicholas appealed, 'Are we to remain as I eagerly desire, on terms of friendship equally profitable to both states, or do you deem it right that the British standard is to wave side by side with the crescent in fighting the Cross of St Andrew?'[15] Victoria returned a cold reply in which she chastised him for his intemperate stance towards Turkey. 'The intentions of Your Majesty have been disregarded and badly interpreted by the form given to the demands addressed to the Porte.'

The last act had at last been played out. On 1 November, Nicholas addressed a solemn manifesto to his people and the world: 'Russia is challenged to fight. Nothing, therefore, further remains for her but to have recourse to arms in order to compel the Ottoman Government to respect treaties, and obtain from it reparation for the offences by which it has responded to our most moderate demands . . . we are firmly convinced that our faithful subjects will join their prayers to those which we address to the Almighty, beseeching Him to bless with his hand our arms in this just and holy cause, which always found ardent defenders in our pious ancestors. *In te Domine speravi, non confundar in aeternum.*'

Before affixing his signature to this declaration, the tsar dispatched a memorandum to the great powers, in which he assured them that he would not take the offensive. Russia would not cross the Danube but its positions in the Principalities would be maintained. Nicholas concluded, 'The situation, altogether of an expectant nature, does not throw any obstacle in the way of continuing negotiations.' Much as Napoleon can be accused of naiveté in pressing for war in the first place, so can Nicholas be blamed, in utterly misunderstanding the temper of the times. Nesselrode was right in saying of his master and of Russia, 'He is going to throw it away.'

9

FIRST BLOOD

During the week preceding the tsar's manifesto, the Turks managed to grab the initiative by advancing their armies across the Danube into the Principalities. Omar Pasha's forces took up positions at four widely distributed points and made preparations to engage the enemy. But it was Russian General Perloff who took the upper hand at Oltenitsa by leading his force in a vigorous attack against the largest body of the Turks which was assembled. Omar Pasha's forces twice repulsed with considerable losses. On 4 November, Perloff launched a fresh attack, but this time with a massive force of twenty infantry battalions, three cavalry regiments and thirty-two pieces of artillery. A prolonged battery of heavy cannon fire cleared the way for the cavalry and infantry.

Despite the massiveness of Russian forces and the determination of the attack, Omar Pasha later reported, 'The well-directed fire from our fortress soon dispersed their right column and the centre gradually fell back . . . the Russian advanced with coolness and resolution almost to the brink of the trench, and on this account, their loss was considerable, amounting to a thousand men killed and double the number wounded.'

The fierce fighting lasted from noon until late afternoon. 'During this interval,' Omar continues, 'wagons never ceased carrying off their dead . . . at five o'clock a total confusion ensued in the Russian ranks; their lines were completely broken and their retreat precipitated. An hour later, some few rallied in the neighbouring villages, but the remainder fled in disorder. Some of our men pushed forward in pursuit of them beyond the lines, but were summoned back by trumpet to their own quarters. Our loss amounted to 105 men. We found on the field of battle 500 muskets, sacs, cartridge boxes, equipment, etc.'

Winter comes early in this southeastern part of Europe, as it did in 1853. So severe had the weather become that all active campaigning in the Principalities was suspended. Nobody could lay claim to victory, but the honours certainly went to Omar Pasha. A shrewd tactician, he deliberately spread his forces all along the Danube, well into westernmost Wallachia, thus forcing the Russians to extend perilously their own lines. Omar knew of the tsar's commitment not to cross the river, a situation of which he took full advantage. The Danube protected the Turks from the Russians, but not the Russians from the Turks. Following Oltenitza and throughout the winter, the Turkish general acquired much satisfaction in ordering brief but deadly sorties across the length of the river into the enemy's territory. The Russians never knew from what quarter next to expect an attack. And always, the attacks came with impunity – no one gave chase. Omar Pasha, comments Temperley, 'irritated Russia just as the swarm of gnats in summer irritate a cow.' The success at Oltenitza and of the forays across the Danube did much to bolster Ottoman self-confidence. While Turks acquired a sense of military strength, Russians felt loss of face, which only further fuelled their anger. The tsar cried for retribution, and this he found at the opposite end of the Black Sea.

Between the Black Sea and the Caspian on Russia's southern fringes, the tsar and the sultan shared a 400-mile (650-kilometre) border within the rugged and spectacular peaks of the Caucasus. It was here, in these remote mountains, far from Crimea, that the first significant blood of the war came to be shed. At the very time that Omar Pasha was darting across the Danube like 'a swarm of gnats', a troop of 5,000 Turks was being transported by barge from Batumi – in what is today southern Georgia – to attack the Russian frontier outpost of Fort St Nicholas. The handful of stalwarts who defended the stronghold – Russian army regulars and local inhabitants – were quickly overcome. To their grief, among the victors was a large contingent of Bashi-Bazouks. 'These troops,' Professor Vulliamy writes, 'They were a murderous and inchoate rabble of Kurds, Albanians, Arabs, Negroes, and every type of unclassified marauder, carrying pistols, yatagans, kinjars, krisses, butchers' knives, or lovely damascene blades, and rifles with decorated butts. They were dressed in dirty barbaric finery, and they were capable of every abomination and of all conceivable atrocities.' These irregulars had flocked to the sultan's service in such vast numbers that 4,000 of the 'picturesque looking vagabonds' were eventually offered for duty among the British and French.

A merciless massacre of the St Nicholas survivors took place. An eye-witness who was fortunate enough to survive the fray describes it: 'The Turks took revenge in a terrible manner. They crucified the customs inspector and then used him for target practice. The priest had his head sawn off. The doctor was tortured to death while being questioned as to the location of the garrison's money. Women and children were slaughtered and, finally, a pregnant woman had her living child cut out of her and, before her very eyes, it was hacked to pieces.'

News of the fall of Fort St Nicholas soon reached the Russian capital and details of the horrible atrocities were vividly and exaggeratedly reported by the press. St Petersburg went wild with indignation, and the infuriated tsar reacted in retribution by ordering Mikhail Vorontzov, Governor General of the Caucasus, to mount a concerted attack on Kars, the principal Turkish stronghold in the Caucasus. Fortunately for Vorontzov thirteen divisions of troop reinforcements had arrived in early September to reinforce the region's numerous tiny garrisons and he was able to direct General Adronikov into action. In mid-November, 7,000 Russian troops marched off towards Kars to engage the Turkish forces, estimated to number 19,000.

The Russian force arrived at the fortified town of Alzuth on 26 November, and Adronikov ordered an artillery barrage of the place. The Turks returned the fire and the duel lasted five smoke-filled hours with little inroads being made by either side. The Russian general then decided to ford the shallow Pashov-Chai River which separated the two forces and to storm the fortification with a bayonet attack. 'Under cover of fire, the infantry crossed the river, chest deep in water,' Adronikov subsequently reported. 'The attack was so singularly determined that the enemy despite stubborn defence, was forced to give way, and the first step of the retreat was the beginning of the final defeat and total derangement.' The shattered enemy was pursued into the surrounding hills. 'By sunset the battle ceased for lack of enemy.'

Some miles away, General Beboutov's troops were following a large Turkish force which had been hastening from
Byandor to reinforce Kars. On 30 November, the Russians
made contact with these Turks and engaged them in battle
near Bshkadyklar. Artillery fire, infantry attacks, counter-
attack and then a general retreat by the Ottoman forces –
the Russians had won another resounding victory.

'I report to Your Excellency,' Beboutov wrote that evening
to Prince Vorontzov, 'that in our forces we had 7,000 infantry,
2,800 cavalry and 32 field guns which we pitted against
20,000 regular infantry, 4,000 regular cavalry plus 20,000
militiamen and 42 field guns, of which we captured 24 . . . the
Russian losses of dead and wounded is approximately 1100
men . . . the Turkish losses, as the counting progresses, nears
6,000 men.' The general further notes that fighting with the
Turks were 'Poles, who in their desperation before death,
hurled grenades by hand, at the heads of our Dragoons'.
These Polish emigrants 'fought brilliantly and nearly all were
cut down'. The Turkish 'artillery was splendidly armed' –
almost entirely equipped by the British.

Here in the Caucasus too winter comes early, and after these
two major engagements, military activities and the advance on
Kars were suspended. The short but brilliant Caucasian campaign fought by the Russians in autumn of 1853, together – as
will be seen – with Admiral Nachimoff's naval success at
Sinope, rekindled a sense of optimism and gave new strength
to the tsar. The victory at Bashkadyklar followed the one at
Sinope by a day, and news of the two events reached European
capitals almost simultaneously. When the British and French
governments came to review the situation, it became clear that
Turkey was in no position to defend itself against Russia
entirely on its own.

*   *   *

On the south side of the Black Sea, some 300 nautical miles (550 kilometres) from Constantinople stands Sinope, a port town, then of 9,000 inhabitants. On 27 November, a Turkish naval squadron on its way to reinforce the garrisons in the Caucasus took refuge here from severe gale-force winds. For three days, the seven frigates, three corvettes and two smaller vessels – together bearing 434 guns – rode out the stormy weather at anchor and then awaited orders to sail on. Shore batteries and guns of the massive castle in the town's centre offered some protective cover to the exposed flotilla.

At mid-morning on the 30th, with the harbour enveloped by a heavy fog, a Russian squadron entered the bay. Three of Admiral Nachimoff's ships, each bearing 120 guns, stealthily came alongside the Turkish vessels while five other vessels moved to take station on the opposite side. The Turkish flagship, the *Nezemiah*, suddenly became alerted to the Russian presence and it opened fire. Guns from both squadrons quickly joined in, with sporadic support of the land artillery. The angry cannonade lasted four hours at the end of which all the vessels of the Turkish fleet were sunk or burning, save one.

'Sinope was in flames,' a St Petersburg newspaper gloated, 'and at two thirty the admiral stopped the firing and sent an officer with a flag of truce to tell the authorities of Sinope that if another gun was fired, either from the town or from strand batteries, he should certainly bombard and utterly destroy the town of Sinope. The officer landed, and stayed about an hour, but he could not find the Turkish authorities. He did not see a single Turk; they had all taken refuge in the neighbouring villages.'

Sinope burned, the Turkish fleet was destroyed and the coast for many miles strewn with dead bodies. Osman Pasha, captain of the *Aon Illah*, was wounded, taken prisoner and afterwards died in captivity. His was the only ship which was not sunk or blown up, and Nachimoff made an unsuccessful attempt to tow it away as a prize of war. An estimated 3,000 Turkish sailors perished that day.

Nicholas was ecstatic over this brilliant vindication of Oltenitza and the humiliations which had been suffered at the hands of Omar Pasha. 'With hearty joy,' he wrote to Menshikov, 'I request you to communicate to my brave sea-men, that I thank them for the success of the Russian flag on behalf of the glory and honour of Russia.' St Petersburg was enraptured by it all – illuminations, balls and festivals were held, and for days to come a succession of toasts were drunk, while the pageant, 'The Battle of Sinope', enthralled capacity audiences.

Nicholas had promised the great powers not to take the offensive against the Turks. Yet he was, after all, at war with them, and the fleet at Sinope was bound for the Caucasus with reinforcements and supplies for the sultan's armies. In Russian eyes, that particular action was totally justified.

The sensational news of Sinope's disaster was received in England, France and elsewhere with cries of indignation. This treacherous massacre of Turks could not go un-avenged; it was outrageous and humiliating. 'The feelings of honour, which this dreadful carnage could not fail to create, have been general throughout all ranks and classes of Her Majesty's subjects in this country,' Clarendon wrote. The Anglo-French fleet lay at Constantinople specifically to protect the capital and the Ottoman coasts. The unexpected hostility of the Russian tsar was in ostentatious defiance of allied naval power. Peace was 'no longer compatible with the honour and dignity of the country', proclaimed *The Times*.

The French demanded that the British forthwith order the combined fleet into the Black Sea. Palmerston urged the same, but Aberdeen and Gladstone wavered. The press clamoured for action – 'Strike down the aggressor,' bannered the *Morning Chronicle*. From Paris, Cowley telegraphed that Napoleon was 'prepared, should it become necessary, to carry it out alone'. Finally, the pacifists within cabinet acquiesced and a majority decision was made to give the allied fleet its sailing orders. On 5 January 1854, the Anglo-French fleets entered the Black Sea.

The fleet, it was explained, was on a peacekeeping mission 'with no hostile design against Russia'. Its sole purpose, according to the announcement, was 'to prevent the recurrence of disasters such as Sinope'. Napoleon's views on the fleet's role were more specific: 'The combined fleets will require and, if necessary, compel Russian ships of war to return to Sevastopol or to the nearest port. It is considered the Turkish fleet should undertake no aggressive operations by sea, so long as matters remain in their present state.' This meant effectively that the Russian navy was to remain bottled up in the north shore ports and that the Black Sea would no longer to be a 'Russian Lake'. Henceforth, Britain and France alone would patrol these waters – *les gendarmes*, as it were.

When the news of the allied penetration of the Black Sea reached Nicholas, together with the declaration of his nemesis, Nicholas ordered the immediate recall of his ambassadors from Paris and London. The governments of France and Britain reciprocated and, on 6 February, diplomatic relations between Russia and the two Western powers were formally ended. In St Petersburg, orders were given to launch preparations for the invasion of Turkey.

A few days prior to this order being issued, there arrived in the Russian capital a curious delegation of three Englishmen, sent there by the Society of Friends to petition the tsar for peace. They requested an audience with his majesty, and, on the 10th, the Emperor of All the Russias received the earnest trio – Messrs Joseph Sturge, Robert Carleton and Henry Pease. He met them alone and allowed a twenty-minute audience, towards the end of which, 'The Emperor shook hands with each of us very cordially and, with eyes moistened with emotion, he turned hastily away (apparently to conceal his feelings) saying, "My wife also wishes to see you."' With that he quit the room, instructing the trio to await the empress. Alexandra Feodorvna met with the three for more than an hour before allowing them to leave the Winter Palace. At the outset of the meeting, the empress had informed them, 'I have just seen the emperor; the tears were in his eyes.' The Quakers tried; a noble initiative it was, but not one that was even remotely destined for success.

In the first days of February, peace between Russia and the allied powers hung by the most fragile of threads. Nicholas in desperation yet again appealed to Francis Joseph by sending his close personal friend, Count Orlov, to deliver a request and specific proposals. Kindly arrange for peace negotiations immediately to be opened in Vienna or St Petersburg. Russia promises not to cross the Danube while the state of war with Turkey continues and its troops would withdraw from the Principalities upon signing of a peace agreement. Austria should remain neutral regardless of circumstance, in return for which Russia promises full assistance in the event of the French attacking any part of the Hapsburg domains. The Balkan states would pass under the joint protectorate of Austria and Russia.

Following Olmütz, Francis Joseph assumed a neutral position with respect to the growing tensions between Russia and Britain–France. But now he was rapidly becoming suspicious of the tsar's sincerity, and sceptical as to Russia's designs on the Balkans. He balked at Orlov's proposals and turned them down. Not only that, but he ordered 30,000 troops to mass in

Transylvania. Austria planned unilaterally to protect the Turkish southern provinces, despite arrangements concluded at Münchengrätz. Orlov returned home empty-handed to explain to his emperor the lamentable turn of events. In the winter palace, the infuriated Nicholas glared at the portrait of Francis Joseph which hung prominently in his personal apartment, and in red-faced rage he turned the painting face to the wall and wrote on the back of the canvas, *'Du Undankbarer'*, or 'ingrate'. In an intemperate letter to his young cousin, he wrote that it was monstrous nonsense 'that you should give even a passing thought to taking no arms against Russia – Russia which had in Hungary so recently given tribute of blood'.

The letter, it seems, had little effect, for on 22 February the Austrian foreign minister summoned Baron de Bourqueney, the French ambassador in Vienna. Count Buol informed the startled envoy, 'If England and France will fix a day of evacuation of the Principalities, the expiration of which shall be the signal for hostilities, the cabinet of Vienna will support the summons.' The surprising message was relayed to Paris and to London. Clarendon immediately requested clarification: did 'support the summons' mean that Austria was now prepared to go to war against Russia? The return answer provided no further elucidation, but again offered assurance that Austria would 'support the summons'.

It seemed decisive. Without waiting for 'the concurrence of the Power which was pressing them into action', Britain and France now set about to prepare 'the instruments which were to bring them into a state of war with Russia'.

From Paris, Napoleon demanded that an ultimatum be sent to Nicholas requiring the withdrawal of Russian troops from the Principalities by a specific date. In Britain, the public clamoured lustily for war – the people longed especially for

naval glory. It was common knowledge that a sizeable fleet
had already been assembled at Portsmouth and that it was
merely awaiting orders to sail for the Baltic. 'Neither the
diplomatic communications between the two governments
[Britain and Russia] nor the correspondence that passed
between the sovereigns could bring about an understanding,'
writes Professor Goryainov. 'The English nation, having enjoyed profound peace for nearly forty years, was suffering
from reaction. Bellicose feeling prevailed, the nation wished
for war; and, on 27 February 1854, Her Majesty's Government delivered its ultimatum to the Emperor of Russia.' If
within six days the tsar did not order the withdrawal of his
troops from the Principalities, Britain would declare war.

The design of such an ultimatum was Austria's, but she was
not consulted as to the date of commencement of war. From
Paris and London, identical notes went to St Petersburg by
messenger, who was instructed en route to stop in Vienna in
order to show the documents to the court. Austria was to be
made aware that, willing or not to secure her own interests,
Britain was irrevocably committed to defending them for her.
Instead of requiring Austria to take part in the very step she
had advised, Her Majesty's Ambassador in Vienna, Lord
Westmoreland, was merely instructed to express a hope that
the directive would 'receive Austrian approval', and that this
would be 'made known to St Petersburg'.

The envoy, having shared the documentation with the
Austrian government, quit Vienna not only with Britain's
message to the tsar, but also with Vienna's orders to its
ambassador in the Russian capital. Count Esterházy was
ordered to support the British ultimatum, and to throw upon
Russia full responsibility for the impending war. What Austria
neglected to do, was to inform Nicholas that a refusal to quit
the Principalities would result in its own declaration of war

against Russia. His country would therefore find itself at war with three of Europe's major powers, and surely Prussia would follow.

And Prussia did. In its own dispatch to St Petersburg, drawn up 'in very pressing language', the Russian government was urged to consider the grave danger to world peace that would arise in the event of a rejection. 'The responsibility of war which might be the consequence of that refusal, would rest with the Emperor.'

On 27 March, the Emperor of the French addressed the *corps législatif*: 'To avoid a conflict, I have gone as far as honour allowed. Europe knows that if France draws the sword, it is because she is constrained to do so. Europe knows that France has no idea of aggrandizement.' And with that, France declared war on Russia.

On the following day, Her Britannic Majesty addressed parliament: 'Her Majesty feels called upon by regard for an ally, the integrity and independence of whose empire have been recognized as essential to the peace of Europe . . . and to save Europe from the preponderance of a power which has violated the faith of treaties . . . to take up arms, in conjunction with the Emperor of the French, for the defence of the Sultan.' Britain too declared war.[16]

The Tsar of Russia addressed his people in a manifesto: 'England and France have sided with the enemies of Christianity against Russia combating for the Orthodox faith . . . Russia fights not for things of the world, but for faith . . . let all Russia exclaim,

'O Lord, our Redeemer! Whom shall we fear? May God be glorified and His enemies dispersed!' On 11 April, Russia formally declared war on France and Britain.

10

THE ARMIES: ALLIED AND RUSSIAN

The allied declarations of war came as surprise to nobody except perhaps Nicholas. In France, only the imperialists in Napoleon's immediate circle held any enthusiasm for it, together with sectors of the army. The French public was apathetic towards it. For Napoleon, the impending war was not unlike a colonial expedition – it would be brief and inexpensive, both in terms of men and resources. 'In this respect he was in agreement with most other observers early in 1854,' remarks Professor Gooch. 'For illusion France was prepared. However, the expedition did not remain a matter of only 10,000 men. Soon the figures were 40,000 and then 70,000.'

In Britain war spirit raged and there appeared to be a collective desire to get on with it. 'A generation had sprung up in England which knew nothing of war and desired to try its mettle by experience,' writes J.W. Fortescue, the chronicler of the British army. 'The government having begun, through its diplomacy, to drift into threats of active hostility, was hurried upon its way by popular clamour.' The English people at this stage were quite simply anxious to start and to be finished with it. Kinglake muses, 'Perhaps it ought to be acknowledged that there were many to whom war for the sake of war was no longer a hateful thought.'

Weeks before the declarations were made, allied preparations had already got under way. In Malta, Britain began to assemble its forces, and in Toulon and Marseilles French armies gathered in preparation for sailing. An advance team of military advisors was sent to Constantinople to counsel the Turkish senior staff, among them Colonel Ardent, the noted French military engineer, and Sir John Burgoyne, hero of the Peninsular War and the War of 1812.

Now that war was officially declared and allied forces were truly on their way to the glorious fields of battle, there remained for Britain and France only two critical matters to resolve: the definition of objectives and the appointment of the joint commanders. As early as 22 February, Napoleon and Lord Cowley, the British ambassador, had started discussions on the matter. The emperor embraced the advice of his august uncle and argued for vesting full authority in one supreme commander. 'When war is carried on against a single power,' Napoleon Bonaparte once declared, 'there should be only one army, acting upon one base, and conducted by one chief . . . long discussions and councils of war . . . will terminate in the adoption of the worst cause.'

As to who that one person should be, not surprisingly Louis Napoleon firmly favoured the appointment of a Frenchman to assume command of the allied land forces. Recognizing British superiority at sea, he allowed that the naval forces might fall under the command of an Englishman. Lord Cowley objected

– to have 'the British army under the French command would, in effect, make the British commander second-in-command of his own men – and for the British estimate of their own pride and importance, this obviously would not do.' In the best tradition of English compromise, the ambassador went on to propose that a loose arrangement of simple cooperation be established – both on land and on sea. And eventually, this was the course adopted with no single person appointed to head either the military or the naval forces.

To command the French expeditionary forces, Napoleon appointed General Leroy de St Arnaud, a sixty-five-year-old veteran of the Algerian campaigns (promoted during the war to Marshal). It was he who took charge of the military aspect of the coup d'état which brought Louis to the throne in 1851. The appointment was certainly a curious one, and in making it Napoleon deliberately overlooked such distinguished and capable officers as Generals Changarnier, Baraquay d'Hilliers, de Castellane, Vaillant and Pélissier – all veterans of the First Empire who fought in such battles as Leipzig, Wagram and Borodino. Louis valued not so much experience and ability, as pliability and unquestionable loyalty to himself – and in St Arnaud he was assured of this.

In his early years, St Arnaud managed to acquire a reputation which was anything but stellar, and in fact was simply dubious. In 1821, as a second lieutenant, he was released from the army after spending fifteen days in a military jail. He travelled to London and there took up the teaching of fencing. 'But when he found no demand for fencing instruction, he became a dancing-master and a "marker at a billiard table",' writes Professor Gooch. 'He also tried his hand at singing, writing poetry and playing the fiddle, but leaving behind unpaid bills, he furtively slipped out of Britain and continued his drifting. With a mastery of four languages, he dabbled in the theatre, as a comedian going under the name of "Floridor". In a lyric troupe in Belgium, Saint Arnaud appeared in a vibrant tenor role.'

In 1831, St Arnaud was reinstated in the army; he married and assumed a more serious outlook on life. Five years later, he was sent to Algeria where his star began to rise. By 1847, he was able to write to his brother, 'I am happy, known, appreciated, a brigadier general commander in the Legion of Honour! My goal is achieved; my children have a name and a position.' In 1851 he was named Minister of War and a year later St Arnaud was made Marshal of France and appointed to the senate.

The marshal was good natured and energetic, but also reckless and vain. He was a skilled administrator, an enterprising officer and an effective, but, we're told, 'not an outstanding commander'. He had 'a more than common willingness to take away human life'. He himself proudly related how in 1845 he dealt with a large body of Arabs who had taken refuge in the caves of North African mountains. 'I had all apertures hermetically stopped up. I made one vast sepulchre. No one went into the caverns; no one but myself knew that under there, there are five hundred brigands who will never again slaughter Frenchmen . . . no one is so good as I am by taste and by nature . . . my conscience does not reproach me. I have done my duty as a commander and tomorrow I would do the same over again.'

At the time that he received his latest commission, St Arnaud was seriously ill. A dozen years earlier he had begun to complain of the illness which finally took his life on the fields of Crimea. By the time he died, the stomach cancer pains became excruciating, and the attacks kept him weak and emaciated. 'He was in such condition of health,' records Kinglake (who knew the marshal personally), 'as to be unfit to command an army in the field. Although during intervals, he was free from pain and glowing with energy, he was from time to time utterly cast down by his recurring malady.'

As divisional commanders for the French Expeditionary Force to Crimea, Napoleon named Generals Canrobert, Bosquet and Forey. Like St Arnaud, the three generals were veterans of North Africa, but they were younger, their average age being forty-six. He also appointed Prince Napoleon, nephew of the iconic emperor and heir to his cousin's throne – a studious young man with little active military experience. Before sailing for the East, Canrobert received from Napoleon a 'dormant commission', appointing him commander-in-chief in the event of St Arnaud's death. This commission was kept secret – even from the marshal – until 29 September 1854. Fifteen days after the allies stepped ashore in Crimea, St Arnaud died, and Canrobert assumed command of the French forces.

To command the British forces, Lord Raglan (Fitzroy Somerset) was appointed. Raglan was an aristocrat through and through – proud, reserved, gallant, urbane and possessing a near self-effacing modesty. In the tradition of his people, he had an allergy to displays of emotion or demonstration, and he was a master of understatement – 'it would be impossible to deduce the full suffering of his army from his letters to the government, either official or private.' 'The silence of Lord Raglan,' complained the Lord Privy Seal, 'was positively excruciating. Nothing came from him but the driest facts!' On the one hand he was persuasive and had the subtle ability to draw men to him: 'Whether he talked to a statesmen or a schoolboy, his hearer went away captive.' On the other hand, his relations with the rank and file were distant and formal, and his rare conversations with soldiers lacked any sort of warmth. During his visit with the Light Brigade, for example, following the sanguinary charge he offered absolutely no comment, no word of appreciation.

Raglan's commission was purchased by his father, at a time when he was still a schoolboy at Westminster College. Early in his career, he married the Duke of Wellington's niece and became the duke's aide-de-camp. At Waterloo he lost his right arm, and in the forty years that followed he held a variety of desk jobs: secretary to the embassy in Paris, and later in St Petersburg; Master General of Ordnance; military secretary to the commander-in-chief at the House Guards; and finally Privy Counsellor. At the time of his appointment, Raglan was the complete civil servant.

'The tragedy of Raglan,' writes Pemberton, 'was that his fine qualities unfitted him for command of an army in Crimea after forty years of peace. The army, shivering on the Heights, did not want the perfect gentleman, the disinterested aristocrat. They did not want, as Layard informed the House of Commons, to be commanded by a "mild, good-tempered old gentleman". They needed a younger man, or, as Captain Higginson declared, "an iron-fisted general who will stand no nonsense," someone who was less of the gentleman and more of the cad; someone who was ruthless, emphatic, energetic, imperious, a slave-driver if necessary, who would feed and clothe and warm his men and keep them in good fettle, would threaten, storm, abuse, act and in the last resource dismiss his dearest friend from office. Raglan at sixty-seven was not and never could be that type of man.'

On receiving his appointment, Raglan's first task was to select his staff. 'He could not have been ignorant of the officers of the army,' editorialized *Fraser's Magazine*. 'He ought not to have been ignorant of the proper elements for making an efficient staff. His choice of instruments was . . . deliberate and systematic. He announced that those who had so long been dandled in peaceful service should have the preference to win their spurs; while those who in India or elsewhere had known war were to be rejected. The new staff was therefore formed of Horse Guards favourites, nephews, and guardsmen. The chief felt himself unspoiled by long years of peace and plenty, and took it for granted that others were as elastic as he was.'

The appointments were eventually posted. Not one division or brigade commander among them had ever taken charge of a large body of troops in battle – for that matter, neither had Lord Raglan himself. Of the four divisional commanders, three had seen action against Napoleon as young officers – Sir George de Lacy Evans, Sir George Cathcart and Sir Richard England. Their average age was sixty-two. The thirty-four year old Duke of Cambridge, grandson of George III and cousin to Queen Victoria, with sixteen years of staff experience, was appointed to command the First Division. Like Prince Napoleon, he was in Crimea 'to pick up whatever prestige might be readily gained for the Crown'. Sir George Brown was given the Light Division and the Earl of Lucan received the Cavalry Division. Lucan had served with the Russian army against the Turks in 1828, but had retired from the military ten years later – fifteen years out of the service. The Earl of Cardigan and James Scarlett were appointed to command the Light Brigade and the Heavy Brigade respectively. Neither had seen active service. The highly-regarded Sir John Burgoyne, veteran of the War of 1812 and seventy-one years of age, was made Chief Engineer.

Such were the senior officers commanding the allied forces which sailed east in the summer of 1854. Professor Gooch points out, 'The amazing degree in which the [French and English] armies differed in both appearance and effectiveness could in large measure be attributed to the fact that essentially, the French were led by officers, the English, by gentlemen.' The

French staff was younger and considerably more experienced – for the most part everyone had seen at least twenty years' active service in North Africa. The Algerian experience, furthermore, had been for the officers one of camaraderie and mutual reliance: 'While differences did exist between them, they were all on cordial terms with one another at the outset.' Such was not the condition of the British staff, where jealousies, quarrels and intense hatreds were manifest off and on throughout the entire campaign. Tales emanating from the savage and protracted feud of Lord Cardigan with his brother-in-law, the Earl of Lucan, are legion. Early in the campaign the commander of the Light Brigade and his immediate superior, the commander of the Cavalry Division, ceased speaking to one another. No one could bring reconciliation between the two men, 'each as proud as Lucifer, the one impetuous, dominant, hard as steel; the other proud, narrow, jealous and self-willed'. 'What a thing war is,' remarked Lord George Paget, 'and what wrangling and jealousies does it engender.'

The French forces on the whole were superior to the British not only from the viewpoint of command and leadership, but in numbers and organization. Initially, France sent 60,000 troops to the theatre of war, while the British committed 26,000 men. As for the operations of the two forces, General Sir Daniel Lysons reported in the earliest stages in the war:

> Our arrangements have been infamous. There is no commissariat, the men are half-starved and officers come on board our steamer to get tea, bread or anything they could get. No generals, except Sir G. Brown, have arrived, and no staff. There are no mules for us, in fact, no organization whatsoever. What a contrast to the French army, which arrived and landed by divisions and brigades with their generals and full staff,

commissariat, provisions, mules for everybody, pack-saddles all complete and ready to march the moment they landed without the slightest confusion . . . The regiments move extremely well and know their work, but the generals and staff are very deficient; it really is wonderful, with the blunders of the staff, how our men can work at all.

Whatever the differences between the two armies, they did share one thing in common: a disdain and distrust of their Turkish ally. 'Beasts,' Prince Napoleon called them. 'No Turk is to be trusted,' declared Cowley. Opinion of the fighting Turk could not have been meaner; he was seen as a primitive and erratic warrior, capable only of holding the enemy at bay from behind the safety of city walls. There was never any doubt at the war council that the Russians would rapidly cross the Danube and would successfully penetrate deep onto Ottoman territory without encountering any Turkish resistance.

The first order of business, therefore, was to attend to Ottoman fortifications. To this end, General Burgoyne and his French counterpart were already busy at work, planning and directing operations. In their reports, the two officers heaped scorn on the modest arrangements the Turks had in place for the defence of the Danube's south bank. The redoubts of Silistra and Schumia were destined to collapse at the first vigorous attack, they warned, and then the floodgates would be open to the Russian horde. Burgoyne counselled that an allied landing be had at Gallipoli in order to set up a preliminary defensive position, and that then the troops should move north. If matters were handled expeditiously, with some luck these positions could be advanced into the Balkans and the security of Constantinople thereby be assured. Napoleon III was 'enchanted' with Burgoyne. At one time, he himself had pondered problems related to engineering, and had in fact produced some pamphlets on the subject. This was essentially a defensive strategy, one that held appeal to engineers, but it has been noted, 'Without engineers actually leading the expedition, the prospects of friction were immediately present.'

Canrobert and Bosquet voiced the strongest objection to the scheme and urged the emperor instead to land at Varna, some distance north on the Black Sea coast. 'Why a defensive position?' they demanded. 'It is an offensive position that we must take . . . why allow the Russians to invade Turkey? Let us place ourselves where we can prevent them not from occupying the last Turkish province, but the whole of Turkey.'

But Napoleon prevailed, and the decision was taken for a landing at Gallipoli. On 19 March, the French advance party was ordered to sail from Marseilles, and twelve days later, the British vanguard force left Malta. Their objective continued disturbingly amorphous: 'to strengthen defences'. All very well, but precisely where? Against what form of attack? From where? And, finally, what then?

The town of Gallipoli is situated on the European side of the Dardanelles, at the southwestern extremity of the Strait where it begins to expand into the Sea of Marmora. An army entrenched there commands simultaneously the entrances to the Aegean and the Dardanelles. Such a force can as easily be marched northwards into the Balkans or to Constantinople, as it can be transported across the water to Asia. Bourgoyne was right, if a defensive stance was to be made or if a springboard to the Balkans was desired. On Wednesday 6 April, the transports bearing the British contingent arrived outside the town's harbour; the French had already arrived. On board the *Golden Fleece* was William Russell of *The Times*, the world's first real war correspondent and he sent home colourful and detailed dispatches. The town, he wrote, was 'a wretched collection of hovels with 10,000 inhabitants, Turks, Jews and Greeks'. He went on to explain that the commanders of the freshly arrived British force received news that their consul had 'gone up the Dardanelles to look for us, but that he would return in the course of the day'. He also reported the un-welcome news that 'horses were not to be had at any price . . . provisions were not very cheap, and . . . the French, being the first comers, had got hold of the best part of town and of the best quarters as well'.

The fleet came to rest at anchor but the troops were not permitted to disembark until Saturday, which left them stoi-cally languishing in boredom. 'Why was this?' demanded Russell, 'Because nothing was ready for them! The force consisted of only some thousands and odd men, and small as it was, it had to lie idle for two days and a half watching the seagulls, or with half-averted eye regarding the ceaseless activity of the French.' Russell went on to report on the admirable completeness of the French preparation: 'Hospitals for the sick, bread and biscuit bakeries, wagon trains for carrying stores and baggage – every necessary and every comfort, indeed, at hand, the moment their ship came in. On our side not a British pendant was afloat in the harbour! Our great naval State was represented by a single steamer belonging to a private company.'

In the weeks that followed the initial landings, the allied forces swelled in number, and new arrivals busied themselves in settling in. Time was spent mostly in foraging for scarce provisions, in making the acquaintance of one another and in coming to terms with the presence of Turkish forces. It was all unhurried, lacking any sense of urgency, or for that matter purpose. The commanding officers arrived on the scene at their own leisure and each such arrival called for a parade and reception. Prince Napoleon arrived on 30 April, Raglan three days later, St Arnaud on the 7 July, and the Duke of Cambridge with his suite on the 9th.

A grand review was held of the joint armies, in which some 22,000 troops paraded. A 'state dinner' was tendered by the sultan in honour of the Duke of Cambridge. One day 'a tremendous storm – lightning, thunder and torrents of rain – broke over the camp,' and a certain Lieutenant Macintosh drowned in the mud. On the day after the storm, the commanders of the allied camps departed by ship for Varna, where the first council of war was to take place with Omar Pasha, the commander of the Turkish army – eight weeks had passed since the declaration. Lord Raglan sailed in the *Caradoc*, Marshal St Arnaud in the *Berthollet,* and the Turkish ministers of war and interior, in the *Cheh-Per* – three separate ships, each under its own flag, and each with creature comforts and well-appointed galleys. Following the council, the foursome returned to Gallipoli in time for the grand celebration of Queen Victoria's birthday: 'A splendid spectacle it was.'

On the appointed day, a parade of 15,000 men was mustered on the plain shortly after noon. 'Lord Raglan and staff, to the number of thirty or forty, appeared on the ground in a perfect blaze of gold lace and scarlet and white plumes . . . the bands played *God Save the Queen*, but not with unanimity.' Lord Raglan took his place at the reviewing stand and after a short pause the naval guns thundered a royal salute while the bands once again struck up the royal anthem and all the regimental colours were solemnly lowered to the ground. Russell describes it:

> . . . the thing was well done and the effect of these thirty-two masses of richly dyed silk encrusted with the names of great victories, falling so suddenly to the earth as if struck down by one blow, was strange and inexpressible. In another minute a

shout of 'God save the Queen' ran from the Rifles on the left to the Guards on the right, and three tremendous cheers, gathering forces as they rolled on with the accumulated strength of a thousand throats from regiment after regiment, made the very air ring, the ears tingle, and the heart throb. Some of the regiments pulled off their shakoes, and waved them in the air in accompaniment to the shouts; other remained motionless, but made not less noise than their fellows.

Relatively few spectators were on hand to observe this spectacular tribute to her majesty. The paucity of attending Turks particularly irritated the British, who from the beginning had been astonished by their ally's apathy towards almost everything. 'There were present some three or four gentlemen on horseback, with their pipe-bearers and two or three carriages full of veiled women; but though Scutari, with its population of 100,000 souls, was within a mile and a half, it did not appear that half a dozen people had been added to the usual crowd of camp followers who attend on such occasions. The Greeks were more numerous, and Pera sent over a fair share of foreigners all dressed in the newest Paris fashions; so that one might fancy himself at a fashionable field-day in England but for the cypress groves and the tall minarets glancing above in the distance.'

During the nine weeks that the allies spent in Gallipoli preparing for battle, the Turks were hot in it on the banks of the Danube, and they held their own against the Russians admirably. Omar Pasha had established his defences from Vadin in westernmost Wallachia to Constanta on the Black Sea, a front of 300 miles (480 kilometres). On the south side of the Danube a number of fortified towns fell under siege, Silistria being the most important, but the positions held. Russian advance was successfully arrested. The 'beastly, untrustworthy and inefficient' Turk was doing impressively well against the 100,000 invaders from the north.

When the allies made their early negative assessments of the Turkish military, they failed to consider that the sultan's standing army was then one of the oldest and most experienced in Europe. Perhaps not the most effective by Western European standards, it was nonetheless one of the largest, numbering 300,000 men. Half these numbers were permanent force and half reserve. Two thirds of the permanent force was stationed in Constantinople and these troops were well armed, thoroughly drilled by foreign instructors and properly cared for. The regulars outside Constantinople were, in the words of St Arnaud, 'poorly clothed, poorly mounted, indifferently armed, disagreeable to look at'. And the reserves for the most part were simply without arms, without officers, and generally poorly trained.

In the event of hostilities, the sultan could often further count on voluntary reinforcement from his dependent vassals, but such assistance was sporadic and inefficient. When, for example, the first Egyptian contingent arrived at Gallipoli, it was found that none of the troops were from the regular forces. Abbas Pasha had conscripted aged veterans from the civilian population. 'Any other factor than having once served was disregarded,' writes Gooch. 'Many had been disbanded for over ten years and some were even veterans of the Greek wars of independence in the 1820s. Many were over sixty; none were under thirty. Without warning, fourteen thousand of these veterans were seized, at work in the fields, in their homes, or wherever they happened to be, chained, and sent to Alexandria where they were clothed and shipped out. Desertion was always a serious problem in units such as these, although in battle theirs was often a ferocity that was unmatched. Destruction of the enemy meant to them not simple death but a vicious mutilation of his corpse.'

The allies furthermore neglected to take into account that the supreme commander of the Turkish army was the remarkable Omar Pasha, a sagacious and enterprising officer and an adept diplomat. In fact he was born an Austrian bearing the name Michael Lattas, and in his younger days he had served as an officer in the Hapsburg army. At age twenty-two, he deserted and fled the country, eventually settling in Constantinople, where he became tutor to the sons of a wealthy Turkish businessman. Michael converted to Islam and assumed a Turkish name. In 1834, Omar Pasha became an instructor at the war ministry, following which he was appointed an aide-de-camp to a Turkish general. By 1839, he had become a colonel in the regular army with the principle assignment of extinguishing the frequent revolts which arose in the empire, 'crushing all effectively and showing particular ruthlessness against Christians'. He eventually married a wealthy heiress, and was appointed Governor of Constantinople. Immediately prior to the Russian invasion, Omar Pasha was promoted to Generalissimo and given the title 'Highness'.

Since October, the singular Omar and 'his beastly, untrustworthy and inefficient' troops held the massive Russian army at bay in Silistria and along the banks of the Danube. Such was the Turkish army.

As for the Russian army, it was an awesome war machine, unquestionably the world's largest. But, ponderous and clumsy, it was permeated with inefficiencies, deficiencies and corruption. At the pyramidal base of the military structure were masses of enlisted men, conscripted from the ranks of factory labourers, peasants and privately owned serfs. In the decades preceding the war, an average of 80,000 draftees were inducted annually, each to serve the mandatory twenty-five years. It was possible to avoid conscription for those with the means to do so, and many did, though class status exemption, bribery, influence or through 'hirelings' – volunteers who took the place of an official draftee. Landowners sent off rebellious serfs and communes arranged for the induction of troublesome peasants. Courts found it convenient to sentence religious offenders to military service, 'schismatics of all sects in general who have been detected in enticement, turbulence or disobedience'. Jews 'of bad conduct who did not pay their taxes' were also relegated to the army together with 'vicious men, vagabonds and criminals'. Not surprising that induction into the army was looked upon as a sort of penal servitude, which to some appeared a life sentence. Russian literature has frequent scenes of broken-hearted parents bidding farewell to distraught sons, as they prepare to depart from home. And if they ever did return home, in what sort of shape were they? One pathetic tale is recounted by Professor Curtiss:

> In 1855 an officer travelling to the rear with a convoy of convalescents had a conversation with a soldier of fifty-five who had re-enlisted after his term of service, as he found he could not live in retirement. He had not heard from his wife and children for twenty years. '. . . when a man becomes a soldier,' he said, 'the first thing that is known to you is that it is difficult to return, and you say farewell to your family as if it were forever . . .' So, after grieving for a time, he had forgotten. As for his wife, she had written several times and had sent him a shirt, and then the letters came more and more slowly and finally nothing at all. 'Indeed, from that time I don't even know if she is alive.' Eventually the army discharged him as too old, and the author met him going home to his village, with seven rubles in his pocket, to live out his days alone in the world.

Lessons in the army were learned by the rod. 'For the Russian soldier, the stick is necessary; he does not understand words,' wrote one commentator. 'To teach and to beat, to beat and to teach were at the time synonymous. If they said: teach him well – they meant: give him a good thrashing. For teaching they put to use fists, scabbards, drumsticks, and so on. Flogging with birches was practised comparatively rarely.'

In 1834, Nicholas decreed a series of military reforms by which service of twenty-five years could be reduced to fifteen through good conduct. In addition, the soldier with a ten-year record of good conduct was granted a leave from 28 to 180 days. For his services, the private in 1850 received an *annual* salary of 2.85 roubles and the sergeant, 4.05 roubles – this, at the time when leather for a pair of boots cost .80 roubles and a sheep-skin coat was worth 2.75 roubles. Officers suffered less: a lieutenant annually earned 238 roubles and a colonel 502.

The soldier was expected to sew his own shirts, boots and underwear. The government did, however, provide the necessary materials: cloth sufficient for two shirts a year, one pair of drawers and leather for two pairs of boots (plus two extra soles). Skilled regimental tailors produced uniforms and overcoats. Regulations, however, decreed that a uniform was to last two years and an overcoat three years; belts, helmets, knapsacks and other such items were expected to last ten years. Pity the poor unfortunate posted to unusually active service or to an especially harsh climate. Likely as not, his kit would wear out well before the stipulated period, especially if through the dishonesty of his regimental administrator he was issued with third-rate materials instead of the first-class stuff. Whatever the circumstances, our soldier was expected to turn out at all reviews in immaculate order. The story is told of one trooper whose boot 'broke open during drill, exposing his toe, whereupon the battalion commander raged against the sergeant, even calling for birches, and the latter was fortunate in escaping with a mere two weeks in the guard house on bread and water'.

Army officers were for the most part either nobles of hereditary families or nobles of lesser status. Most were of humble origins, men who had risen through the ranks having given exceptional service as sergeants for at least twelve years. The majority of officers were *jünkers*, young men who had received little formal military education, but who qualified for commission after having served as volunteer apprentices in a regiment. A mere ten per cent of the officer cadre were university graduates or possessed a higher education in special cadet schools. Thirty per cent had completed secondary school, but the majority was with minimal formal education, barely literate. At the time of the war, a network of cadet schools provided the army with approximately one-fifth of its officers.

Depending on the regiment and where it was stationed, an officer's life might have been one of carefree ease or of primitive privation and hardship. A guards officer from a wealthy family, finding himself in the capital, could look forward to splendid balls, fine dinners and other amusements such as drinking bouts and hob-knobbing with the fashionable of St Petersburg. The impoverished officer of a lesser infantry regiment, on the other hand, stationed in some insignificant provincial outpost might expect little more than extreme isolation, boredom and privation: 'Cast off in winter to a distant village, sometimes in a chicken-house, he sees no one but the parish priest; and even this does not fall to the lot of all of them.' Little wonder that many an officer, isolated in one of the empire's distant stations or another, took to drink and sunk into apathy.

Despite abuse, brutal treatment and privation, the army

managed to develop a strong esprit de corps. Regimental traditions, old soldiers' tales, inspirational exhortations by commanders and a system of awards and decorations all helped to instil pride in the service. The Orthodox Church, always so closely tied to Russian patriotic and nationalistic sentiment, was a powerful vehicle in the swaying of masses, no more so than in the army. Military authorities made skilful use of the Church in instilling submission and a sense of devotion to the cause. The love and loyalty the common soldier had for his 'little father', the emperor, was resolute. When in 1855 the troops of one station were informed of the death of Tsar Nicholas, they 'crossed themselves, many uttered prayers, others fell to their knees and bowed to the ground, praying for the repose of the soul of the departed!' as one contemporary reports. 'When I began to read the manifesto, the soldiers, officers, generals – all wept.' The soldiers' catechism which all learned by heart, defined the oath he took as 'a pledge given before the face of God on the Cross of the Saviour and on His Holy Gospel: to serve God and Sovereign with faith and truth: unconditionally to submit to commanders; patiently to endure . . . not to spare the last drop of blood for Sovereign and Fatherland'. The catechism went on to read, that whoever 'is true to the holy oath and lays down his life on the field of battle, will receive from God the Heavenly Kingdom; and who returns from war alive will have the glory and the grace of the Sovereign.' As in certain parts of today's world, so then in Russia: unquestionable obedience, cloaked in semi-religious fervour.

The army marched to war almost cheerfully. The same chronicler claims somewhat cynically, 'The Russian soldier always goes joyfully in a campaign, because on the campaign there is no tiresome drill, and at times there flows an extra drink of vodka; change of place and lodging cheers the glance;

finally, because, where you are going always seems better than it was where you came from.' Despite all, particularly tactical errors, successes in battle were won through the bravery and steadfastness of the enlisted man. 'The Russian soldier is an astonishing person: he goes to sleep with a cobblestone under his head, he is well fed with black biscuits and water, and he sings a song in a cow-shed – that is his superiority,' writes another observer. Helmuth Von Moltke, the famous German general, writes of the Russian soldiers who fought in the 1829 campaign against the Turks: 'Their brilliant moral qualities, which never left them, served as guarantees of success in the grave minutes of trial.'

The backbone of the army was the infantry, and here the bayonet was the favoured weapon. A determined bayonet charge in massed strength was deemed far more effective than any small-arms manoeuvre. Russian muskets were poorly constructed and badly mistreated by the troops, who generally regarded their weapons as essential only for mounting the bayonet or for display at glittering parades or reviews. Professor Curtiss tells of the 1318 smooth bores of the Moscow Regiment that were inspected during the Crimean War. 'Seventy were so badly rusted as to be unusable, while 464 had damaged locks. Many of the others had damaged or defective barrels, defective breeches, or worn and loose bayonets. In the Butyrskii Regiment, 1400 out of 1991 muskets received had similar defects. These were extreme cases, but other units had the same experience on a lesser scale.' The newly developed French breechloading musket was deemed unsuitable for Russian infantry. 'With us troops having this weapon would cease to fight [hand-to-hand], and there never would be enough cartridges.' The Prussian needle gun was also discounted: 'The rifleman, in the confusion of battle, has the possibility of firing all his cartridges in an instant and will be defenceless.'

In the decades preceding the war, the Russian cavalry, like the infantry, was an instrument of delight for the parade square. In the event that the emperor, while on a tour of inspection, unexpectedly called for a field training manoeuvre, the general staff always held in readiness a well-programmed sequence of battle evolutions. 'We rehearsed manoeuvres exactly like a ballet.' But Nicholas saw through this and vainly tried to impress on senior officers that their purpose was, first and foremost, the business of war and not dress parades. Nevertheless, many regimental commanders continued to frown on strenuous military exercises and on weapons training, outpost work, scouting and battle tactics. Standing apart from all this were the Cossacks, who inspired universal admiration and fear by their boldness, horsemanship and shrewdness.

Although the Russian infantry and cavalry were ill-prepared for war, the artillery and engineering services were in good shape. The gunners were well trained, properly equipped, and better educated and paid than others within the tsar's army. Marksmanship and manoeuvres took priority over parade square work. One British general wrote during the war, 'If it were not for the [Russian] artillery, we could drive them out of the country, but in that branch they are far superior in every way to us.' Another Englishman agreed less generously, 'I think they are equal, if not superior to us.'

Russian engineers were perhaps the most professional in attending to their task. In the business of fortification, siege, mining and bridge building, every advantage was taken of the latest technical innovations which were cleverly adopted to local conditions. It was Russian engineers who first put the electric spark to use in detonating explosives and it was they who during the war so efficaciously introduced the land mine. The sea ports of Sevastopol and Kronstadt were impressive examples of Russian engineering skill. United States Major Delafield, a member of a three-man commission sent by President Pierce to report on European military developments, wrote as follows of these fortifications: 'Such were the formidable defences that for two years set the allies at defiance and protected the city of St Petersburg. It cost the Russians great exertions and some treasure, and the allies far greater. Russian skill and ingenuity kept pace with that of the allies. Every new expedient on the part of the latter soon became known to the former, and her engineers, as capable in every way as those of France and England, with a ready talent to turn everything to advantage, were not long in adopting some counteracting defensive means.'

Such was the state of the tsar's army at the time it faced the allied invasion of Crimea.

II

SILISTRIA AND DEBATE

The Russian forces Omar Pasha faced on the banks of the Danube in spring 1854 were infantry and cavalry – not artillery and engineers. Against such an enemy he could for the moment hold his own, but not indefinitely, and before long he sent out pleas for reinforcement by the massed Anglo-French forces which had assembled at Gallipoli. With such reinforcements, they could together 'hurl' the enemy back across the Danube and save Turkey, he declared. Raglan was 'much pleased with Omar Pasha', and surprised that the Turks were 'making such a good show of it'. Anglo-French estimation of Turkish capability was reassessed and in time relief was promised.

On 22 May, General Bosquet, commanding a troop of Zouaves, marched out of Gallipoli and headed north to Adrianople. There he was to set up headquarters and command the left wing of the combined allied forces. Shortly after the start of the march, however, plans were changed and the general was now ordered to march on to the port town of Varna. Six days after Bosquet's departure, Raglan, St Arnaud and a contingent of the combined armies sailed out of Gallipoli also to buttress the besieged Turks by joining up with Bosquet just north of Varna. The advance force arrived at its destination on 2 June, and took up positions in the town and in its immediate vicinity. In the days which followed, vessel after vessel arrived in the harbour, bearing yet more troops, some freshly sent out from England and France. The town's population of 13,000 suddenly tripled in size. Russell, who found quarters with an Armenian in the village of Aladyn on Varna's outskirts, describes the scene shortly after the initial landing:

After a few days at Aladyn, I rode down to Varna and was astonished at the change which the place had undergone, owing principally to the French. Old blind side walls had been broken down, and shops opened, in which not only necessaries, but even luxuries, could be purchased; the streets, once so dull and silent, re-echoed the laughter and rattle of dominoes in the newly-established cafés. Wine merchants and sutlers from Algeria, Oran, Constantine, Marseilles, Toulon, had set up booths and shops, at which liqueurs, spirits, and French and country wines could be purchased at prices not intolerably high. The natives had followed the example. Strings of German sausages, of dried tongues, of wiry hams, of bottles of pickles, hung from the rafters of an old Turkish khan, which but a few days before was the abode of nothing but unseemly insects; and an empty storehouse was turned into a nicely white-washed and gaily painted 'Restaurant de l'Armée d'Orient pour Messieurs les Officiers et Sous- Officiers'.

The names of the streets, according to a Gallic nomenclature,

printed in black on neat deal slips, were fixed to the walls, so
that one could find his way from place to place without going
through the erratic wanderings which generally mark the
stranger's progress through a Turkish town. One lane was
named the Rue Ibrahim, another Rue de l'Hôpital, a third Rue
Yusuf; the principal lane was termed the Corso, the next was
Rue des Postes Françaises. As all these names were very
convenient, and had a meaning attached to them, no sneering
ought to defer one from confessing that the French manage
these things better than we do. Where at this period was the
English post-office? No one knew. Where did the English
general live? No one knew. Where was the hospital for sick
soldiers? No one knew. Did any one need to find General
Canrobert? He had but to ask the first Frenchman he met, and
he would tell him to go up the Corso, turn to the right, by the
end of the Rue de l'Hôpital, and there was the name of the
general painted in large letters, over the door of his quarters.
The French post-office and the French hospital were sufficiently indicated by the names of the streets.

The cosiness of these arrangements, however, was short-
lived, for by the end of June Varna's population had further
swelled with the arrival of an additional 15,000 troops. 'The
whole plain around Varna for the distance of two or three
miles, was covered with tents. Grass, herbage, and shrubs
disappeared, and the fields were turned into an expanse of
sand, ploughed up by araba wheels, and the feet of oxen and
horses, and covered with towns of canvas. There could not
have been less than 40,000 men encamped around the place,
including French, English, Egyptians and Turks, and the town
itself was choked in every street with soldiery. Upwards of 300
vessels were at anchor in the bay, and were kept in readiness to
sail at a moment's notice.'

On 24 June, the allied commanders were taken by surprise by the arrival to their headquarters of a Tartar horseman. 'Like bomb' he brought the sensational news that the siege of Silistra was over – in the early hours of the previous day the Russians had quietly withdrawn; Omar Pasha had prevailed. A cavalry reconnaissance team was dispatched to confirm this news, which in short order they did – no enemy troops were to be had anywhere on the left bank of the Danube.

The Russians had viewed Silistria as pivotal to their invasion – control of the fortress-town meant the control of Wallachia. It was essential to take it, not only for the continued penetration into the interior, but for any significant offensive action against the Turks. When the Russians crossed the Danube in March, there appeared to them no great obstacle in attaining this goal. The allies were encamped at Gallipoli, with not a sign of a single Frenchman or Englishman in Varna, and Omar Pasha was garrisoned 60 miles (100 kilometres) away at Shumla. 'Either Silistria will be left to its fate,' observed Engels at the time, 'then its fall will be assured . . . or the allies will come to its rescue. If this happens, a decisive battle will take place, for the Russians cannot retreat from Silistria without a fight if the army is to avoid demoralization and considerable loss of face. Actually, it would appear that they have no intention of doing so.'

How is it then that after three months' siege the massive Russian army was unable to dislodge the lone, stubborn Turk at Silistria? Furthermore, why did it fail even to cut off the flow of supplies into the city? Twenty-five years earlier, 'Prince Bragation with 14,000 troops found the means to isolate Silistria and render it impotent,' observes one military observer. But in 1854, 'General Paskevitch with an army of 100,000 was unable to do so.' This seems all the more incredible inasmuch as General Schilder, the brilliant engineer who masterminded the 1829 fall, was again supervising the siege of the town whose defences were so familiar to him.

That the siege of Silistria failed was the fault of one man, and one man alone – the commander-in-chief of the Russian forces, Field-Marshal Ivan Feodorovich Paskevich. After the death of Grand Duke Michael, it was Paskevich who stood closest to Emperor Nicholas. The tsar had implicit trust in the general and his respect for him exceeded even that given to his brother. Paskevich was the Commanding Officer of the Guards Division in which the emperor had served as a young man, and to the end of his days Nicholas referred to the general as 'Father-Commander'. The marshal was an unusually clever individual, reasonably well-read, efficient, conscientious and reserved. He came from wealthy but un-illustrious provincial nobility, and after completing the Corps des Pages he embarked on a military career of instant brilliance. By 1810, at twenty-eight years of age, he was already a major general, commanding the Orlov Regiment. He distinguished himself in the war against Napoleon, and in 1826 he brought to a successful conclusion the war against Persia, which Nicholas had previously all but forsaken as a lost cause. In 1829 he was presented with a field-marshal's baton, and two years later, after crushing the revolt of the Poles, he was awarded the title Prince of Warsaw. He was the administrator of the Kingdom of Poland until the start of the Crimean War. It was he, incidentally, who lead the Russian forces against the Hungarians in 1848 on behalf of the Hapsburgs.

From the very start, Paskevich did not favour this new war against Turkey and he vehemently counselled against crossing the Danube. Having crossed the river, he urged that the Russian troops be removed – particularly after Francis Joseph declared his neutrality in the pending conflict. Above all, the cautious Paskevich feared French and British intervention. To fight a coalition of these two powers, plus Turkey, and possibly Austria and Prussia, would be suicidal madness.

On 4 May, the field-marshal met with Nicholas and reviewed the situation. 'We cannot occupy the Principalities if Austria with its 60,000 appears on our rear. In such case we will be forced to abandon Wallachia and Moldavia and have on our hands 100,000 Frenchmen and Turks. We cannot rely on the Bulgarians. From the Balkans to the Danube, the Bulgarians are oppressed and unarmed. Like negroes, they live in slavery. In the mountains and beyond they are reportedly more independent, but between them there is no unity and little armament. To unify and to arm them requires time and our presence. From the Serbs – under their present ruler, we may expect nothing. Perhaps two or three thousand troops but not more – and Austria will be aggravated. In Turkey we can eventually expect an uprising, but thus far there has been no evidence of such.'

The field-marshal concluded his briefing by declaring that the Russian army must immediately be cleared out of the Principalities; the forces must re-cross the Purth, and there await developments. 'Austria's anger is so fierce,' Paskevich warned, 'that she might well bring claim on us, evacuation of the Principalities or not.'

It is evident that Paskevich's efforts on the Danube, from the outset were focused on an avoidance of any form of action that might hasten Austria's entry into the fray. As Soviet historian Tarlye points out somewhat cynically, 'Paskevich at Silistria wanted nothing, commanded nothing, ordered nothing. He did not wish to take Silistria, and indeed, he did not wish anything.' It got to the point where members of his staff plotted for his recall home. All of the field-marshal's urgings for a withdrawal fell on deaf ears.

Reluctant as Paskevich was, Engineer General Schilder

tackled his work with energy and enthusiasm, commencing siege operations on 24 March. In short order a pontoon bridge resting on the hulls of twenty-six sailing boats, was thrown across the Bortchin River. Fourteen batteries began to take shape – bunker-like structures, twenty feet (six metres) thick, constructed, according to Schilder's unique design. 'The soldiers worked with incredible diligence. It seemed to them that now, after crossing the Danube, war will progress in earnest.' As work proceeded, the general not only became increasingly 'fired up with determination to take Silistria' but also 'convinced . . . that if the field-marshal would not interfere with him, the fortress would inevitably fall, and fall soon'. On 10 April, the Russian siege guns commenced firing.

Unfortunately for Schilder, not two days had passed when Paskevich appeared on the scene for a personal inspection of the siege operations. Not one word was passed between the two ranking officers and within a couple of hours the field-marshal had departed. On the following day, however, a flow of orders flooded in from the headquarters of the Commander-in-Chief – remove certain baggage wagons, pack up this and that gun, send regiment such-and-such away from Silistria, leave in the garrison camp only so many pieces of artillery, dispatch the following specific support guns to Kalarash, etc. The most crippling order read as follows: 'In the event that the batteries are ordered abandoned, blow up the foundations of the embrasures so that the Turk will not discover the secret for the new method of battery construction.' The effect of this last order was devastating for the sappers. Why continue their exertions if on the next day the fruits of their labours might be blown sky high? The flow of Paskevich's orders was quite simply sabotaging the siege. Schilder was crushed; under such circumstances Silistria would never be taken. The weakened and dispirited siege continued on painfully for three more weary months. Finally, with Austria's posture assuming menacing proportions, orders were issued for a withdrawal not only from Silistria but from the Principalities; all work halted.

News of the Russian evacuation was received in Varna with astonishment. The *raison d'être* for the allied expedition had suddenly dissipated, and the prospect of war itself suddenly seemed to have dissipated. Eighty days had passed since the Anglo-French armies disembarked on Turkish soil in order to rescue their besieged ally from the barbarians of the North. And now the Turks had done it by themselves without a single English or French gun having been fired. 'I cannot recover from the shock of the disgraceful retreat of the Russians,' a frustrated St Arnaud complained to his wife. 'I would have infallibly beaten them, flung them into the Danube.' Among the assembled troops the same feel of disappointment dominated. They had come so far, waited so long, and now it seemed they would not even be 'having a go at it'. Sir George Evans paraded his troops and said a few words 'in order to soothe their spirits upon this point'.

Correspondent Karl Marx, writing for the *New York Tribune*, chided, 'There they are, eighty or ninety thousand English and French soldiers at Varna, commanded by old Wellington's late military secretary and by a marshal of France . . . there they are, the French doing nothing and the British helping them as fast as possible.' The Turks graciously thanked the allies for the aid they had received, and Minister of War Riza Pasha complimented the British on their delightful appearance. To his attendant, however, the Pasha commented drily, 'very fine to look at, but . . . probably they would run away'.

The allies arrived in Varna on 2 June, and the evacuation of Silistria took place three weeks later, but the Anglo-French army remained on the spot for more than another ten weeks. Two problems preoccupied them: first, strategizing for the future. What next: an evacuation for Gallipoli, or possibly a return home? But the more immediately pressing concern was how to cope with every sort of shortage, with boredom and sickness, and, above all, with the ravages of cholera.

When the allied armies disembarked at Gallipoli in early April, the expedition was committed to one objective: the defence of Turkey and particularly of Constantinople. No definite plans had been formulated for future operations. Now that Austrian pressure had successfully squeezed the Russians from the Principalities, Constantinople and Turkey were no longer threatened. 'The objectives for which the Western powers undertook the war had been already attained.' Three years later, as the war was drawing to a close, Queen Victoria told her uncle, King Leopold: 'I repeat now what we have said from the beginning. . . if Austria had held strong and decided language to Russia in 1853, we should never have had this war.'

By mid-summer, 'England had become so eager for conflict that the idea of desisting from the war merely because the war had ceased to be necessary was not tolerable to the people.' Military contact with the enemy simply had to be made. And then, quite unexpectedly, word was received in Varna that 10,000 Russians remained on the south shore of the Danube, north of Constanta. For St Arnaud, the opportunity of giving battle was too rich to miss, and without further ado, he dispatched an expedition to seek out and destroy the wretched Russians. Should the diplomats achieve success in restoring peace without further military action having been taken, France at least would return home in glory, having met the enemy face to face. In Bosquet's mind there was little doubt that, if the enemy were engaged, success would follow 'a good cannonade and a bayonet charge'.

'The result of this expedition was one of the most fruitless and lamentable that has ever occurred in the history of warfare' Russell wrote. Even before the start of the month-long march north, on the very eve of departure from Varna, 'Cholera declared itself among them with an extraordinary and dreadful violence. Between midnight and eight o'clock next morning 600 men lay dead in their tents smitten by the angel of death!' The expedition nevertheless pressed on, at last reached the Danube and found the south shore void of any Russians – they had long departed. The sick and dispirited troops took the long way home, along the same path they had just trod. By the time they reached Varna, over seven thousand men had succumbed to cholera.

What, then, was there to do? In London, Paris and Varna, alternatives were discussed. An invasion of Russia through Poland was possible only if Prussia actively sided with the allies – but Frederick William had already declared his neutrality. An attack by sea through the Baltic was proposed. There the allied fleets, under Sir Charles Napier and Vice Admiral Deschenes, were already carrying out operations against enemy fortresses, but with mixed results. A full-scale invasion of Russia through St Petersburg, it was decided, would require the support of Sweden and to bring that power into the war was deemed undesirable. 'If Sweden joins us,' Aberdeen cautioned, 'it will be for objects of her own, to which we shall become more or less pledged. Sweden is not moved, as we are, by a regard for a balance of power in Europe, or any desire to redress the wrongs of Turkey.' An alliance with Sweden would serve only to complicate further the possibility of full-scale war. By a process of exclusion, the sole remaining 'point of contact with the enemy' was the north coast of the Black Sea. Russia's great naval base at Sevastopol, 'the eye tooth of the bear', was the symbol of her power in the Black

Sea. Here, there was a mammoth arsenal with an enormous supply of stores, 'fortified seaward by more than 700 guns, and sheltering Nicholas Black Sea Fleet'.[17]

The 'stupendous naval and military establishment' at Sevastopol was not necessary to protect Russian maritime trade or to guard against an enemy. It was useful 'only for aggression', Clarendon declared. 'The taking of Sevastopol and the occupation of Crimea,' urged *The Times*, 'would repay all costs of the war and permanently settle in our favour the principal questions in dispute.' It went one to say that peace with the tsar would 'leave Russia in possession of the same means of aggression and would only enable her to re-commence the war at her pleasure'. From Varna, St Arnaud argued, an invasion of Crimea would be a 'beautiful climax that would end the war'.

The notion of invading Crimea and of taking Sevastopol had been bandied about in London and Paris as early as November 1853. The Duke of Argyll advanced three good reasons for such action:

In the first place, it would fulfil, as nothing else could, our avowed object of relieving the Turkish Empire from the most imminent danger to which it was exposed. In the second place, Sevastopol was the point in the Russian dominion most accessible to the assault of fleets, and affording the most secure naval base for military operations, however prolonged. In the third place, it was that point of Russian territory which, at the extremity of her dominions in Europe, would call for the greatest drain on her resources, both as to men and materials of war.

But arguments against an invasion of Sevastopol were equally strong. No one knew the Russian strength and estimates of troop concentration varied wildly. 'It is very curious that neither the government nor the commanders have the slightest information as to Russian forces in the Crimea or the strength of Sevastopol,' Grenville observed. 'Some prisoners they took affirm that there were 150,000 men in the peninsula, but nobody believes that.' London was warned against any such attack. 'An attack on Sevastopol,' reported Major General Shaw-Kennedy, a veteran of the Peninsular War, 'was so desperate and reckless an adventure that no commander-in-chief would attempt it. The place is invulnerable on the side of the sea. To force the line of defence on the side of the land would be very difficult, and the besieging force would be exposed to attack by all the forces in the south of Russia.'

The debate in cabinet continued. On 6 April, Sir James Graham, First Lord of the Admiralty, received a persuasive letter from the highly regarded Sir Edmund Lysons, Commander-in-Chief of the British fleet in the Black Sea. 'I remember that when you spoke to me of the defences of Sevastopol in October last, I said it appeared to me that people in general thought too lightly of them, and an opinion is gaining ground that the place is invulnerable. To me the bare idea of our not striking a successful blow at Sevastopol is painful. It haunts me in my solitary evening walks on the deck of this splendid ship, for I am convinced that if we do not leave our mark in the Black Sea this time we shall have to do the work over again before many years elapse.' Graham was converted to the invasion proposal, and the peace faction lost another voice of moderation.

The Times continued to clamour for an attack on Crimea. 'Day after day in that month of June, the authority of the newspaper kept gaining and gaining upon the Queen's Government.' The bellicose urgings of Palmerston and Newcastle fell on increasingly receptive ears. Eventually, towards the end of the month, Lord Aberdeen lost control of the cabinet And, despite his deep personal commitment to peace, gave his consent for the invasion of Crimea.[18]

The cabinet gathered at Lord Russell's home at Richmond Park to consider the war situation. 'It was the habit of ministers at that time to have cabinet dinners, as well as the usual and more regular meetings in Downing Street. At the dinners the least serious work was done – such, for example, as the final reading of dispatches, which in substance had been already agreed to,' reminisces the Duke of Argyll. 'It was midsummer, and the air was full of the smell of all blossoms,' and the dinner they had just consumed was a heavy one. Vintage port was passed around and soon some of the ministers were found to have dozed off in the comfort of the deep leather armchairs. The final dispatch was read and the assembled guests muttered their approval. 'In this way, after many and long discussions,' concludes Argyll, 'we had unanimously agreed to send out a dispatch to Raglan, directing him to employ our army in an attack on the Russians in Crimea.' The British mind was made up.

In Paris, news of the British decision was received by Napoleon with delight. He had himself frequently promoted the idea of a Crimean invasion. Now, more than ever, the French desperately required a military victory, especially after the Dobruja debacle. The emperor endorsed British resolution, and heartily agreed to the dispatching of orders to the allied joint staff in Varna. The document provided for an invasion of Russia, but left it up to the allied command to determine the most prudent date for such action.

12

ON TO CRIMEA

When word was received in Varna of the decisions taken in London and Paris, the council of war immediately assembled to deliberate on the course of action next to be taken. The full assembly of ranking officers came together: Marshal St Arnaud, Lord Raglan, and admirals Hamelin, Dundas, Lyons and Brant.

In the British camp, troop morale had reached its lowest ebb; in many quarters, men suffered from depression. Most of the soldiers had been in the East for over four months without as much as laying an eye on a Russian; they were bored. The roe deer, boar and game birds, which had at one time been so plentiful, were now hunted out. Food was available, not plentiful and barely tolerable. 'The doctors thought a pound of meat a day was not enough for each man in such a climate, especially as the meat was rather deficient in gelatine and in nutritious quality.' As summer progressed the bread 'served out of the Varna bakeries became darker, more sour and less baked'. Large quantities of sometimes un-ripened apricots ('kill johns') were devoured by the men, as was other hard fruit. The resultant diarrhoea served to weaken the men, and this, no doubt, contributed to the spread of ever-present cholera. Temperatures hovered in the mid-nineties, and the physical exercises that were the rule of the day were made tolerable only by permitting soldiers to shed most of their heavy kit.

In the interest of sanitation, the French battalions changed camp sites every fortnight. Not only did this arrangement periodically permit a gainful employment of troops, but it allowed them a physical change of scene. No such luck for the British; concern over sanitation arrangements was a back-burner issue. In addition, their tents were more cumbersome – shared by numerous wives and sweethearts – and this made camping and de-camping a reasonably arduous enterprise. It may be noted, furthermore, that a British officer's baggage was of significantly greater volume than that of his opposite number in the army of France. French officers 'live in their uniform, while everybody knows that no real British soldier is quite happy without his mufti. He must have his wide-awake and shooting jacket and dressing gown and evening dress, a tub of some sort or another, a variety of gay shirting, pictorial, and figurative, while the Gaul does very well without them.'

Perhaps those who suffered most but complained least were the stolid women of the camp. In the British army of the time, 'Queen's Regulations' allowed six married women for every hundred men, excluding non-commissioned officers. Such women were officially recognized; they received barrack ac-commodation; and their children were entitled to accompany them and to attend regimental school. With this particular expeditionary force, however, only four women for every hundred men were permitted to embark in Malta, and because children were prohibited far fewer women found themselves in Varna than otherwise might have been. Sharing the squalor, shortages and illnesses of their men-folk, for the most part they attended to cooking, laundry and mending. The women were 'unacknowledged', and in order to survive, they had for the most part to scrounge and scavenge. 'The poor women are most to be pitied,' observed Lieutenant Stirling of the Highland Brigade, identifying them as 'miserable wretches and a most depraved set'. Another observer comments, 'Their morality seems to have been of the mottled or variable sort; they were doubtless indulgent and often tempted.' The Minister of War, the Duke of Newcastle, eventually concluded, 'It was a misfortune that any went.'

Wives of officers, however, were quartered in considerably greater comfort away from the camp, either in Pera or Constantinople, with a few even living on board husbands' yachts. A small armada of such vessels, some quite luxurious, arrived in the area and followed the armies along the shores of the Black Sea, where they provided a more tolerable 'home way from home' for a select few.[19] Madame St Arnaud for example, lived in Pera and entertained with great elegance *l'élite des dames*. One of the more adventuresome 'ladies of quality' was Lady 'Fanny' Duberly who distinguished herself by following her husband everywhere, even onto the actual battlefields. Writing to a friend, she says:

> You ask how I really endure what I do? . . . by never thinking of it for one moment. I never, if I can avoid it, have one idle moment. Work – wash – write all the morning – ride from four till seven every day – and then dinner and rum and water till bedtime, or the very strongest Turkish coffee. You must have just as much pluck as the men – it is no place for women. Men

are so eager for their own health and lives – their sports and amusements, that if you cloy them they leave you behind, if you go with them it's all very well . . .

Her colourfully written Journal offers a glimpse of the prevailing attitudes towards the hardships being endured by one and all:

I was out in the evening when stragglers [from heat and cholera] came in; and a piteous sight it was – men on foot, driving and goading on their wretched, wretched horses, three or four of which could hardly stir. There seems to have been much unnecessary suffering, a cruel parade of death, more pain inflicted than good derived; but I suppose these sad sights are merely casualties of war, and we must bear them with what courage and fortitude we may.

By far the most pressing concern in the East was cholera. From the very beginning, this dread disease indiscriminately plagued Englishmen, Frenchmen, Turks and Egyptians alike. Despite precautionary measures, men died at rapidly increasing rates not only in Varna but at Gallipoli and on board ships. At first it was thought to be diarrhoea – transmitted by the wine and fruits of the country – but when the sickness took on the added complications of severe vomiting, cramps and high fever, the true diagnosis was confirmed. Death became a commonplace thing. Captain Jocelyn of the Scots Guards, for example, recalls: 'We buried three this morning and this afternoon I have three more to bury. I have read the burial service over their bodies – it is a very sad duty, and when one sees the strongest cut down in a few hours, it impresses upon one the uncertainty of all life . . . it is most depressing being here.'

Canrobert's First Division numbered nearly 8,000 men – eventually 5,000 of these were affected with cholera and 1,500 died. Bosquet's and Prince Napoleon's divisions lost approximately 1,700 each. The navies did not escape. One midshipman records:

> the sailors suffered even more acutely from its ravages by being crowded so closely together, as all crews must be on board ship. One man would scream out in pain on the lower deck at night, and his cries were generally followed by those of others. Thus the flagship lost 109 men in a few days, and on board some of the French ships the mortality was even greater.

Correspondent Russell describes a visit to a French hospital:

> Men sent in there with fevers and other disorders were frequently attacked with the cholera in its worst form, and died with unusual rapidity, in spite of all that could be done to save them. I visited the hospital, and observed that a long train of araba carts, filled with sick soldiers, were drawn up by the walls. There were thirty-five carts, with three or four men in each. These were sick French soldiers sent in from the camps, and waiting till room could be found for them in the hospital. A number of soldiers were sitting down by the roadside, and here and there the moonbeams flashed brightly off their piled arms. The men were silent; not a song, not a laugh! A gloom, seldom seen among French troops, reigned amid groups of grey-coated men, and the quiet that prevailed was only broken now and then by the moans and cries of pain of the poor sufferers in the carts. Observing that about fifteen arabas without any occupants were waiting in the square, I asked a sous officier for what purpose they were required. His answer, sullen and short, was, 'Pour les morts – pour les Français décédés, Monsieur!'

Burials were hasty and often loads of bodies were taken out
to sea, where they were expeditiously and unceremoniously
dumped. Russell continues:

> Horrors occurred here every day which were shocking to think
> of. Walking by the beach one might see some straw sticking up
> through the sand and on scraping it away with his stick, he
> would be horrified at bringing to light the face of a corpse,
> which had been deposited there, with a wisp of straw around it,
> a prey to dogs and vultures.

Of the bodies buried at sea, Lieutenant Colonel Edward
Hamley writes:

> . . . after a time the corpses, sewed in blankets or hammocks,
> and swollen to giant size, rose to the surface and floated upright
> among the ships, their feet being kept down by the shot used to
> sink them. One of these hideous visitants lingered about the
> foot of the accommodation ladder of one of our transport, till a
> man going down the side passed cords with weights attached
> over its neck, when it slowly sank.

Sickness, death, boredom, ennui. Discipline went by the
board. 'Drilling and tight stocking began to fall into disuse
and by general order, towards the end of July, moustaches were
allowed to grow.' Soldiers fearing cholera took to drink, ratio-
nalizing that brandy was a preventive. 'They might be seen lying
drunk in the kennels, or in the ditches by the wood sides, under
the blazing rays of the sun, covered with swarms of flies . . . the
conduct of many of the men, French and English, seemed
characterized by a recklessness verging on insanity.'

It would be impossible, the allied commanders reasoned
when they met as a council of war, to remain in Varna without

eventually losing the entire force. The need to do something was urgent; the armies simply had to move. And, it was unanimously decided to move on to Crimea.

The momentous decision had at last been taken, and now attention became focused on the preparations. The urgent problem: no maps of Crimea were available and the coast was relatively unknown. The first task, therefore, was to find a landing place, close to Sevastopol, which could safely accommodate an invasion of 60,000 soldiers, over 3,000 horses and 130 heavy field guns. The second problem was to acquire the necessary boats and rafts to execute such an amphibious assault. The French insisted that there be immediate availability of heavy artillery support. This meant that flat-bottomed lighters had to be constructed to enable the guns to be run out straight from the boat onto the beach.

Varna suddenly became animated as frenetic preparations got under way; everyone looking forward to quitting the miserable country. From Constantinople there arrived a large number of Turkish boats that commonly plied the Bosphorus. These vessels, 50 feet (15 metres) long, 8 feet (2.5 metres) wide and drawing less than a foot (30 centimetres) of water, were fastened together in pairs and planked over, and thus rafts were formed, each one capable of carrying over 150 troops or two heavy guns with crews

At first only the highest-ranking officers knew their true destination was Sevastopol. Rumours were rampant, some supposing that they were bound for Odessa, while others wishfully laying bets that they were returning to Portsmouth or Toulon. Actually, to most it did not matter where they were going. 'Tired of the monotony of life in the wretched country and depressed by the influence of illness and laborious idleness,' all were happy at last to be on their way.

On 20 July, Generals Brown and Canrobert, accompanied

by artillery and engineering experts, set off in HMS *Fury* to reconnoitre Sevastopol and to explore the neighbouring coastline for a suitable landing place. The *Fury* 'stood off Sevastopol quietly at night, and about two o'clock ran in softly, and stopped within 2,000 yards (1,800 metres) of the batteries.' There she remained till six o'clock in the morning. As General Brown counted the guns, an officer observed a suspicious movement in the muzzle of one, and a moment afterwards a shot roared through the rigging. An undeniable signal to quit, and the *Fury* did so, steaming out of the harbour at full speed – but the shot came after her still faster. A shell burst close to her, and one shot went through her hull; fortunately, no one was hurt.

On the 28th, the *Fury* returned to Varva. Brown and Canrobert, now more optimistic than ever, were in agreement that the most 'perfectly practicable' landing place was at the mouth of the Katcha river, 7.5 miles (12 kilometres) north of Sevastopol.

The decision to invade Crimea was made on 18 July; the embarkation was completed and the last of the ships cleared Varna's harbour some nine weeks later. Fifty-two days, more precisely – time that slipped by for every sort of reason to delay or, indeed, to suspend the departure. First it was St Arnaud: cholera losses were so great that the weakened force was in no position to move out. It was rumoured, furthermore, that the Russians had halted their withdrawal eastwards from the Principalities and now they might well return to invade Turkey. In addition, the season was far too advanced for opening such an ambitious campaign. Raglan would hear none of these arguments. But as August wore on, things changed – French enthusiasm for the invasion waxed and Raglan's eagerness waned; the English were unable to secure flat-bottomed boats for the landing of troops, horses and artillery. 'Earlier Dundas had refused the opportunity to buy many of these because he regarded the price too high. The French had immediately paid the price and now the British were paying any amount for the same things. Virtually everyone blamed much of the delay of the British force on Dundas' haggling over a few hundred pounds at a time when each day's delay cost thousands.' And now it was Raglan who argued that the season was too late for the massive undertaking. St Arnaud would hear none of these arguments. The English wish 'not to take part', he scorned. 'I will make them go to Crimea in spite of themselves.'

In the meantime, the mounting invasion of Crimea ceased to be a secret. Russian intelligence agents in London and Paris worked assiduously, attending to their task with brilliant results. All the while *The Times*, together with other papers, reported on the details of the comings and goings at Varna, and in St Petersburg everything was read with more than passive interest. Much valuable intelligence was thus gained and the tsar's staff lacked knowledge only of a few minor details.

In the hiatus of those fifty-two summer days, Russia poured vast reinforcements into Sevastopol, and the garrison there worked tirelessly in buttressing the defences. Parapets were constructed, embrasures installed, and abatis of felled trees and pointed stakes put into place. Gun emplacements were constructed for a variety of artillery pieces, including navy guns of 68 pounds; arsenals, barracks and warehouses were made bomb-proof. Directing this gigantic effort was General Eduard Ivanovich Todleben, the brilliant engineer, who not only oversaw virtually every detail of construction, but personally drew up the overall master plan for the gigantic enterprise. During the siege itself, it was he who directed the strengthening of redoubts, the re-positioning of guns and the improvisation of other defensive measure. Out of the 'very stones and earth of Sevastopol', there arose 'an immortal monument to his genius and his glory'.

If Britain could lay claim to a true hero of the Crimean War, undeniably it would be Florence Nightingale; in Russia's case, it would be Todleben. It was this simple son of a Riga merchant who so successfully confounded the enemy. For very nearly a full year, the allied forces besieged the port city, and it was only after a loss of 185,000 lives that the exhausted Sevastopol finally capitulated. His genius and originality consisted in a totally fresh view of the nature of defence. 'He may justly be called the originator of the idea that a fortress is to be considered, not as a walled town but as an entrenched position, intimately connected with the offensive and defensive capacities of an army and as susceptible of alteration as the formation of troops in battle or manoeuvre.'

When Todleben arrived at Sevastopol, he found the situation in disgraceful need. A mere 39,000 men were available for the defence of the stronghold. Of the 1,944 guns deposited in the arsenal, only 931 were usable and the total number of serviceable pieces, including those of the anchored fleet, was 2,822. A little less than 90,000 round of shot and shell were available in the stores. There were no building materials, few supplies in the depots, and tools for but two hundred men. The commissariat was without money and the troops had not received salaries for months. It was estimated that the food stores would last no more than five months. 'Sevastopol was intended to strike a blow, not to receive one. For all aggression its resources were ample, though for resistance it was wanting in many respects,' comments W.H. Russell in his history of the siege.

Todleben's genius and inspiration quickly reversed Sevastopol's inadequate situation. Long after the mid-August landing at Eupatoria and into October, as the battles of Alma, Balaklava and Inkerman were being fought, efforts within Sevastopol were redoubled in strengthening further the powerful line of defence. The entire population took part in the effort as man, woman and child toiled alongside soldiers and sailors. By day, and by torchlight at night, women conveyed earth in their aprons and children pushed wheelbarrows. 'One battery was known as "the women's battery" and the builders were presented with a silver medal. A child of ten, whose father was killed in the early days of the siege, actually fired guns and received a military decoration. Even younger boys helped in the work of defence and those of fourteen and over performed regular military duties, encouraged by their mothers.'

From the north there continued to flow reinforcements and additional supplies, and soon the garrison had doubled in numbers. The Moscow Regiment took its position in the city after a forced five-day march of 160 miles (260 kilometres). By 17 October, at the time the allies commenced the actual bombardment of the town, fortifications stood completed, redans were finished, gun emplacements occupied strategic positions, abatis were in place, and the Russian batteries stood armed with every sort of heavy gun. All was in readiness for the lengthy siege.

On 24 August, as the early work of defence preparations was getting under way in Sevastopol, another council of war convened in Varna. It was a long session, with St Arnaud mostly commanding the floor, arguing for a decision to invade Crimea. He spoke passionately and with a 'clarity and precision of language and a firmness of conviction which rendered him truly eloquent'. It was here that victory would be had, where the combined forces would achieve 'success and glory'. Eventually, after several hours of debate, the marshal's view prevailed, and the decision was taken to launch the invasion, with the embarkation to commence immediately.

On the day following, St Arnaud issued a lengthy, inspirational proclamation to his troops:

> Soldiers, you have just given fine examples of perseverance, calmness and energy, in the midst of painful circumstances which must now be forgotten. The hour has come to fight to conquer . . . Providence calls us to Crimea . . . the enterprise is good and worthy of you . . . I see in it success itself . . . we shall soon salute the three united flags floating together on the ramparts of Sevastopol with our national cry, '*Vive l'Empereur*!'

Lord Raglan issued no such stirring message to his troops; he satisfied himself by dictating the following terse memorandum: 'Mr Commissary-General Filder to take steps to ensure the troops should all be provided with a ration of porter for the next few days.'

That same evening the work of embarkation began. When finally the fleet did weigh anchor, the French had shipped 28,000 soldiers, 1,437 horses and 68 guns. The Turks, who were attached to St Arnaud's forces, loaded nearly 6,000 infantry on to their own vessels. Admiral Lyons took charge of the British embarkation. At first, 60 guns, each with six horses for drawing, were loaded on board the transports. There then followed 28,800 soldiers and finally the cavalry's 1,110 horses were swung aboard.

The entire procedure was painfully slow. The slightest movement of the sea hampered the stowing away of guns and horses. Any mild surf brought the operation to a standstill. It took the British fourteen days to complete the embarkation, but at last, on the evening of 6 September, all was in readiness for departure. The French contingent had already left harbour. Their work had been completed two days earlier and St Arnaud adamantly refused to wait further for what he considered the intolerable delay of the British operations.

On the moonlit early hours of 7 September, a gun shot from HMS *Britannia* broke the stillness. At this signal, 104 vessels readied to weigh anchor and make way. Soon the *Agamemnon*, flagship of Admiral Lyons, moved through with signals and colours flying. By mid-morning the last of the ships had cleared harbour. Listen to the correspondent Russell:

> It was a vast armada. No pen could describe its effect upon the eye. Ere an hour had elapsed it had extended itself over half the circumference of the horizon. Possibly no expedition so complete and so terrible in its means of destruction, with such enormous power in engines of war and such capabilities of locomotion, was ever yet sent forth by any worldly power. The fleet, in five irregular and straggling lines, flanked by men-of-war and war steamers, advanced slowly, filling the atmosphere with innumerable columns of smoke, which gradually flattened out into streaks and joined the clouds, adding to the sombre appearance of this well-named 'Black Sea'. The land was lost to view very speedily beneath the coal clouds and the steam clouds of the fleet, and as we advanced not an object was visible in the half of the great circle which lay before us, save the dark waves and cold sky.

Some thirty nautical miles (fifty-five kilometres) from the coast, the Royal Navy made its rendezvous with the French fleet. Signals were had, 'hurrahs!' exchanged, and then they together sailed north – to Crimea to fight the war which, in the words of E.J. Hobsbawm, was nothing more than a 'notoriously incompetent international butchery'.

13

THE WAR ON THE BALTIC

Challenging as it may be to appreciate the full complexities of conditions and events that finally triggered the invasion of Russia, the task of following the progress of the war itself is relatively straightforward. It must, however, be understood at the outset that the war which took place on that peculiarly-formed peninsula, jutting prominently into the Black Sea, was not a localized struggle.

Most certainly, the peninsula was the focal point of the struggle, beginning in September 1854 with the allied landing at Kalamita Bay on its western coast, and terminating in January 1856 with the Russian bombardment of Sevastopol. It was on these shores that the celebrated battles, such as Alma and Balaklava, were fought. It was here that reputations were made and unmade of such familiar names as Florence Nightingale, Lord Raglan and the Earl of Lucan. Here too Tennyson found inspiration for his immortal 'The Charge of the Light Brigade'.

The Crimean War was a struggle global in scope – one might be tempted even to consider it the *first* world war. As pointed out earlier, blood was shed in more than one part of the world, and the vibrations of war were felt in such unlikely places as Australia, Canada, Hawaii and India. After Crimea itself, the second most noteworthy theatre of war – uncelebrated by song and story – was along the shores of Finland on the Baltic Sea. Squadrons of the Anglo-French fleet were bombarding Russian installations at Bomarsund and other centres of those northern waters long before gunfire resounded in Crimea, and efforts did not let up until near the war's end.

And finally, there were the ancillary theatres of war, which all too frequently escape notice of historians – garnering no more than footnotes at best. Places close to Crimea, that is Romania, the Caucasus and Armenia, and utterly remote locations, such as the Kola Peninsula, just below the Arctic Circle, and Kamchatka on the Pacific Ocean. In all these places battles also were fought and lives were lost.

So, when and where did the Crimean struggle actually start? France would say that it began with its declaration of war on 27 March 1854. Britain would argue for the following day, with its own declaration. The Russians declared on Britain and France on 11 April. It would probably be most accurate, however, to accept the Turkish declaration against Russia as the start of the war: 5 October 1853. A month later, with Omar Pasha's resounding victory over the Russians at Oltenitza, the first blood was shed.

Five months preceding the allied landing at Kalamita Bay, the Anglo-French fleet had entered the Baltic. In tracing the progress of the Crimean War, therefore, it would be appropriate to begin with the arrival of that naval force.

When word was received in London of the Russian invasion of the Danubian provinces, alarm was raised by Vice-Admiral

Sir Charles Napier who warned that with the inevitability of war, Britain would do well to shore up its naval defences. The Tsar had some twenty-eight ships of the line in the Baltic, he argued, plus an extended number of auxiliary vessels. Such a force might readily threaten the British coastline, which at the time was left defenceless – the bulk of the Royal Navy had by then been dispatched to the Mediterranean. Prime Minister Aberdeen at first scoffed at Napier's warnings, sensing no urgency in the situation, but within a couple of months as developments grew more alarming, he acquiesced and approved the assembly of a fleet at Spithead, the ships being drawn mostly from the Lisbon station.

France at that moment was in no position to take action in the Baltic. All its available ships had been sent to the eastern Mediterranean under Vice-Admiral Hamelin and it would be some time before another fleet could be assembled. France was, however, able to offer immediate token support in the form of the 100-gun battleship *Austerlitz*.

The hastily gathered force was put under Admiral Napier's command and ordered to the Baltic – fifteen ships of 882 guns with 8,500 men. It was the largest exclusively steam-ship fleet ever to assemble – augmented later by sailing vessels. Its mission was to set up a blockade at the entrance to the Gulf of Finland in order to deny a Russian sea lane to the North Sea. Sir Charles was further ordered to provide protection to the coastlines of Sweden and Denmark – really, a show of strength to reassure those two countries before they gave thought to siding with the Tsar. The Admiralty's orders were clearly focused: 'establish a strict blockade of the Gulf of Finland . . . to prevent the Russian fleet from passing this line'. It is important to note that at this stage no mention was made of possible offensive action, for, as we shall see, Napier eventually suffered severe censure from the government and the British public for not having pursued the enemy more aggressively.

The squadron passed through Kiel and came to anchor at Kjöge Bay, just south of Copenhagen. It was here that Sir Charles first determined he could most effectively dominate any Russian exit into the North Sea. When the news of Britain's declaration of war was received, the admiral issued a resounding call to his men, which later came to haunt him:

> Lads, war is declared with a common and bold enemy. Should they meet us in battle, you know how to dispose of them. Should they remain in port, we must try to get them. Success depends upon the quickness and precision of your firing. Also, lads, sharpen your cutlasses, and the day is your own!

Within a couple of weeks, however, he moved out of Kjöge and sailed for the entrance to the Gulf of Finland, arriving there on 19 April. Since the days of Peter the Great, the Gulf of Finland was (and continues to be) of critical strategic importance for Russian security and commerce. The 200-mile (320-kilometre) channel leads directly to St Petersburg, the Russian capital at the time, and its defence rested on four heavily-fortified strong-points. Northwest of the entrance, between Sweden and Finland lay the Åland Islands with the massive Bomarsund fortress. On the southern coast stood Revel (Tallinn), while on the north coast Sveaborg guarded the entrance to Helsingfors (Helsinki). The final approach to St Petersburg was strongly defended by the massively fortified port town of Kronstadt.

The Russian Baltic Fleet was larger than Napier had been led to believe. There were, in fact, twenty-seven ships of the line, eight frigates and ninety other vessels – corvettes, paddle-steamers, schooners and gunboats. Initially, the Russian Baltic

Fleet was superior to that of the allies in terms of both numbers and firepower. It was, however, un-centralized and its ships were scattered about in a number of Gulf locations, principally at Sveaborg and Kronstadt. By steadily patrolling the waters between these points, Napier was successful in denying the enemy an opportunity to gather forces in one major concentration, thereby always assuring an upper hand. The Russians faced two additional problems: ice and uncertainty in leadership. Since early winter, the fleet had been ice-bound and in the first weeks of Napier's unexpected entry of the Baltic, it remained locked up. By the time the ice had given way in early May, the issue of leadership had become severely exacerbated – there was no united command. The 27-year old Grand Duke Konstantin Nikolayevich, to whom command of the Kronstadt Division was entrusted, was inexperienced and indecisive, while the authority of the 77 year-old Admiral Pyotr Ivanovich Rikord, aboard the 110-gun *Imperator Pyotr I*, was generally in question, particularly by the Sveaborg Division.

Napier's arrival at the entrance of the Gulf coincided with a period of heavy fogs and gales. With landmarks made invisible by the weather, lighthouses destroyed or extinguished and an unavailability of pilots, he found himself in a tenuous position. Further problems beset the fleet: most of the ship's crews were untrained and inexperienced raw recruits or elderly men who had been hastily pressed into service. It took at least half a year of hard training for a recruit to acquire a degree of effective seamanship; the men of the Baltic fleet were lacking it. For the shortage of trained signalmen, for example, station-keeping was problematical thus making manoeuvring at sea hazardous at best. The shortage of experienced gunnery officers was even more critical. The commanding officer of HMS *Princess Royal*: 'Daily did we practise at the target, and what with the noise of the guns, and the hammers of the artificers, of whom there were about 100 on board, for a fortnight we were in the confusion of Babel; but still we could not get men, men, men!' And lastly, most of the British ships were of deep draught, which prevented them from entering the shallow waters of many ports and coastal areas. It was clear to Admiral Napier and his senior officers that they were painfully unprepared to carry out any meaningful offensive action.

The unending thick fog was particularly distressing. Reviewing the overall unhappy situation, rather than any particular hazard, he ordered the fleet to about turn and make for the safety of Stockholm – and there he languished for nearly two weeks, waiting for the weather to change. During that forced sojourn, he sought and received an audience with King Oscar I, whom he tried to persuade to come over to the side of the allies. All without success – his majesty remained adamant in his neutrality. Sweden's relations with Russia were excellent and he was quite unprepared to jeopardize them at the behest of Britain or France.

In early May, the weather cleared sufficiently for the fleet to reconnoitre the small town of Hangö on the Finnish mainland, across from Stockholm, where a few rounds were haphazardly exchanged – the first exchange of fire on the Baltic. The ships then moved on to Sveaborg where, it was determined, the fortifications were too formidable for an effective engagement; little might be done, other than to maintain surveillance.

Nearly three months had passed since Napier's arrival to the Baltic. The French by then had joined him with a good-sized fleet, Vice-Admiral Parseval-Deschènes in command – twenty steamers and sailing vessels with a combined force of 1,200 guns. Napier's own fleet had by then nearly doubled, with the arrival from Spithead of additional. The blockade effectively held its ground, but apart from the token engagement at

Hangö, little had been achieved to quench the public's developing yearning for glory in the field.

On 21 June, however, a singular engagement did take place within the Gulf. Captain William Hall, commanding a small squadron of three ships, *Hecla, Odin* and *Valorous*, had been ordered to lay off Bomarsund to observe Russian movements. This formidable fortress, strategically situated in the Gulf of Bothnia midway between Sweden and Finland, was vital for the defence of Finland, then a duchy of Russia. The fortifications consisted of three round towers and a citadel of thick brick walls faced with huge granite blocks. It was in its twenty-second year of construction and had been nearly completed. Its garrison consisted in excess of 2,200 men manning sixty-six guns, and it dominated the harbour.

After days of idly riding at anchor, and having managed to lure on board an experienced pilot, the impatient Hall decided he could no longer remain inactive. He skilfully manoeuvred his vessels through the shallow waters, close enough to hit the fortress with his guns, yet too distant for the majority of Russian guns to hit him. For the next eight hours, Hall's three ships bombarded the fortress, all the while suffering minimal damage to themselves. Only after the stores of ammunition had been completely exhausted did Hall order a withdrawal, pleased with his success. In fact little strategic harm came to Bomasund, with only the roofs of some out-buildings set on fire, but since they were undercoated with thick bomb-proofing, the damage was more cosmetic than anything else. Four defenders were killed and fifteen were wounded, while the British suffered five wounded. In due course, Hall was severely reprimanded by Napier: 'If every Captain when detached chose to throw away all his shot against stone walls, the fleet would soon be insufficient.' The Admiralty also rebuked Hall not only for having expended large quantities of ammunition, but for having put his ship into unnecessary danger. The tsar, on the other hand, was well pleased with the performance of his troops – they had fought bravely and the enemy had been repulsed. A silver rouble was awarded to each defender.

The British public, however, now long starved for battle honours, greeted the news of Hall's action with unbridled jubilation. Particularly inflaming the nation's imagination was the heroic action of Midshipman Charles Davis Lucas of the *Hecla*. During the engagement a live shell managed to land on the ship's upper deck. The cry went up for everyone to take cover, but the twenty-year old Lucas jumped forward, grabbed the fizzing round, carried it to the railing and dropped it overboard. Just before hitting the water, the shell exploded with some force, superficially injuring two seamen. In gratitude for having saved his ship, Captain Hall promoted the quick-witted young man to Acting Lieutenant, and at the war's end, Lucas was received by Queen Victoria who awarded him the first ever Victoria Cross – he finished his career as a rear admiral.

By early June cholera had spread among the British ships as they continued to lie off Sveaborg. The French also felt the sting of the debilitating sickness, but it seemed to have hit them more forcefully. Despite this handicap, the allies determined to attack Kronstadt, and on the 22nd they set sail for that strategically placed fortress. They arrived four days later and gave over the next three to a studied reconnaissance of the citadel island, the results of which proved overwhelmingly discouraging. In the first place, they found that they were outnumbered: their eighteen capital ships to the Russians' twenty-two – and the enemy's fleet was manned by seasoned crews. The fortification, furthermore, bristled with daunting mortars and guns. After consultations with his ranking officers, Napier concluded that an attack on Kronstadt would be an act of sheer madness, even without the burden of cholera. He ordered a withdrawal, and the ships stood off Kronstadt in order to return to Sveaborg.

All the while, Rear Admiral Arthur Corry remained at Sveaborg with a force of sixteen British and French ships, with orders to observe Russian movements and to survey the defences. He found that a formidable array of guns was in place at strategic points, and he estimated that at least 8,000 troops were garrisoned there. Booms had been constructed at the entrances to the island and the approaches had been mined with the 'infernal machines'. Sveaborg, Corry reported to the Commander-in-Chief, was not for taking without profoundest risks.

By early August, Napier's forces had been greatly augmented with the arrival of 10,000 French soldiers and marines, under the command of General Baraguay d'Hilliers. They had been boarded at Boulogne and Calais on British transports, and after a long, cramped voyage of enforced activity, by the time they arrived were a disgruntled lot, on the verge of mutiny. It was the fare from the British galleys that proved to be the prime source of complaint; the Frenchmen viewed English cookery with unabashed disdain. One of their senior officers reported laconically, 'Soldiers have the habit of moaning in such a way that they complain constantly: the chocolate is not thick enough or is too thick, the soup too salty, the tea insipid; they've always got something to say . . . I've adopted the policy of putting all who complain on bread and biscuits; it is the only way of making them see reason.' A singularly Gallic reaction – get at them through the stomach – but it worked, and discipline was enforced.

With this fresh influx of troops and the further arrival of a thousand British military engineers and marines, Napier now felt himself sufficiently strong to launch a concerted offensive against Russia, and since Kronstadt and Sveaborg both seemed unattainable, he decided on Bomarsund. The impromptu attack eight weeks earlier of Captain Hall proved of no real consequence to the defenders; Napier's assault would be different.

The plan of attack was simple: station the fleet in such a way as to prevent Russian reinforcement from intervening, and then bring ashore artillery and marines to the north and to the south to lay siege, all with the support of the ships' guns. And it all went according to plan, with British engineers paving the way for French marine brigades. They landed on 8 August, and the siege began five days later, with guns firing simultaneously from sea and shore (including the land-based French 16-pounders, which required a team of 150 men to pull into place). The sustained firepower had its effect, for on the third day the Russian commander, Vladimir, ordered the white flag of surrender hoisted over the mortally wounded fortress. In the days that followed, some pillaging took place and the fortification's church was blown up – but only after its clock was removed and packed off to London. The remainder of the building was also destroyed, including the towers. Blazing fires were set along the granite walls, bringing them to intense heat, after which they were doused with cold water, causing the stones to crack and break apart – the walls would now be useless. The take of prisoners was massive – 2,225 officers and men, including Vladimir, and all were conveyed to internment camps in France and England.

Napier was jubilant with this splendid success and the British public applauded enthusiastically – the Åland Islands had been captured; the first great victory over the enemy had been won, and now surely the war would soon end.

According to the practice of the day, the British Baltic Fleet was accompanied by a number of privately owned yachts that carried the idle rich and the curious – in today's terms, they 'embedded' themselves with the troops. During the day, these 'war tourists' saw, heard and smelled the unfolding battle from appropriately distant anchorages. During the evenings, within the plush quarters of the more elaborate vessels, they sipped champagne and enjoyed the splendid offerings wrought by their chefs.[20] To take in the battle from a safe distance was one thing; to walk the ground in its aftermath was an altogether different matter. Following Bomarsund's surrender, most of these good folk came ashore to examine the field, and they were appalled by what they found – the full reality of the horrors of war struck forcefully. The Reverend R.E. Hughes of Magdalene College, Cambridge, was one such, and in his diary he wrote of the 'cold, clean silent forms of the dead,' and lamented:

> The shock of the surprise was fearful; the light linen cloths that shrouded the stiffened figures wavered and flickered in the draught, as if stirred by the breaths of those who could breathe no more. What did these fellows know about the Turkish question? And yet they fought and trembled, they had writhed in agony, and now father and brother, maid and mother were weeping, and breaking their hearts for them, and all about the Danubian principalities.

In early September orders were received by Napier and Parseval-Deschènes to withdraw their fleets from the Baltic and return home at a time of their own selection. A conference of senior Anglo-French commanders was convened, and it was unanimously decided that the lateness of the season precluded any further offensive action – nothing could be attempted that year against Sveaborg without gravest risk There was little to do but to return home, which the French did immediately.

The success at Bormasund had been a gratifying start in quenching the public's insatiable thirst for honour and victory – but it was insufficient. The clamour for a decisive encore continued to sound, and the government rapidly caved in to the rising pressure. Within a week of Parseval-Deschènes' departure, a fresh dispatch was received by Napier from the Sir James Graham, the First Lord of the Admiralty, which in effect reversed the earlier order. With a series of caveats, he was now informed that conditions were ripe for an attack on Sveaborg:

> We are always reminded that the Russians are most unwilling to navigate the Gulf of Finland in line-of-battle ships when autumn has commenced; and Kronstadt is always locked up by ice formations fourteen days before Sveaborg is closed. The attack, therefore, on Sveaborg might be made towards the end of October . . . The final decision must rest entirely on yourself. If the attack on Sveaborg, in present circumstances, be desperate, it must on no account be undertaken by you. If, calculating the ordinary chances of war, and on full consideration of the strength of the enemy's fortresses and fleets, you shall be of opinion that Sveaborg can be laid to ruins, it will be your duty, with the concurrence of the French Admiral, not to omit the opportunity.

The anxious Admiralty was in essence ordering an attack, but with qualification, and it left the ultimate decision up to the Commander-in-Chief. Sir Charles received the dispatch with no little dismay, which was only exacerbated three days later with the arrival of yet another dispatch. It was a counter-order – there was to be no attack on Sveaborg. Little wonder that the exasperated admiral lost his temper. Winter comes early in the Baltic, and atrocious weather was setting in. He replied to the Sea Lords with an intemperate note:

I should consider myself unfit for the command I hold were I much longer to expose [the fleet] to the violent gales of the north – more particularly as their Lordships have directed me in their letter of the 23rd September, confirmed by their letter of 26th – to withdraw when in the opinion of the French admiral and myself, the presence of the combined fleet is no longer safe.

The exchanges between Napier and the First Sea Lord had grown increasingly heated, 'disrespectful in tone', and Graham finally had enough – he ordered the admiral home. So Napier returned to England, arriving with his fleet at Spithead on the 16th. Two days later he held a stormy interview with the First Sea Lord, shortly following which curt orders were delivered to him: 'You are hereby required and directed to strike your flag, and come ashore.' After sixty years of dedicated service to the Royal Navy, Napier had been dismissed and forced into retirement.

Thus ended the naval campaign in the Baltic that first year of the war. On the surface, little had been attained by the allies, apart from the destruction of Bomarsund. The honour and glory so sorely demanded by the British public had been undelivered. Yet, it is undeniable that the Anglo-French campaign had successfully bottled up the Russian Navy for the entire first summer of the war. The tsar had been denied an opportunity to reinforce his Black Sea fleet with additional ships. The 30,000 Russian troops posted in the Gulf, furthermore, had also been prevented from joining the army in Crimea. (Who knows what the outcome in the Crimea might have been had they been there?) All this, together with the neatly executed Bomarsund action, was achieved despite manifold logistical shortcoming suffered by the fleet, the prevalence of cholera, and the confusing orders and counter-orders issued by the Admiralty. In the process, not one ship had been lost.

There is no denying that the Admiralty made the embittered Napier a scapegoat for the perceived failures of the campaign. Every sort of negative accusation flew at him: he was ignorant of steamship tactics; his men lacked confidence in him; he was timid and drank too much; at seventy-seven, he was simply too old. Others, however, came firmly to Sir Charles' defence, pointing the finger squarely at the Admiralty – it was the Sea Lords who had bungled the campaign from the very start by its interference and micro-management. The first half of the Baltic campaign ended messily, indeed.[21]

The following summer, the British fleet returned to the Gulf, this time commanded by Rear Admirals Dandas and Peno. Not only was it ordered to re-establish the blockade, but it was to take and destroy Kronstadt. The new fleet of thirty-eight ships included twenty propeller-driven vessels and four frigates, which greatly outdid Russian forces. The citadel, however, had been refurbished during the winter and strengthened with additional guns. New, improved mines were laid in its waters, insufficient perhaps to penetrate the thick hull of an armoured vessel, but powerful enough severely to shake the enemy psychologically – four British ships on reconnaissance were severely damaged by them. Like Napier and Parseval-Deschènes in the previous summer, Dundas and Peno, after a studied examination of possibilities, concluded that Kronstadt could only be taken with unacceptable losses. It was unrealistic to contemplate an attack, and therefore prudent to withdraw.

The fleet moved on to Sveaborg, where a success appeared more certain, and there, on 9 August, the greatest gun battle of the Baltic campaign was fought. The allies manoeuvred their ships into range of the fortress, and over a two-day period they bombarded it with over 20,000 rounds, all the while persistently receiving return fire from more than a thousand guns. Russian defences held firm; Sveaborg was not for taking. With little more to be done, the allies withdrew and resumed station at the mouth of Baltic where they remained until early December. One chapter of the Crimean War had come to a close in an apparent stalemate. The Black Sea blockade, however, had been successfully enforced.

Although the conspicuous exit to the North Sea had been closed to the Russians, there existed another, less likely avenue: through the White Sea and around the northern tip of Norway and Finland – by what in the Second World War was called 'the Murmansk run', not far from the Arctic Circle.

On the eastern side of the White Sea, at the mouth of the Dvina River, stands the port city of Archangel, which by the mid-nineteenth century had developed into a nascent commercial centre. Since its port could potentially service Russian needs in Crimea, the allies decided to extend their blockade to these northern waters. Three ships under the command of Captain Erasmus Ommaney were dispatched, in order to hammer in the blockade's final nail, joined by two others of the French navy, Captain Pierre Guilbert commanding. The small squadron that sailed up the Norwegian coastline that July, therefore, numbered five ships, carrying ninety-eight guns – two sailing frigates and three corvettes, two of which were under steam power.

Having stopped briefly at Hammerfest – where delighted merchants eagerly rushed to service the flotilla – the allies arrived at Archangel, to find the town heavily fortified and garrisoned by 6,000 troops. Rather than risk an attack on that imposing target, the squadron moved to the nearby Solovetsky Islands where they bombarded a fifteenth-century monastery and its periphery. When all the ammunition had been spent, Ommaney demanded an unconditional surrender, which the defenders summarily rejected. With nothing further to be done, the British sailed away. During the brief engagement, one Englishman was killed and five had been wounded; the Russians suffered no casualties; the French did not participate – they stood off Solovetsky.

With Archangel a non-starter and Solovetsky a disappointment, the fleet next set sail for the small fishing port of Kola on the north side of the White Sea, near present-day Murmansk. In the early morning of 24 August, they bombarded the small settlement which was defended by one battery and dozens of muskets. Captain Edmund Lyons of the fourteen-gun *Miranda*, penned a rather naive account of the engagement:

> . . . the guns were shortly dismounted, and the battery reduced to ruins, but our shells burst well into the loop-holed houses and stockades. An obstinate fire of musketry was kept up from various parts of the town. This allowed me no alternative, and I was obliged to destroy it. It was soon in flames from our shell and red-hot shot, and burned furiously, being fanned by a fresh breeze. The ship at this time became critically situated. The violence of the tide caused her to drag the bower stream anchors, and the two kedges laid out to spring her broadside; and, the passage being too narrow for her to swing, she grounded at less than three hundred yards from the burning town, fragments of which were blown on board. However, by keeping the sails, rigging and decks well wetted until the ship was hove off, no bad consequences ensued . . .

Nothing of significance had been achieved by the attack, save the burning of some warehouses and three-quarters of the 128 wooden houses. The one hole in the northern blockade, however, had been stopped up. With winter rapidly setting in, Ommaney withdrew from the sub-Arctic waters for a return home. The blockade 'season' was over for the year – in the Baltic and in the White Sea

In early summer of the following year, a fresh allied squadron returned to the White Sea to renew the blockade, with Sweden unsuccessfully pleading for exemption from restrictions on commercial shipping. During the entire length of the season that the allied ships were in the area, nothing much happened. The few tiny settlements along the shore suffered no damage, but sixty small trading vessels were put to the torch. By mid-August, the allied squadron had joined the fleet of the Baltic station, and all returned to their home ports, bringing to an end the allied campaigns in Russia's north, some 1,800 miles (2,900 kilometres) from the fighting in Crimea.

14

FIRST CRIMEAN STEPS

On the Black Sea, the euphoria of departure from Varna subsided, and the routine of life at sea settled in. The allies were now taking the war to Russia itself – but the objective of the war remained clouded in obscurity. They knew they were off to Crimea, but of Crimea had only scant knowledge, either of topography or of defences. 'Common, sensible, fanciful men – men wise with the cynic wisdom of London clubs – were now by force turned into venturers, intent, as Argonauts of old, in gazing upon the shores of a strange land to which they were committing their lives. From the crowded decks they strained their eyes to pierce the unknown,' Kinglake observes wryly.

The expedition's immediate course of action, however, had been defined: land northwest of Sevastopol at Eupatoria on Kalamita Bay, and then march the armies the 30 miles (50 kilometres) to the fortified city itself. Earlier on, the allies had made a reconnaissance of the south coast, and after debating views on the ideal landing ground, they finally agreed on Kalamita's flat shores. During that search, the *Caradoc,* accompanied by two ships of the line, approached Sevastopol so closely that, amid the clear sound of Sunday church bells, Admiral Lyons was able to raise his hat to a mounted Russian officer. It was all uncannily peaceful, with no hostility in the air, as the Russians carried on in their business seemingly unconcerned with the passing warships.

By noon of 13 September, the British fleet had drawn up to Eupatoria on the western shores of Crimea. This vast peninsula is an irregular land formation of some 27,000 square miles (70,000 square kilometres) – nearly the size of Belgium. The southeast coastline is flanked by mountains, but the southwest coast, where the allies landed, is generally of rolling hills. The interior of the landmass, into which the allies never sallied, is substantially semiarid prairie lands.

From the ships' decks, the straining eyes seeking 'to pierce the unknown' beheld only a lone road paralleling the shore, upon which a horse-drawn cart lazily made its way, followed by a horseman at full speed – both equally unconcerned by the vast armada crowding the lapping waters. No troops, no guns; only the tranquillity of the seaside. An advance party was landed at Eupatoria, and the town's chief administrator was summoned, an individual who proved to be the quintessential bureaucrat. 'The governor or head man of the place was an official personage in a high state of discipline. He had before his eyes the armed navies of the Allies, with the countless sails of their convoys. And to all that vast armament he had nothing to oppose except the forms of office. But to him the forms of office seemed all-sufficing, and on these he still calmly relied.' Colonel Steele explained through an interpreter that the allies planned to disembark their forces. The little man replied that 'decidedly they might do so', but, according to strict health regulations, before moving on into the interior all those who came ashore would have to spend the stipulated time in quarantine. He much regretted the necessity of this inconvenience, but after all, rules were rules.

Quarantine shunted aside, the advance forces landed and took over Eupatoria. Apart from a handful of officials and bureaucrats, there were very few Russians about the place. The inhabitants were Tartars, who within days became willing purveyors of every sort of fresh produce and supply to the new-arrivals. The market, however, got off to a slow start for lack of Russian coins; unfamiliar British sovereigns proved suspect. In the planning of the expeditionary force, the commissariat had neglected to provide for this important detail. Fortunately, however, one war tourist accompanying the fleet had demonstrated greater foresight – aboard Sir Edward Colebrooke's yacht was a goodly supply of Russian gold roubles that he had obtained in Constantinople, and the quartermaster gratefully accepted the civilian's advance.

By the end of the day, the French and Turkish fleets had joined up, and the united armada now lay in Kalamita Bay in its full strength, extended in line, parallel to the coast – the French and Turks at the south side, and the British north off Eupatoria. The formidable task of disembarking the armies began at half past eight on the following morning with sunny blue skies and calm waters. The process continued until the evening of the 18th, stopping only for extreme darkness of night and unduly rough seas. The absence of enemy and ideal weather conditions greatly favoured the work, despite the cholera which continued to plague soldiers and sailors alike. Of the crew of the *Britannia*, for example, 139 of the 985 men had died of the sickness. Back at Scutari, hundreds lay stricken in dismal physical surroundings, poorly attended – two months would pass before Florence Nightingale would arrive with her team to bring comfort to the suffering.

The first ashore were ordered to take positions at the top of a commanding hill overlooking the bay, which they did, scrambling up all the way. The sudden, unaccustomed exertion in the heat of the day took its toll and many collapsed from pervasive sickness. 'Of those who only this morning ascended the hill with seeming alacrity, many now came down sadly borne by their comrades. They were carried on ambulance-stretchers, and a blanket was over them. Those whose faces remained uncovered were still alive. Those whose faces had been covered over by their blankets were dead. Near the foot of the hill the men began to dig graves.'

That gloomy spectacle aside, the days went 'merrily on' in an almost festive atmosphere, with everyone showing 'zeal, abounding zeal' in completing the task at hand. They were off the cramped, unsteady ships; they were physically engaged, and finally, they were about to meet the enemy. 'The toil went on with strange good-humour – nay, even with thoughtful kindness towards the soldiers. The seamen knew that it concerned the comfort and the health of the soldiers to be landed dry, so they lifted or handed the men ashore with an almost tender care. Yet, not without mirth – nay, not without laughter far heard – when, as though they were giant maidens, the tall Highlanders of the 42nd placed their hands in the hands of the sailors and sprang by his aid to the shore, their kilts floating out wide while they leapt.'

In reading the graphic description of disembarkation submitted to *The Times* by William Russell, it is difficult to see how a Highlander, or for that matter any other soldier, could possibly have 'sprung' or 'leapt' ashore, in view of the clumsiness and weight of his gear:

A gig or a cutter, pulled by eight or twelve sailors . . . would come alongside a steamer or transport in which troops were ready for disembarkation. The officers of each company first descended, each man in full dress. Over his shoulders was slung his haversack, containing what had been, ere it underwent the process of cooking, four pounds and a half of salt meat, and a bulky mass of biscuit of the same weight. This was his ration for three days. Besides this, each officer carried his greatcoat, rolled up and fastened in a hoop round his body, a wooden canteen to hold water, a small ration of spirits, whatever change of underclothing he could manage to stow away, his forage-cap, and, in most instances, a revolver. Each private carried his blanket and greatcoat strapped up into a kind of knapsack, inside of which was a pair of boots, a pair of socks, a shirt, and, at the request of themselves, a forage-cap. He also carried his water canteen, and the same rations as the officer; a portion of the same mess cooking apparatus, firelock and bayonet of course, cartouche box and fifty rounds of ball-cartridges for Minié, sixty rounds for the smooth-bore arms.

On the first night of disembarkation, a heavy, prolonged rain fell, and the British suffered pitifully for lack of tents. 'Lying in wet pools or in mud, their blankets clinging heavy with water, our young soldiers began the campaign.' (Sir George Brown slept under a carriage, while the Duke of Cambridge gave up all hope of sleep, and wrapped in a mackintosh, he remained on horseback all night steadfastly jollying along his men.) The French troops, on the other hand were well provided. Every man carried in his kit a lightweight *tente d'abri* – or, as the English had it, 'dog-tent' – into which he could comfortably crawl.

The weather improved on the following day and the landing continued on the beaches, although hindered by a high swell. From the deck of the *Himalaya*, the irrepressible Fanny Duberly observed the proceedings: 'The beach is a vast and crowded camp, covered with men, horses, tents, general offi-cers, boats landing men and horses, which latter are flung overboard and swum ashore . . . eleven were drowned today.'

By the time the five-day disembarkation had been com-pleted, the allies had landed a force of 67,000 infantry, 1,200 cavalry and 137 pieces of artillery – two-fifths of those landed were British, with the remainder French and Turkish. What land transport vehicles they brought with them and the bulk of ammunition together with sustaining supplies were to follow. It had all gone smoothly – not a shot had been fired, not a life lost – and hopes were high for a speedy advance on Sevastopol.

The Turks seemed to have completed their task with the greatest efficiency. Embarkation and disembarkation from ships was a practised procedure: 'They had an advantage over the French and English in their more familiar acquaintance with the mode of life proper to warfare.' When on the morning after the rain, British officers called on the Turkish comman-der, they were received in style. Well-pitched tents surrounded his elaborate tent, and there was a large concentration of horses, some grazing, others standing by saddled and ready for instant use. Biscuits, sweets, coffee and tobacco were offered the guests, all within dry quarters. 'His whole camp,' Kinglake comments, 'gave signs of a race which gathers from a great tradition, going on from father to son, the duties and simple arts of a pious and warfaring life.'

Throughout the whole five days not a Russian was to be seen, and those coming ashore, whose only anxiety was to 'show the confounded Russkys a thing or two', remained disappointed. All too soon, however, Russian troops would be met, and estimates of their numbers varied widely – any-where from 50,000 to 100,000. The British guessed that in Sevastopol alone, there were 75,000. Whatever the exact numbers, it would be a force not to be taken lightly – well-trained, disciplined and above all committed. The advance from the Kalamita's beaches began on the 19th, amid much grumbling by the French – they had been ready to set off two days earlier, as were the Turks, but they were prevented by 'British dawdling'. The contemporary French historian, C.L. Bazancourt explains, 'An immense quantity of impedimenta retarded their operations interminably.' While the columns proceeded south, the fleet glided slowly along the coast paralleling them, all the time sending out advance reconnaissance parties. The French positions were to the right, closest to the sea, and they were formed up in diamond-shaped divisions, in the centre of which were Turkish battalions. The British made their advance to the left, inland from the sea.

> Thus marched the strength of the Western Powers. The sun shone brightly, as on a summer's day in England; but breezes springing fresh from the sea floated briskly along the hills. The ground was an undulating steppe alluring to cavalry. It was rankly covered with a herb like southernwood; and when the stems were crushed under foot by the advancing columns, the whole air became laden with bitter fragrance. The aroma was new to some. To men of the western counties of England it was so familiar that it carried them back to childhood and the village church. They remembered the nosegay of 'boy's love' that used to be set by the Prayer-Book of the Sunday maiden too demure for the vanity of flowers.

With colours flying and bands playing, the vast assembly made steady progress, marching in columns and divisions to the cadence of drums. The hot sun beat down mercilessly on the heavily-equipped troops, and before long the effects of cholera and diarrhoea began to hit them. 'The pain of weariness had begun; few spoke, all toiled . . . before the first hour of march was over, the men began to fall out of the ranks. Some of these were in the agony of cholera. Their faces had a dark choked look. They threw themselves on the ground and writhed, but often without speaking and without a cry.' There was concern for the drop-outs, that if left behind they would be taken prisoner, but for lack of transport little could be done – the unfortunates were abandoned where they had fallen. That evening, with the trickle of fallen having during the day developed into a stream, there was a change of heart. Crews were dispatch to retrieve the stricken.

There was a further problem. 'An army marches on its stomach,' Napoleon Bonaparte once quipped. Feeding an army has always been a logistical challenge for the planning of any war, and for the Crimean invaders it was as great as any. The fleet transports carried limited provisions, insufficient for the full requirements, especially those of a lengthy engagement; the land would have to provide. The French were quick off the mark and without losing a moment upon landing, patrols were successfully sent out into the countryside to forage for food. The settlements and farms in the immediate vicinity were soon stripped of all edibles – sometimes paid for, but more often expropriated.

It was the Tartars who proved instrumental in relieving the problem of provisions for the British. Before the first transports had discharged their loads onto the beaches, Lord Raglan had met with their headmen. 'They approached him respectfully, but without submissiveness of an abject kind . . . they spoke with truthfulness and dignity, allowing it to appear that the invasion was not distasteful to them, but abstaining from all affectation of enthusiastic sympathy. They seemed to understand war and its exigencies, for they asked the interpreters to say that such of their possessions as might be wanted by the English army were at Lord Raglan's disposal.' It had been an amicable meeting and surprisingly productive for in short order, vegetable and fruits, sheep and cattle, wagons and carts were being delivered to the wanting armies. Within days the accommodating Tartars had sold not only copious quantities of food, but 350 wagons together with sufficient horses and camels to pull them. Raglan's army had made a good start in meeting its supply requirements.

Waiting for the advancing invaders somewhere not far, were the Russians, whose numerical strength continued in uncertainty – somewhere around 75,000, it was thought. By early afternoon of the 19th, the first cohorts of the vast military machine had reached the Bulganik, called a river but really more of a stream. Up to then, the allies had not encountered Russians, other that a lone cavalryman or two sent to scout out the invading force. But now a report reached Lord Cardigan that units of his Light Brigade had discovered 2,000 Cossacks stationed at the ready on the river's south side. A closer inspection of the situation resulted in a skirmish and a few fruitless musket shots were exchanged. Just as Cardigan's cavalry was about to attack the enemy formation, Lord Raglan spotted the glint of bayonets at the rear, together with a mass of enemy horsemen. The force which the Light Brigade was set to attack was significantly greater than the reported 2,000 Cossacks; he ordered the charge broken off. As the horsemen were wheeling about in response to the command, they were fired upon by Russian artillery – two men were wounded and five horses killed. The British quickly replied with shots from their heavy nine-pounders, and this discouraged the Russians from further action – they moved off. Perhaps not a notable exchange, but it was the first exchange of fire in Crimea.

That night the allies bivouacked north of the Bulganik, within sight of the enemy on the opposite shore. Within the

Russian encampment, Captain Chodasiwicz passed a sleepless night. He recalled:

> As it became dark, we could plainly see the enemy's fires . . . I lay down in my hut of branches and tried to sleep, but in vain, notwithstanding the fatigue of the previous day. I rose at three o'clock . . . went up the hill (for our own battalion was stationed in a ravine), to take a peep at the bivouac of the allied armies. Little was seen but the fires, and now and then a dark shadow as someone moved past them. All was still and had the appearance of coming strife. These were two armies lying, as it were, side by side. How many, or who would be sent to their last account, it would be impossible to say. The question involuntarily thrust itself upon me, should I be one of that number?

Unrealistic to believe that our Russian chronicler was alone in pondering the solemn question. One imagines thousands of weary, on both sides of the river, tossing restlessly in the coolness of that still September evening, also wondering, 'Will I be one of that number?' They had arrived from Lyon and Istanbul, from Liverpool and Smolensk; they left families behind in Marseilles and Newcastle, in Moscow and Scutari. On that Crimean night of 19 September, they rested, enveloped together in the peace of the starry heavens flickering above. With morning's sunrise, a new day and many would be 'sent to their last account'. And they were – thousands upon thousands.

Sunrise, but the Russians were gone. They had deserted the Bulganik and moved south four miles, entrenching themselves on the further bank of the Alma, 'where they awaited their destiny'. In command of the awaiting troops, and of Crimea itself, was Prince Menshikov – the same who stormed out of

Constantinople on board the *Thunderer* four months earlier. From his Sevastopol headquarters he had tracked the progress of the allied landing at Kalamita, but made no attempt to impede it. It was possible that the enemy's appearance so far north was merely a feint. Had he moved to prevent the landing at Kalamita, Sevastopol would have become vulnerable. The enemy's steam-powered vessels could move down the coast considerably faster than an army returning to the rescue.

While the allies were disembarking at Kalamita, the Russians had busied themselves in establishing positions on the Alma's south bank. By the 20th, the defenders were well and truly dug in, and artillery pieces had been strategically placed. The forces marching in from the Bulganik reinforced those already in place, bringing the total numbers to 39,000 men, including infantry, cavalry, Cossacks – plus 104 light and heavy guns.

The five-mile (eight-kilometre) front established by Menshikov along the Alma was a strong position. The meandering river flows east to west, nearly perpendicular to the coastline and to the road that connects the north with Sevastopol. It runs swiftly, but is 'generally fordable for troops', in Raglan's words. 'Its banks are extremely rugged and in most parts steep. The willows along it had been cut down in order to prevent them from affording cover to the attacking party. In fact everything had been done to deprive an assailant of any species from shelter.'

From the allies' viewpoint looking south, three villages were situated on their side of the river – to the right, Almatamak; to the left, Tarkhanliar; and at the centre Burliuk, where the only bridge connecting the two banks had been partially destroyed by the Russians. There were two hills, one to the left, the Kourgané, and one at the centre overlooking Burliuk and the main road, Telegraph Hill. To the right, by the sea, steep 300-foot (90-metre) cliffs rise to dominate the mouth of the Alma.

On their side of the river, the ground is reasonably even, but at the time it was covered with low stone walls, terraces and vineyards. On the opposite side, the irregular ground is broken by hills, ravines, knolls and gullies – ideal topography for defensive works.

In blocking the invader's march south, Menshikov decided that the sheer seaside cliffs were inaccessible, and he therefore left that flank minimally defended. Instead he massed the bulk of his infantry and artillery on the slopes and heights of Kourgané and Telegraph Hill, and stationed the remainder between them. Two massive defensive earthworks had been constructed – the 'Greater Redoubt' and the 'Lesser Redoubt'. The former was situated three hundred yards from the river, on the lower slope of Kourgané, while the latter was behind it to the right where the heaviest guns had been mounted.

It was 10:30 by the time the allied troops got under way from their overnight encampment at Bulganik, with St Arnaud once more grumbling about 'Messieurs les Anglais' – additional time was required to bring British battalions into position. On the previous evening, the two commanders had conferred on the plan of attack. St Arnaud had pressed for a French thrust from the seaside, supported by naval guns and the Turks. His scouts had reported that the steep cliffs were passable and sparsely defended, and the marshal was confident that they could be taken. He further proposed that the British push forward upon the enemy's centre and right positions. Throughout St Arnaud's animated presentation, Raglan sat passively, 'with governed features, restraining – or only perhaps, postponing – smiles, listening graciously, assenting, or not dissenting, putting forward no plan of his own, and, in short eluding discussion.' The conference ended with agreement on St Arnaud's plan, and with Raglan assuring the 'vigorous cooperation' of the British could be counted upon.

The allies reached the Alma by 11:40 and took up station on the north side. Across from them 39,000 Russians were dug in and 126 guns had been strategically placed. Menshikov's army was facing a trilateral force nearly double the size of his own. 'The Russian officers,' writes Kinglake, 'had been accustomed all their days to military inspections and vast reviews, but they now saw before them that very thing for the confronting of which their lives had been one long rehearsal. They saw a European army coming down in order of battle – an army . . . with a mind to carry their heights and take their lives.' Despite the disadvantage of lesser numbers, the Russians remained confident. 'God does not abandon the righteous and we therefore await the outcome calmly and with patience,' wrote Vice-Admiral Kornilov in his diary on the eve of the battle.

At 13:25 the allied squadron of eight French steamers and one Royal Navy vessel, opened fire on the scant Russian defences along the heights of the seaside cliffs. Additional rounds were lobbed at Telegraph Hill and the low flat ground at its base. Within moments of this opening volley, a round ripped up the ground near Raglan's command post, followed by a continuous rain of Russian cannonade that sprayed the full length of the British line. The first great battle of the campaign in Crimea had started; within three hours it would be over. For many of those who on the previous night had tossed under the starry heavens, the 'wait for their destiny' had ended. In the battle's brief time span, an estimated 5,000 men were killed, or subsequently died of their wounds.

Following up on the heavy naval bombardment of the right flank, and supported by the Turks, Generals Bousquet and Canrobert landed battalions of chasseurs and Zouaves, and successfully expelled the few Russian infantry and artillery that defended the cliffs. They then managed to cross the river, but became bogged down in a futile attempt to haul their heavy guns into place. In the meantime, Prince Napoleon's light infantry regiments had come under a continuous heavy fire from Telegraph Hill – so much so that they were unable to ford the river.

On the left and at the centre, Sir George Brown and Sir George de Lacy Evans advanced the British infantry and artillery, leaving the cavalry under Lord Lucan in reserve. The 'thin red line' was greatly extended but it started off with parade square exactitude – not since Waterloo, forty years earlier, had such a stirring sight been had. From one awed Russian:

> Our hearts pounded at the sight of the endless mass of troops marching steadily towards us, but when our artillery, which occupied good commanding positions, opened fire, the shells fell short as the enemy was still out of range . . . as the enemy got closer our shells began to blow great holes in his ranks; but the many gaps were immediately closed up and the enemy strode on, apparently indifferent to his loss. Soon afterwards we began to feel the terrible effects of his rifle fire.

Because the line was lengthily extended over the terraced ground, and what with the deadly fire it was receiving, all semblance of orderliness quickly dissipated, and the formation broke up and developed into a jumbled mass. To sort out the confused tangle of men was unrealistic, and they were therefore ordered to press forward in whatever order, helter-skelter as it were, to ford the river and capture Kourgané.

Sergeant Timothy Gowing of the Royal Fusiliers recalls:

> Up to the river we rushed and got ready for a swim, pulling off knapsacks and camp kettles. A number of our poor fellows were drowned, or shot down with grape and canister – which

came amongst us like hail – while attempting to cross. Our men were falling now very fast. Into the river we dashed, nearly up to our armpits, with our ammunition and rifles on the top of our heads to keep them dry, scrambled out the best way we could – the banks were very steep and slippery – and commenced to ascend the hill.

From the Russian side, the determined advance of the British redcoats was breathtaking. General Oleg Kvitsinsky describes it:

The mass of English troops, notwithstanding our devastating force of shot and shell that made bloody furrows through their ranks, closed up once more and, with new forces, protected by swarms of skirmishing riflemen and supported by a battery firing from behind the smoking ruins of Berliuk, crossed the river and drove back the brave Kazan, forcing our field battery to limber up and depart.

Somerset Calthrope takes up the English viewpoint with colourful editorial comment. Once over the river, the sodden troops rushed forward:

. . . driving the Russian skirmishers and riflemen before them at the point of the bayonet. But the most terrible was yet to come: directly they got out of the vineyards double the number of guns opened upon them with grape and canister. In spite of the numbers mowed down, the remainder never flinched, but kept up a telling fire upon the Russian gunners. On they went, and after a time actually reached the Russian battery: then commenced a regular hand-to-hand encounter, the Russians defending themselves with great bravery, but our men fighting with that English determination which almost invariably overcomes every obstacle.

For a minute a Russian gun was captured by the 23rd Regiment, but immediately after our men were overpowered by numbers. A fresh column of Russian infantry had come up in support of their beaten comrades, and the English, being reduced to half their former strength, were obliged to relinquish the hold they had gained, and the division was compelled to give way before the overwhelming forces of the enemy. Still, however, although retiring, these brave men never turned their backs on the Russians, but kept up a regular and effective fire; and whenever the enemy attempted crossing bayonets with them.

Beaten down by the heavy fire, the retreating British regrouped and a second spirited assault was launched against the redoubt. Amid cries of 'Hurrah!' and 'Forward!' they pressed up the hill, all the time receiving the same heavy fire as before. Within the melee, as Kinglake relates, a singular incident took place that greatly inspired the attacking force. 'Then a small child-like youth ran forward before the throng, carrying the colour. This was young Anstruther. He carried the Queen's colour of the Royal Welsh. Fresh from the games of English school-life, he ran fast; for, heading all who strove to keep up with him, he gained the redoubt, and dug in the butt-end of the flagstaff into the parapet. And then for a moment he stood, holding it tight, and taking a breath. Then he was shot dead, but his small hands, still clasping the flagstaff, drew it down along with him, and the crimson silk lay covering the boy with its folds.' A certain William Evans ran forward, grabbed the fallen standard, raised it and 'laid claim to the Great Redoubt'.

Sergeant Gowing relates, 'We had re-topped the Heights, routing them from their batteries . . . the enemy had bolted – the Heights of Alma were ours! The enemy was sent reeling from then in hot haste, with artillery and a few cavalry in pursuit. If we had only three or four thousand cavalry with us, they would not have got off quite so cheaply. As it was they got a nasty mauling, such a one as they did not seem to appreciate.' The French on the right flank in the meanwhile continued in a state of confusion. Much to the frustration of the generals, St Arnaud appeared reluctant to pursue an attack, cryptically claiming that his men 'had left their packs in the valley below.' Eventually, however, the forces of Canrobert and Prince Napoleon did successfully link up, and artillery fire was directed against the enemy positions on Telegraph Hill. The Russian commanding officer there, General Kiriakoff, had been witnessing the progress of the battle that raged on Kougane. With the British victory over that height and the resultant retreat, he deemed the overall situation hopeless, and ordered his forces to pull out. 'The French continued their onset, and three agile soldiers running forward in advance of their comrades, reared the colours of their three regiments.'

Through most of the engagement on the Kourgane, the British cavalry under Lord Lucan had been stationed on the left flank, standing by in readiness to receive an attack by the Russian cavalry, which outnumbered them four to one. The attack never came; it was as though Menshikov had completely forgotten that formidable force. Perceiving the unfolding drama on Kourgane and itching 'to get on with it', the impatient Lord Lucan, on his own initiative and without orders from Raglan, rode his men up the Kourgané's western slope to help relieve the pressure on the infantry.

With young Anstruther's planting of the colours atop Kourgané, and the Russians in retreat, the battle of the day had come to a close. Lucan's cavalry division, fresh to the struggle, gave a brief, spirited chase to the retreating forces. Regimental Sergeant Major George Smith writes of it:

On arriving at the brow [of Kourgané], before us was a vast plain. In the distance could be seen the Russian army in full retreat, with many stragglers. We now sent pursuers to make prisoner of all that could be overtaken. A number were brought back – most of them unwounded. One (a Pole, not wounded) appeared rather glad he was taken. The ball part of the grenade of his helmet had been shot through, which I appropriated and now have in my possession. Sergeant Bond, during the pursuit, received a bayonet wound in the face from a prisoner he had taken who pretended surrender, then treacherously made a point at him. Bond would have cut him down, but an officer galloped up and told him to spare the scoundrel. At this moment it was perceived that a swarm of Cossacks were rapidly approaching, so that the pursuers had to retreat and this Russian escaped. It is singular that Bond was the only man of the cavalry that was wounded, and not a single horse – although we had, during the day, at three different times been exposed to cannonade – and once under rifle fire.

For the exhausted and dispirited Russians the retreat was a pathetic journey of death and pain, as described by one witness:

The scene was so agonizing and sorrowful that a man of a weakened condition and nervous disposition might easily have gone mad. It was impossible to watch with indifference the hundreds of mutilated soldiers gasping for breath, dragging themselves after their comrades in a state of near unconsciousness, letting out dreadful and unbearable cries at each step. But it was an inevitable consequence of war. Some soldiers had several wounds – six or seven, on all parts of their bodies, principally from rifle shots. Fatal infections and inflammations set in rapidly. In addition, the troops were parched with thirst, but there was no water. The retreating army [had no] doctors, medical assistants or carriages. The wounded had to look after themselves – flaps of coats and ragged shirts were used as bandages. They pleaded for help from the passing soldiers . . . [it was] the last spark of life . . .

One rather pathetic Russian fared significantly better than those escaping south. A poignant vignette of Victorian warfare, as related by Lieutenant-Colonel Calthorpe:

On the more distant heights now occupied by the British troops a Russian General named Shokanoff was taken prisoner, and, when Lord Raglan and his Staff came up, he was sitting on one of the gun-limbers of Captain Wodehouse's battery, looking perfectly comfortable. On being questioned, he said that he was a General of one of the reserve brigades, and that he had been thrown from his horse, and being an old man could not get on again without help, and as his men were all then retreating as fast as possible he could obtain no assistance, so he lay down on some straw, where he was taken prisoner by some of our artillerymen. He stated that the Russians had about 42,000 infantry on the ground, about 80 or 90 guns and 6,000 cavalry; that they had come to fight against 'men', not 'devils', and finished his account by saying that, as he was an old and almost useless man, he hoped the English General would send him to Sevastopol, or allow him to follow his comrades. Lord Raglan replied that was impossible, but that he would be taken great care of, and every respect shown him. As the accommodation in camp would not be first-rate, he would go immediately on board ship, and he would send him to the English Admiral, who would receive him with all hospitality. The poor soul said he had never been on board ship in his life, and had a particular aversion to the water. Nevertheless, that evening he was sent down to the shore and taken on board the *Agamemnon,* where Sir Edmund Lyons put him up and treated him as a friend.

The first great battle in Crimea had been fought and quiet descended on the Alma. Two day were spent by the allies in burying the dead, attending to the wounded and resting. Calthorpe continues:

Going over the field of battle was a dreadful sight, everywhere torn and mangled bodies of brave soldiers, English, French and Russians, but three of the latter to one of the former. In some places where the fight had been hotly contended, the dead and dying were lying on one another, and their groans and piteous cries for water were heartrending. Lord Raglan, till a late hour of night, was giving orders and instructions for the accommodation of the wounded. One of his two tents was given up for the use of some wounded and sick officers. The remaining houses of the village of Burliuk were turned into field hospitals, and here might be seen the surgeons hard at work at their terrible but merciful duty, their arms covered in blood, the floors strewed with limbs just amputated, and slippery with gore. The enormous number of wounded quite overpowered the unceasing efforts of the medical officers, who worked all night without rest, and many were quite knocked up, and had to give in for a certain time. The first night between 400 and 500 wounded were brought into the field hospitals, but this was only a third of the British. There were from 900 to 1000 Russians lying about in all directions. The cholera was also at work and swept off many who had taken part in the battle.

Two days following the Russian retreat were given over to burying the dead, attending to the wounded and in resting up. The ranks were then were formed up more, and the armies pressed forward towards their ultimate objective. Sevastopol soon loomed before them.

15

ON TO SEVASTOPOL

Twenty years before the Anglo-French alliance came to be, an adventuresome Scotsman with a fondness for foreign travel had made his way to Crimea as a simple tourist. For years Sevastopol had been a closed port, out of bounds to Europeans. However, 'An obstacle of this kind was sure to be overcome by the spirit of enterprise, and Mr Oliphant not only found means to enter Sevastopol, but succeeded in informing himself of the state of the land defences on the south side of the harbour.' Upon his return home, Oliphant published an account of his travels, dwelling on Sevastopol and offering the following salient detail:

> . . . but of one fact there is no doubt, that however well fortified may be the approaches to Sevastopol by sea, there is nothing whatever to prevent any number of troops landing a few miles south of the town in one of the six convenient bays with which

the coast as far as Cape Kherson is indented; and marching down the main street – provided they were strong enough to defeat any military force that might be opposed to them in the open field – and sack the town and burn its fleet.

As the issue of the far away holy shrines heated, Oliphant's observations on Sevastopol's vulnerability struck a cord with Britain's War Office, and the strategic planners of the day began focusing on it as the point of attack in the eventuality of war. The means of gathering updated information on the protected city was tenuous at best, but by 1853 there appeared little evidence of significant changes having been made to the inland defences. Lord Raglan interviewed Oliphant at length before leaving England, and subsequently made up his mind that any attack should come from the south.

Sevastopol is situated on the south side of a narrow bay, half a mile wide and nearly four miles long, with a small suburb spreading on the opposite side. At the time the allied armies gazed at it, the city was defended by a set of strong fortresses along the shoreline, and a network of redoubts, earthworks and batteries on the inland side. Thirteen batteries housed 611 guns, many of them high calibre. The northern side of the bay was sparsely populated, but it did have three major fortifications, the centrepiece being the 'Star Fort', situated on a height that dominated not only the harbour but the city itself. Seven ships of the line, eight frigates and twenty other vessels were stationed in the harbour, together mustering massive firepower. Founded seventy years earlier, Sevastopol had grown to become one of three most formidable naval citadels in Europe – Gibraltar and Kronstadt being the other two.

After months of deliberation and planning, the allies had at last arrived at their destination – the laborious journey of preparation was over, and now was the moment of truth. Since their resounding victory at Alma, three days had passed, and in that brief time Raglan and St Arnaud failed twice to grasp golden opportunities to bring the entire campaign to a rapid end, and presumably therefore the war.

In the first place, rather than giving chase to the enemy retreating from Alma and destroying its forces, the allies dallied two days on the spot. Menshikov, therefore, was given the chance to regroup and reinforce the Sevastopol garrison with impunity – the infusion of 34,000 troops returning from Alma significantly buttressed of the city's defences and proved critical in the following months. The two day hiatus, furthermore, allowed the city's defenders to strengthen earthworks and to bring more guns into place.

Why the delay in the allied camp to move forward? The French and British blamed one another. 'The English are not ready!' exclaimed St Arnaud. 'I am detained here.' Bazancourt, who was at the scene, records:

> The English, intrepid and indefatigable in action, appear not to understand the vast importance of a day, or an hour of delay, in warlike operations. They either know how not to hurry themselves, or they will not do it. 'I have lost fewer men than they,' writes the Marshal [St Arnaud], 'because I have been more rapid. My soldiers run; theirs march . . .' the English army . . . was completely wanting in pliability (mobility) . . . the 22nd was another day lost.

Kinglake, on the other hand, declares, 'Lord Raglan desired to press forward,' and he urged St Arnaud that they do so. 'The answer was that any further advance of the French on that day was "impossible"; and the necessity of returning to where the knapsacks had been laid [on the banks of the Alma] was once more used as the reason which forbade all movement forward.' Additionally, Kinglake tells us, St Arnaud claimed that 'his troops were tired, and that it could not be done'. The probable truth is that both sides were to share in the blame for the delay in immediately pressing the vanquished enemy. An opening lost by the allies; an opportunity gained by the Russians.

But by the 24th, the allied forces had made the eleven-mile (eighteen-kilometre) march from Alma and they now stood on the northern heights overlooking Sevastopol and Star Fort. And here the second blunder was committed. Long before the landing at Eupatoria, Raglan and St Arnaud had agreed that an attack on the citadel-city would be made from the south. Now, however, they found themselves on the north side, and having lost two days, Raglan was unprepared to waste more time – he pressed for an immediate attack from where they stood.

St Arnaud disagreed and adamantly argued against a change of plan – the attack must be launched from the south. Russian defences on the north side, he argued, were significantly more formidable than they promised to be in the south. Star Fort in particular caused him concern. In addition, news had been received that the Russians had scuttled seven vessels at the mouth of the harbour which now blocked entry of allied ships – fleet support for a northern land attack would thus be denied. After much bitter argument, Raglan acquiesced and went along with St Arnaud. As a result of the decision, they now faced a 13-mile (21-kilometre) route inland over rough terrain no longer open, with forests and heavy brush – all this in the heat of day, and with primitive, unreliable maps. They would be cut off from the fleet, thus losing not only a direct line of supply but also the cover of naval guns. In giving way to St Arnaud, Raglan acted partially in deference to the marshal's deteriorating health. No doubt about it, St Arnaud was rapidly failing. 'Did you observe St Arnaud? He's dying.' Raglan remarked to an aide, as they were leaving the French camp.

That the allies failed to launch an attack from the north was a strategic mistake that bewildered not only the Russians at the time, but subsequently a cross-section of the public in Britain and France. A year later, *The Times* accused Raglan of lacking 'sufficient spontaneous energy' to carry an immediate assault. What the allies had failed to appreciate at the time was that the Star Fort and northern defences were not at all strong. The stout walls of the fortifications which St Arnaud found awesome were in fact made of brick, albeit three layers thick and they were certainly vulnerable to a concentrated cannonade. No great arsenal guarded these walls – only 198 guns, mostly light calibre, and clumsily distributed.

Admiral Kornilov, commanding the Russian naval forces, remarked in wonder at the lack of a northern attack: 'It must be that God did not abandon Russia. Without a doubt, had the enemy immediately advanced on Sevastopol after the battle of Alma, they could have easily taken it.' General D.E. Osten-Saken: 'Had the enemy acted with decisiveness then an entire army would have been insufficient to defend [Sevastopol].' Another missed opportunity.

With the arrival of the allies at the town of Balaklava, the Crimean campaign got underway in earnest. In the cabinet rooms and drawing rooms of London, Paris and Constantinople there was confidence that it would all be over in short order, and a general feeling of optimism prevailed. Little was anyone prepared that the siege would drag on for nearly a year, seemingly interminably. To be precise it lasted 347 days, and in that time the city endured six major bombardments, and suffered from every conceivable hardship. On Sevastopol's periphery a succession of battles were fought. Their names are familiar and they resonate in the pages of history, as well as in song and story – Balaklava, Inkerman, Eupatoria and Malakoff, for example. But the most memorable of all is Balaklava.

To call Balaklava a 'town' is presumptuous, for at the time it was no more than a string of houses along the eastern side of an S-shaped harbour nestled among some steep hills, the largest of which was called Mount Hiblak. When the British arrived there, its defences were limited to an old fort on the east side of the harbour – one of its mortars lobbied a shot at the advance party which managed to land harmlessly close to Raglan's feet. The fort was quickly occupied, with the officer in charge surrendering without resistance.

While this small skirmish was unfolding, the Royal Navy took up station offshore with its guns trained on the harbour. Balaklava was now firmly in British hands. Its tiny harbour, however, proved even smaller than indicated on the primitive maps – too small to meet adequately the needs of the allies. When, therefore, the French fleet arrived on the following day it took possession of two bays slightly to the west, Kamiesh and Kazach. The result of these arrangements was that when the attack on Sevastopol did take place, the French found themselves on the left, with the British to the centre and the right, in the thickest part of the bloody engagement.

St Arnaud's failing health had been deteriorating at an alarming rate and by the 26th he was in critical condition. With the French fleet's arrival, the ailing marshal was transferred to the *Berthollet* for a return to Constantinople and hospitalization, but within a few hours of sailing, he died. Days earlier the marshal had turned over command of the French forces to General Canrobert.

Yet more days passed as the allies reconnoitred, conferred, argued and prepared. Raglan push for an immediate attack, but Canrobert would have nothing of that. Artillery had first to be brought into place, he argued, and for that to be effective, appropriate earthworks had first to be constructed. And once more Raglan gave in to his French counterpart.

By 17 October, nearly a month had passed since the Eupatoria landing. Following the allied failure to launch an attack on the northern shore, it was clear to the Russians that the assault would come from the south, and they rushed to fortify that quarter of the city. Virtually the entire population – soldiers, sailors and civilians – laboured feverishly night and day to strengthen the existing defences and to create additional earthworks. Guns and ammunition were relocated from the bay-side to the new lines. In September, the garrison's defenders numbered 16,000 men – mostly sailors and militia, save for one battalion of regular troops. By mid-October, twelve additional battalions had arrived from the Danube thus more than doubling the numbers of defenders, including the returned Alma forces. The artillery covering the southern approaches was increased from 172 guns to 341, many of them heavy calibre.

Finally everything was at last in place for the allies to get on with the siege. Orders had been issued on the 16th for the cannonade to commence on the following morning at 06:30, with the off shore fleet firing at the same time. The Russians, however, surprised everybody by grabbing the initiative – at 05:30 they opened fire on the Anglo-French positions. For lack of proper coordination, the joint fleets began their bombardment four hours late. And when they did finally join in, it was all for naught. The French vessels found themselves too far from target to be effective and withdrew, while the British were too close to target and, because of the fierce fire they were sustaining, also withdrew. The land bombardment, however, continued throughout the day with the Russians returning an effective cannonade. In mid morning, a lucky Russian shot hit the largest French magazine and in the enormous resultant explosion, not only represented a critical amount of ammunition lost, but all fight was taken out of the instantly demoralized artillery. 'For those who had witnessed the scene of havoc,' writes Kinglake, 'it may well have been appalling to see half a hundred human beings before, now changed by one blast of fire into mere blackened corpses or maimed and helpless sufferers.' The French guns went quiet, and they remained so for the balance of the day with the British carrying on, on their own. By nightfall, the result of the day's bloody exchange was a standoff – but it did mark the start of the siege.

Actually, it would be more correct to say that the 17th was a preview of things to come, for in the week that followed there was hiatus – a calm of sorts descended on the field. During that interlude, the Russian General Pavel Liprandi brought together 25 infantry battalions, 34 squadrons of cavalry and 78 gun – a force of 23,000 men. At 05:00 on the 25th his army moved forward into the valleys north of Balaklava, and very quickly engaged an allied force of 20,000.

The fighting took place in two valleys which were separated by an east-west causeway that carried Vorontzov Road, the supply route connecting Sevastopol with mainland Russia. The North and South valleys – each approximately a mile and a half long – were defined on the west by a sharp-rising bluff, the Sapouné Heights, and on the east by a height which came to be called 'Canrobert's Hill'. The allies had established a series of redoubts along the north and south sides of Vorontzov Road, manned principally by the Turks but supported by British artillery. The cavalry was stationed on the road's south side. Turkish battalions stretch along the base of the Sapouné Heights, and at the top of the heights General Bosquet was stationed.

Initial success lay with the Russians – they quickly captured

Canrobert's Hill and the strategically important Fedioukine Heights north of it. It was the Turks who suffered most in these engagements, with 170 of 500 being killed. The remainder fled in panic and ran in the direction of Balaklava crying, 'Ship! Ship! Ship!' The flight of some of these unfortunates was short-lived, for their path brought them face to face with 'a stalwart and angry' wife of a Highlander sergeant who brandished a large stick. In her fury over the apparent cowardice, she flayed out vigorously at those retreating. Kinglake describes the scene, as reported by witnesses from the Duke of Cambridge's 2nd Battalion, 'The blows dealt by this Christian woman fell thick on the backs of the Faithful. She believed, it seems, that, besides being guilty of running away, the Turks meant to pillage her camp, and the blows she delivered were not mere expressions of scorn, but actual and fierce punishments. In one instance, she laid hold of a strong-looking, burly Turk, and held him fast until she had beaten him for some time and seemingly in great fury.' Such was the indomitable spirit of the 'ladies of the camp'.

In addition to Canrobert's Hill and Fedioukine Heights, the Russians also took possession of three of six redoubts. As they were establishing themselves on the captured heights, Liprandi's infantry began a slow advance onto the Anglo-Turkish positions. In response, Lord Lucan moved his Heavy Brigade forward to meet them – more correctly, to threaten them. The Russians appeared to be unimpressed with this manoeuvre for they continued in their measured advance. Lucan then veered left towards the causeway in order to reinforce Sir Colin Campbell's Highlanders at its western end.

In the meantime, fearing a successful thrust at Balaklava itself, Raglan had ordered the divisions under the Duke of Cambridge and Sir George Cathcart to move in that direction in anticipation of an attack by fresh forces from Sevastopol. The start of that mission was slow in getting under way because the troops were at breakfast following a full night in the trenches; eventually they did move on. This left the western flank lightly defended, mostly with British and Turkish infantry and virtually no artillery. For the Russians, the opportunity to break those defences was too good to miss and General Rijov grasped it – he formed up a battalion of his Hussar Brigade and prepared for a charge. One British infantry battalion now faced a charge by 400 horsemen. Under normal circumstances, an infantry about to receive a cavalry charge would form itself into a compact square formation in order to withstand the attack by a 360° concentration of firepower. In this case, however, there was insufficient manpower to do so effectively. The Russian attack would be met by an infantry line – 'the thin red line' as it subsequently came to be known. 'Remember,' Sir Colin Campbell told his Highlanders, 'there is no escape from here. You must die where you stand.' William Russell in his dispatch to *The Times* relates what happened next:

The ground flees beneath [Russian] horses' feet. Gathering speed at every stride, they dash on towards that thin red streak topped with a line of steel. The Turks fire a volley at 800 yards, and run. The Russians come within 600 yards, down goes that line of steel in front, and out rings a thundering volley of Minié musketry. The distance is too great; the Russians are not checked, but still sweep onwards with the whole force of horse and man, through the smoke, here and there being knocked over by a shot of our batteries above. With breathless suspense everyone waits the bursting of the wave upon the line of Gaelic rock, but ere they come within 150 yards, another deadly volley flashes from the levelled rifle, and carries death and terror into the Russians. They wheel about, open files right and left, and fly back faster than they came.

In the meanwhile the main body of Rijov's cavalry was beginning to cross over the causeway and Vorontzov Road, seemingly with nothing to check them. Brigadier James Scarlett spotted this movement, and without a moment's hesitation swung his Heavy Brigade to meet the Russians. With no idea of the enemy's strength, he divided his force into two columns and had the bugler sound the attack. He, himself, at age sixty-one led the charge of the left squadron, plunging fearlessly into the centre of the Russian Hussars. Horsemanship gave way to swordsmanship. Sabres flashed, thrust, pierced and slashed, with the frenzied Scarlett outperforming many who were half his age. Sergeant-Major Henry Franks describes the scene:

> Some of the Russians seemed to be rather astonished at the way our men used their swords. It was rather hot work for a few minutes; there was no time to look about you. We soon became a struggling mass of half frenzied and desperate men, doing our level best to kill each other. Both men and horses on our side were heavier than the enemy, and we were able to cut our way through them, in fact a good many of them soon began to give us room for our arms, and to quote Mr Russell's words, 'The Heavy Brigade went through the Russians like a sheet of pasteboard.'

Soon three British artillery pieces came into action, and quickly finding the range of the Russian rear, they opened fire, an action that proved critical to the outcome of the fierce engagement. The speed, vigour and determination of the British attack, coupled with the gun fire, proved too much for the Russians, who sounded retreat and withdrew temporarily into the North Valley. The engagement that Scarlett precipitated was as brief as it was unexpected – the outcome was negligible. No territory was exchanged, no positions were gained, few were killed – insufficiently sharpened sabres, it was claimed, on the British side – but numerous wounds were sustained, many proving fatal. Scarlett himself suffered five wounds and his aide-de-camp, sixteen. It was, however, an outstanding achievement for the British – Scarlett had brought his 800 horsemen into battle against an enemy force of 1,600 and he had won, sending the Russians packing.

The Crimean War records a number of instances of outstanding heroism wrought by individuals – hark back to Midshipman Lucas on board the *Hecla* in the Baltic. There are also notable instances of collective heroism – the bold French assault of Malakoff for example, to which we shall come shortly, and the resolute Russian defence of Sevastopol. For the British, the charge of Scarlett's Heavy Brigade at Balaklava on that October day is the dominant example of such heroism. It was a genuine victory, albeit with a careless lack of immediate follow-up.

History, however, can be fickle. The daring charge of the Heavy Brigade pales in notoriety to the charge of the Light Brigade – undeniably the most famous incident of that unfortunate war. As the Heavy Brigade pressed the attack, Lord Cardigan observed its progress from a gap in the heights, but did nothing to shore up Scarlett's forces, despite the orders he carried to attack everything and anything. His 675-strong horsemen remained still, even during the subsequent retreat of the Russian Hussars. Raglan was stationed at the highest point where he viewed the entire unfolding scene – not only Scarlett's attack but Cardigan's inactivity. During a brief lull, the general sent an order to Lucan to occupy the ground vacated by the retreating Russians: 'Cavalry to advance and take advantage of any opportunity to recover the heights. They will be supported by the infantry which have been ordered to advance on two fronts.' Lucan received the order but made no immediate move in the indicated direction, preferring to wait for the appearance of the promised infantry – an arrival that never occurred. He did, however, move the Light Brigade closer to the North Valley, where he had a better view of the situation. In that same lull, the Russians made good their retreat with impunity.

With the retreat successfully completed, General Rijov was pleasantly surprised by the quiet which had befallen the field. So much so that he sent out sortie parties to retrieve the guns which remained in the redoubts the Russians had captured earlier. This too Raglan observed from the heights, and furious that the enemy would make off with 'the fruits of victory', he ordered his Quartermaster General Airey to write down fresh instructions to Lucan. The officer hastily scribbled these on an odd bit of paper, resting it on his scabbard, 'Lord Raglan wishes the cavalry to advance rapidly to the front, and try to prevent the enemy carrying away the guns,' signed 'R. Airey'. The Quartermaster General then handed the note to his aide-de-camp, Captain Sir Louis Nolan, for delivery. Before the officer had actually set off, Raglan called him and ordered him to tell Lucan to attack immediately. The choice of messenger, on the one hand, was judicious – Nolan was an excellent horseman and if anyone could get through to Lucan expeditiously, it was he. On the other hand, the selection was singularly unfortunate for the relay of oral instructions. The contempt Nolan had for Lucan and for Cardigan was no secret. Both officers irritated him to the extreme – one he openly and contemptuously called 'Lord Look-on' and the other, 'The Noble Yachtsman'.

Nolan plunged down the steep cliffs, skilfully manoeuvring his horse and, galloping up to Lucan, he handed over the tattered note with Raglan's instructions. Lucan received the note with suspicion – it was after all, signed not by Raglan but by Airey whose very own ADC delivered it, a man considered by Lucan to be an 'unreliable prig'. With the breathless, sweating and impatient ADC standing by, Lucan examined the paper with studied deliberation, pausing long moments in thought, which only irritated Nolan further. Lucan then openly voiced his hesitancy in undertaking the dangerous and probably useless mission, certainly without infantry support. This was too much for the excited Nolan, who then cried out indignantly, 'Lord Raglan's orders are that the cavalry should attack immediately.'

'Attack, sir! Attack what? What guns?' Lucan sputtered angrily.

'There, my lord, is your enemy,' replied Nolan contemptuously. 'There are your guns!' As he spat out these words, he pointed with a vague wave of the hand not at the causeway where the Russians where salvaging guns, but to the North Valley, at the end of which a mass of Rijov's cavalry had re-formed, protected by a redoubt of Russian guns. Exasperated with Nolan's insolence, Lucan, in the words of one historian, 'tottered off', to order Cardigan to attack the Russian position, approximately one and a half miles away. The Earl, smartly saluted his commanding officer and replied, 'Certainly, sir, but allow me to point out to you that the Russians have a battery in the valley in our front, and batteries and riflemen on each flank.' Lucan concurred, and with a shrug of the shoulders moved on, as though to indicate that there was nothing to be done. In every war, situations arise when a few are called upon to make sacrifices for the good of the whole – this, it seemed, was one such moment, and an order was an order. There was no option; it had to be followed. Or, as Tennyson wrote poignantly, 'Their's not to make reply, / Their's not to reason why, / Their's but to do and die.' The fate of the Light Brigade was sealed.

Standing up in his stirrups, Lord Cardigan called out in his strong, hoarse voice: 'The Brigade will advance!' The trumpeter sounded, first 'Walk,' then 'Trot,' and finally 'Gallop,' and with that, 'Into the valley of Death / Rode the six hundred.'

It took them twenty-five minutes to ride the stretch of valley, all the time receiving scorching fire from heavy guns and rifle. Despite greatly-thinned ranks, the frenzied horsemen, amid yelling and cheering, charged the redoubt, dispatched the gunners and pressed on into the thick of Russian cavalry. It then dawned on Cardigan that his forces had plunged into enemy forces which wildly outnumbered his own, and it became clear that it would be suicidal to press the charge. There was nothing to be done but to fall back and retrace the route by which they had come. And this they did. A Russian cavalry officer witnessing the event:

> It is difficult, if not impossible, to do justice to the feat of these mad cavalry, for, having lost a quarter of their number and being apparently impervious to new dangers and further losses, they quickly reformed their squadrons to return over the same ground littered with their dead and dying. With such desperate courage these valiant lunatics set off again, and not one of the living – even the wounded – surrendered.

Through it all, the helpless French watched with horror at the surreal drama unfolding below them. 'C'est magnifique, mais ce n'est pas la guerrre,' mumbled General Bosquet. And another officer pronounced, 'Je suis vieux! J'ai vu des batailles: mais ceçi, est trop!' The Chasseurs d'Afrique, who had been stationed at the base of the escarpment, did, however, charge forward, through the Russian riflemen to the guns on the west side which were raining such havoc onto the galloping horsemen. They successfully silenced them and thus significantly eased the way for the retreat. Ten of these gallants were killed and twenty-eight were wounded – a noble French sacrifice for their allies, one of which little is heard.

Thus came to a conclusion this mad-cap feat of valour – a heroic but futile effort to capture the wrong battery of guns. The charge of the Light Brigade is legendary, and as with all legends fact is clouded by fiction. The notoriety given over to this particular engagement creates the impression that six hundred men charged into the valley and only a handful survived. This was not the case. According to Kinglake, 673 horsemen went into action, and of these 113 were killed and 134 were wounded. The brigade, in other words, was reduced in mounted strength by one-third – additionally, 475 horses were killed. One officer who came out only lightly scathed was Lord Cardigan, who in the battle's aftermath mixed with the bleeding survivors. Approaching one of the gravely wounded, he remarked as though in apology, 'It was a mad-brained trick; but it was no fault of mine.' To which the reply was, 'Never mind, my lord, we are ready to go again.' With that the Lord rode away towards the bay where his yacht awaited him. There he bathed, changed into comfortable clothing and enjoyed the dinner that his French chef had prepared. It was all in a day's work.

Balaklava was a draw. The Russians had failed to re-possess the port town, the entry point of allies supply, and the allies had failed to take control of Vorontzov Road, the supply route to Sevastopol. Both forces retired for the moment, the British and French above all to attend to their wounded and to catch a second breath.

16

THE FIRST WINTER

From mid-September reinforcements had been pouring into Sevastopol. With Austria having declared neutrality, the Russian high command felt free to transfer troops from the Danube to the Crimea. Battalion after battalion flowed 'with great vigour' by a circuitous route into the besieged citadel. By the end of the month, Menshikov had amassed an aggregate of 120,000 defenders, nearly double the numbers the British and French had at the time. Also at the side of the allies was a contingent of 11,000 Turkish troops, but these in the estimation of the British were useless – or, as Kinglake puts it, 'Notwithstanding their warlike capacity, it would be illusory to reckon the Turks, in unqualified words, as components of the "effective" strength now possessed by the Allies.'

Ten days had passed since Balaklava, and now the opposing armies were face to face once more, this time at Mount Inkerman slightly east of Sevastopol and not far from the mouth of the Chernaya River. In fact, it was anything but a 'mount' – a large plateau, really, broken with ridges and gullies in the centre of which rose a 650-foot (200-metre) hill. General B. McClellan, an American sent by President Pierce to observe the war and its weaponry, observed that it was 'the most elevated ground in the neighbourhood, and is susceptible of string defence from whatever direction it may be attacked . . . could the Russians have anticipated a siege of Sevastopol, it would have been an unpardonable error not to have occupied the Inkerman by a small permanent force . . . It was still more inexcusable on the part of the allies to have omitted the occupation of the position in force.'

The allies had in fact long established themselves on these heights. At dawn on 5 November, under cover of dense fog and drizzle, they were assaulted by 30,000 Russians. The plan was simple: launch a false attack on Balaklava which would draw the French away from the British. Then advance two columns onto the heights from the centre and the right, and thrust the British down onto the plateau below, where another force would await to help drive them south or into the sea. The immediate object was not so much to destroy the enemy as it was to prevent or to delay an attack on Sevastopol. Although the fortress-city was becoming stronger by the day, it was judged insufficiently prepared to receive a concerted assault – additional time was required to strengthen the earthworks, build up the redoubts and bring more guns into place.

The *New York Times,* founded three years earlier, carried a report on the event in its edition of Sunday, 5 November 1854:[21]

And now commenced the bloodiest struggle ever witnessed since the war cursed the earth . . . We have been prone to believe that no foe could ever withstand the British soldier wielding his favourite weapon [bayonet] . . . but, at the battle of Inkerman, not only did we charge in vain – not only were desperate encounters between masses of men maintained with the bayonet alone – but we were obliged to resist bayonet to bayonet the Russian infantry again and again, as they charged us with incredible fury and determination.

The battle of Inkerman admits of no description. It was a series of dreadful deeds of daring, of sanguinary hand-to-hand fights, of despairing rallies, of desperate assaults – in glens and valleys, in brushwood glades and remote dells, hidden from all human eyes . . . [eventually] our old supremacy, so rudely assailed, was triumphantly asserted, and the battalions of the Tsar gave way before our steady courage and the chivalrous fire of the French. No one, however placed, could have witnessed even a small portion of the doings of this eventful day, for the vapours, fog and drizzling mist obscured the ground where the struggle took place to such an extent as to render it impossible to see what was going on at the distance of a few yards . . .

The plan the Russians had put into place was, in General McClellan's words, 'excellent in conception . . . the difficulty arose in the execution'. General Pavlov advanced his column to the right, and Lieutenant General Soimonov moved up the centre. McClellan goes on to report what happened next:

It would appear that in the orders [Soimonov received] the expression *left of the Careening Bay ravine* was used for *western*. Soimonov improperly interpreted this as meaning his own left, and thus brought his own and Pavlov's columns into a state of confusion which paralysed the efforts of both, so that but a portion of either command was at any one time engaged.

The feint planned to draw the French forces off the heights did not work. General Bosquet had observed Prince Gorchakov's army and quickly realized that the Russian initiative was limited to a long-range artillery bombardment; there were no attacking cavalry or infantry. He therefore remained where he was, and turned his attention to the nearby British. Quickly sizing up the confusion and disorder in which the redcoats found themselves, and perceiving the resultant progress the Russians were making, he ordered his two reserve battalions into a counter attack. One witness's account:

> About 10 o'clock a body of French artillery had already begun to play with deadly effect on the right wing of the Russians. Three battalions of the Chasseurs d'Orléans rushed by, the light of battle on their faces. They were accompanied by a battalion of Chasseurs Indigènes – the Arab Sepoys of Algiers. Their trumpets sounded above the din of battle, and when we watched their eager advance right on the flank of the enemy, we knew the day was won.

The heated struggle continued to ebb and flow, generally in favour of the Russians, but the tide quickly changed when Bosquet entered the fray. The confusion of battle was eloquently described by General Sir Edward Hamley:

> On our part it was a confused and desperate struggle. Colonels of regiments led on small parties and fought like subalterns, captains like privates. Once engaged every man was his own general. The enemy was in front and must be beaten back. The tide of battle ebbed and flowed, not in waves, but in broken tumultuous billows. At one point the enemy might be repulsed while, at a little distance, they were making the most determined rush. To stand on the crest and breathe awhile, was to our men no rest, but far more trying than the close combat of infantry, where there were human foes with whom to match,

and prove strength, skill, and courage, and to call forth the
impulses which blind the soldier to death and peril.

The fierce fighting continued all day, finishing at eight
o'clock in the evening, with the Russians having been routed
and driven 'pell-mell down the hill towards the valley, where
pursuit would have been madness, as the roads were all
covered by their artillery. They left mounds of dead behind'.

To describe with precision the ins and outs of the fighting is a
challenging assignment for any historian – Kinglake gives over an
entire volume to its description, and breaks it up into six convoluted periods. Suffice to note that Inkerman was a battle unlike
Alma or, more importantly, Balaklava. Whereas Balaklava was
principally a cavalry engagement by sabre, Inkerman featured
infantry with bayonet. At Balaklava, it was the English who took
whatever honours were had; at Inkerman, it was the French.
Balaklava produced inconclusive results; Inkerman had a decisive outcome. And at Balaklava, 1,300 were killed or wounded; at
Inkerman, 17,500 – without any doubt, the bloodiest engagement of the entire war. Staff Captain Pyotr Alabin, aide-de-camp
to General Pavlov, was in the retreat and he describes it:

In the Quarry Ravine I saw a terrible picture. The whole ravine
was full of dead and wounded. The French skirmishers were
sitting in many places behind rocks on the opposite side of the
ravine and were exchanging fire with our skirmishers. There were
many killed and wounded . . . it was a terrible mess. The officers
were trying to sort out the soldiers into their regiments but in
vain . . . I took more than ten carriages and loaded them with the
wounded under the aqueduct. What bloodcurdling scenes I
witnessed! The medical attendant of the Okhotsky regiment,
Danilov, was dressing the wounded under a rock . . . the French
overthrew us totally and . . . every minute we expected the French

to follow our troops to the Quarry ravine and cut off our retreat. In that case disaster would have happened! [The retreat progressed under continued French bombardment].

The last shell caused terrible scenes. Many doctors and priests took to their heels. The wounded who could move followed them, among them one man from the operation table with a partially amputated leg. It was a very sad picture.

The Russians had retreated and the allies rejoiced over their victory, close as it was. As the generals conferred on the following day, they were under no illusion of what lay ahead – they 'were aware now of having to commit to a long, drawn-out siege operation which nobody really wanted,' Fletcher and Ishchenko write. 'The defences of Sevastopol had stood up to the first bombardment whilst the Russian army still hovered increasingly in the interior. Inkerman had demonstrated just how fragile the allies' position was. It was even worse now, with casualties having reduced the British forces to fewer than 15,000 fit men. Indeed, from now on Raglan's army would be the junior partner in the enterprise, the main burden of responsibility falling heavily upon the more numerous French.'

With winter rapidly setting in, the invaders occupying the open spaces around Sevastopol were becoming threatened with dangerous exposure. Even in Crimea, 1,600 miles (2,600 kilometres) south of Moscow, winters could be harsh. In 1812, Napoleon Bonaparte was forced to retreat from Russia, defeated, he claimed, by 'generals January and February'. What would these same generals bring in 1855? In the churches of Sevastopol, the prayers of the faithful mixed with the clouds of incense rising into the cupolas – may the Almighty send down a crippling winter of the harshest sort; may the British and French be confounded.

*   *   *

The allies had come before Sevastopol on 25 September to begin the year-long siege. On the day before that, Anglo-French guns had blazed in an exchange of fire with the Russians in entirely different part of the world – some 5,300 miles (8,500 kilometres) distant from Crimea, in the remote northwest corner of the Pacific.

During the preceding decade rivalry between Russia and Britain for supremacy in that corner of the world had come to boiling point – France and the United States had also become players in the match, albeit to a lesser degree. In 1842, Britain assumed control of Hong Kong, and shortly thereafter Count Nikolai Muraviev, Governor-General of Eastern Siberia, headed an expedition to occupy Chinese territory north of the Amur River. British reaction to this move was unequivocally negative, and the concern exacerbated after learning of St Petersburg's plans to send a high-profile diplomatic mission to the Mikado of Japan with the view of persuading him to open up his closed country to Russian trade. The outbreak of the Crimean War provided the British a golden opportunity to deal with the troublesome Russians.

On 29 August, an Anglo-French squadron entered Avacha Bay on the east coast of Kamchatka Peninsula. The six-ship flotilla, commanded by rear admirals David Price and Auguste Fébvrier-Despointes, sailed the seven miles (eleven kilometres) inland to Petropavlovsk where they found the 44-gun *Aurora* and an armed transport, the *Dvina* blocking the passage to the harbour, guns facing outwards. Half the ships' armament had been removed and placed ashore in the batteries overlooking the harbour, and substantial earthworks had been erected in anticipation of an attack that was sure to come. The Russian garrison, bolstered by sailors from the ships, numbered 1,013 men, while the seaborne squadron carried over 2,000. On arriving, the ships opened fire on the Russian defences in a brief and inconclusive cannonade, with the Russians returning in good measure. So severe was the Russian response, that the allies were forced to retire, with the resolve of returning on the next day in a new formation.

On the following morning, they again approached Petropavlovsk and at ten o'clock started a fresh cannonade in an attempt to silence the active shore batteries. Gunfire from ships and shore continued for a couple of hours, until the totally unexpected happened. At the hour of noon, Admiral Price retired to his cabin for lunch, and there he committed suicide. It is supposed that under the strain of the cannonade he thought Petropavlovsk to be more heavily defended than he had anticipated and that the 'proper account of the Russian frigates' he had promised to deliver would not be. Command of the fleet was assumed by Fébvrier-Despointes, who brought a halt to the cannonade, and withdrew once more. Rather than engage in a fruitless bombardment, he decided to try a landing on the following day.

On the 31st, the landing did take place but it was quickly repulsed by a Russian counter-attack. For four days, Anglo-French forces tried repeatedly to gain the upper hand, but they were rebuffed each time by the single-minded defenders. On one occasion, a concerted attack was made by 400 Frenchmen and 300 Englishmen who laboriously won the height of a hill, only to be ambushed and thrown back by Russian sharpshooters. Nothing was achieved, and it appeared nothing could be gained. During these engagements, the Russians lost 165 men and the allies, an estimated 350. On the 5th, Despointes called off the siege and withdrew his ships from the embattled scene – the French sailed off to San Francisco, and the British to Vancouver; the Russians filed into churches and held services of thanksgiving. God was with them.

*   *   *

Would the Almighty now stand by the defenders of Sevastopol? The battles of Alma, Balaklava and Inkerman had failed to stop the advance of the allies; they were at the city's doorstep. The depletion of troops through death, wounds, sickness and winter freeze weighed heavily on the besieged. It became certain that Russian forces could not prevail in the field without further reinforcements – and of that, there was no immediate promise. Massive numbers of troops had already been transferred from the Danube, and Paskevich would not risk releasing any additional. The war in the Baltic also required men – there would be no relief from that quarter.

For the allies, it was clear that the anticipated rapid victory would not be – estimates of enemy strength and determination had been gravely miscalculated. In the days of Varna, it had all seemed so certain, but now they found themselves bogged down with no end in sight and with a morale that was rapidly plunging. Whatever hardships the Russians were suffering, theirs were the same, but worse. A severe November storm of hurricane proportions had struck the coast and thirty French transports loaded with supplies were wrecked, with a calamitous loss of provisions and ammunition. The scarcity of forage for horses had greatly weakened transport arrangements – supplies unloaded at Balaklava were delivered to the front over the muddy road with profound effort. All they could do now was to maintain a continuous shelling and unremitting pressure in an effort to exhaust the defenders, and hopefully also to draw them outside the defensive lines. Underground mining operations were being put into place, and sooner or later the earthworks and ramparts were bound to collapse. It was merely a question of time and patience, and the Russians would give in. Little did the allies expect that a full eight months would pass before their objective would be attained.

For the Russians, it was a matter of exhausting the enemy by inflicting the greatest amount of physical and psychological wear and tear they could – in a weakened condition the invader would be glad to make peace on favourable terms. What was left unappreciated by the defenders was the tenuous situation in which the allies found themselves. Had Menshikov been fully aware of their condition, rather than thinking defensively, he might well have launched a concentrated attack at a particularly vulnerable point and quite probably brought the entire Crimean campaign to a rapid and satisfactory conclusion. But that was not to be; both sides continued in preparing for the siege.

The word 'siege' in the classic sense conjures pictures of massive stone walls bristling with armament, being shelled and then scaled or breached by a patiently persistent foe. At Sevastopol there were no massive stone walls – merely earth-works reinforced by stone and timber taken from the town's buildings. On the surface the defences might have appeared more of a statement than a reality. But the ingenious design of these lines proved as effective as any fortification constructed by Vauban, Louis XIV's iconic military engineer – at least, such was the case for nearly a year.

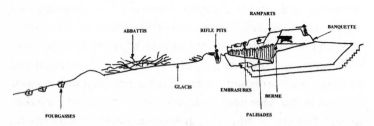

The above sketch illustrates Todleben's design for the de-fences, back-breakingly dug and assembled by soldiers, sailors and citizens of the city. A trench-like ditch seven feet (two metres) deep was dug, with the excavated earth being carefully formed into a rampart on the defensive side. A wooden palisade of sharpened stakes was erected on the rampart side of the ditch, with a *berm*, or narrow passage, in between to enable personnel to carry out repairs. On the inner side of the rampart was a *banquette*, or a step, upon which defending marksmen could take up position when under attack. Another line of infantry could also take up position in 'rifle pits' – trenches dug in front of the ditch. Between these rifle pits and the potential path of attack was a *glacis*, or cleared bank of open earth, to expose advancing troops – advancing, that is, if while under fire they first man-oeuvred through the *abatis*, or tangle of felled trees and sharpened stakes, firmly planted in the ground. The *glacis* was usually 100 yards wide and often served as a primitive minefield – a series of *fourgasses*, or funnel-like holes, dug in the earth with rocks piled at the bottom. An electrically-fired charge set from the rifle pits detonated at a strategic moment flung the rocks upward and wrought havoc on the attackers. Between the *fourgasses*, planks were scattered about with protruding nails. The artillery was mounted in embrasures within the ramparts and these were reinforced with *gabions*, or heavy sheets of padded wicker, skilfully woven by the sailors. The defences were so manned that whatever damage was sustained by heavy guns during the day, was repaired at night. Little wonder that the allies encountered difficulty in breaking through these formidable and regenerating defensive lines.

Conditions inside Sevastopol had rapidly deteriorated and become more strenuous – bombardment, unending repairs, cold, sickness, shortages and little hope of relief. 'A kind of apathy has set in with all our commanders,' wrote Captain Pyotr Lesli in despair, 'and seeing this all your energy disappears too. In general it's time to finish this terrible bloodletting war . . . with every hour that passes it gets harder and harder. Everything has become so loathsome that, oh, oh – there's no strength left! And I would be prepared to leave for

Siberia at once to do hard labour, even for a lifetime, if only I could get out of Sevastopol.'

Shortly after Alma, a young artillery officer arrived to the besieged city and in a series of vividly written articles he described the life of the place and what he saw. Leo Tolstoy was twenty-five years old at the time, and the pieces he wrote for the *Russian Veteran*, a newspaper independent of the official army gazette, were eventually brought together in his *Sevastopol Sketches*. He was particularly struck by the heroism of the defenders:

Not even in the time of ancient Greece was there such heroism. As he inspected his troops, Kornilov would say to them, not 'Good health, men,' but, 'If you are called on to die, will you die?' And the soldiers would cry back, 'We will die, your excellency. Hurrah!' And they shouted this not for the sake of effect, for on every face you could see that they uttered these words not in jest but in earnest, and indeed 22,000 men have already fulfilled this promise.

A wounded soldier almost on the point of death told me how on the 24th [the date of Inkerman] they had taken a French battery but had been given no reinforcements. He was sobbing out loud. A company of sailors nearly mutinied on being told that they were to be relieved from the battery on which they had held out for thirty days under fire. Soldiers tear the fuses out of shells with their bare hands. Women take water to the men at the bastions. Many of them have been killed or wounded. Priests enter bastions bearing crosses and recite prayers under fire. On the 24th, in one brigade there were 160 wounded men who refused to leave the battlefront. Extraordinary days!

Incredible as it may seem, it never occurred to the allies to block off access from the north, the supply lines to the besieged garrison. Food therefore continued to arrive into the city with regularity, albeit with considerable difficulty. It had to be transported from afar on wagons in need of repair, pulled by horses undernourished for lack of forage, and driven by men often afflicted by cholera or other illness.

The siege in those early winter months seemed to have become bogged down with no notable engagements having taken place. In February, however, Menshikov did initiate an offensive by dispatching General Wrangel with a force of 20,000 (including 600 Greek volunteers) and 108 guns to re-take Eupatoria. The allies' disembarkation point had just received another landing, that of Omar Pasha's Turkish troops from the Danube. A segment of that force had been marched south, but the larger part continued on at Eupatoria, and was on hand to meet Wrangel's attack. Siding with the Turks were small contingents of British and French forces, joined also by local Tartar inhabitants – off shore two French frigates were anchored with guns strategically trained.

On the night of the 15th, a Polish deserter brought word to Omar Pasha of the planned attack, and as a result the Turkish defenders were well prepared to receive it. When the Russians did attack on the following morning, it proved to be a two-day debacle. The French naval guns almost immediately knocked out their artillery, and Omar Pasha's troops encountered little trouble in repulsing Wrangel's forces as they attempted to cross a deep, water-filled ditch and mount the defensive walls. Russian troops on the flanks who had taken cover first in a Jewish burial ground and subsequently in a Russian cemetery – tomb stones offer fine protection – were quickly routed by 200 horsemen of the Turkish cavalry. The attack on the town was called off, and the Russians retreated into the Crimean countryside.

It was Nicholas himself who had urged Menshikov to take some form of offensive, and the catastrophe of Eupatoria caused him 'intense mortification and disappointment'. That the defeat was at the hands of the Turks was particularly galling – 'the very Turks whom he had loved to imagine less warlike than his own highly-disciplined troops'. Menshikov was relieved of his command, and Prince Gorchakov was appointed Commander-in-Chief. Shortly after Eupatoria, Nicholas fell ill, and on 2 March died of 'a paralysis of his lungs' complicated by a 'want of heart-power'. Rightly or wrongly, it was postulated that the tsar died of grief. 'A want of heart power we know, is a kind of bodily ailment not infrequently brought on by grief . . . [in this case] it sprang from a sense of humiliation, entailing bitter anguish of mind,' wrote Kinglake. The tsar's first-born, Alexander II (1855–81) came to the throne and continued the war entered upon by his father.

The official Russian account of the Eupatoria debacle would gladden the heart of today's spin masters:

> . . . thus the principle object of our attack had not been attained. Eupatoria remained in the possession of the enemy, but the affair in itself was productive of advantageous results in our cause. The attack obliged the allies to be always on guard and in readiness to repel others. It was from apprehension on this point that they always maintained at Eupatoria a large garrison and that they established here a vast entrenched camp.

Gorchakov had written to the minister of war at the time of his appointment, 'It is a deadly heritage that I have received . . . I am exposed to being turned, cut off and perhaps broken, if the enemy has a little good sense and decision.' Fortunately for him, however, the allies were indecisive as they continued in their inability to strategize effectively. Raglan and Canrobert recognized that the siege was not airtight – supply lines for the defenders remained open. They agreed, however, that under the circumstances little could be done and that the siege therefore had to continue in its porous state. By March, Napoleon's confidence in Canrobert had nearly evaporated, and he threatened that he himself would travel to the front to take charge of the campaign. To the relief of the French War Office, this did not happen. The emperor did, however, order the transfer of General Pélissier from Algeria to the Black Sea as an eventual replacement to Canrobert, and also sent General Adolphe Niel, the country's expert on siege warfare. These two quickly persuaded the Council of War to reorganize its forces. Much to Raglan's chagrin, it was the French who ended up with the greater share of the responsibility, including the lines opposite Malakov and the Little Redan. His own disseminated forces were to assume a reduced role – the sector in front the Great Redan. Furthermore, it was decided to transfer from Constantinople 12,000 Egyptians being held in reserve – troops that would be stationed in Eupatoria, thus enabling Omar Pasha's Turks to join up the besieging forces at the front.

This last decision particularly displeased Raglan, who judged the Ottoman troops unreliable and dirty. In fact, Raglan had little use for any troops other than his own. The French he held in an esteem only slightly greater than that of the Turks – their troops, he judged, were incompetent and not as courageous as the British. Weeks earlier Napoleon had suggested to Lord Cowley, the British Ambassador in Paris, that since 80 per cent of allied sea power was British, it was they who should be given sole command of the fleets. Conversely, because four-fifths of the land forces were French, command of the armies should be assigned to them. Napoleon's proposal was summarily rejected – no way might French generals ever command British forces, whatever the numbers.

And when rumour was heard that Napoleon might personally take charge of the Crimean campaign, the prospect became even less acceptable. Under no circumstances would the dignity of the British crown or the prestige of the nation be compromised.

In April another heavy bombardment of Sevastopol was begun – the second in a series of six. This one lasted nine days, during which time 168,700 rounds were fired at the city, with the Russians returning about half the number. Stockpiles of ammunition had diminished within the city and batteries were limited on the number of rounds they could fire per day. As fast as damage was sustained, it was repaired at night by the driven defenders. Casualties among the Russians were heavy – 6,000 killed or wounded, mostly from the nocturnal repair parties. Tolstoy gives a description of a visit to one the dressing stations:

Now, if you have nerve strong enough, go through the doorway on the left: that is the room in which wounds are bandaged and operations are performed. There you will see surgeons with pale, gloomy physiognomies, their arms soaked in blood up to the elbows, deep in concentration over a bed on which a wounded man is lying under the influence of chloroform, open-eyed as in a delirium, and uttering meaningless words which are occasionally simple and affecting. The surgeons are going about their repugnant but beneficial task of amputations. You will see the sharp, curved knife enter the white, healthy body; you will see the wounded man suddenly regain consciousness with a terrible, harrowing shrieked cursing; you will see the apothecary assistant fling the severed arm into a corner; you will see another wounded man who is lying on a stretcher in the same room and watching the operation on his companion, writhing and groaning no less with physical pain than the psychological agony of apprehension; you will witness fear-some sights that will shake you to the roots of your being; you will see war not as a beautiful, orderly and gleaming formation, with music and beaten drums, streaming banners and generals on prancing horses, but war in its authentic expression – as blood, suffering and death.

This second bombardment produced little tangible result and proved to be as great a failure as the first one. One British officer's pessimistic reflections:

This is the fourth day of the second bombardment, and we seem to be doing no good. The enemy keeps up his fire well, no one is in the least sanguine as to the result. Some talk of storming, but I hardly think this likely . . . if the bombardment fails, which there is every reason to suppose it will . . . I fear we shall never do anything so long as Sevastopol can communicate with the country.

At the same time another discouraged witness, a Colonel Charles Windham gives a more critical view not only of the bombardment but of the campaign's leadership:

How true that 'War' is usually a series of mistakes. The conduct of the allies, since we arrived in this country, has been one continued piece of blundering stupidity . . . We have now fired upon the place for four days, have lost many hundreds of men [in fact: British, 260 and French 1,500] and, unless we follow it up with bloody assaults at different places, we shall never take it. Should we lose a large amount of men in doing so (which is more than probable), we shall have thrown away more life and more money, for a useless object, than was ever done before.

At the time of the bombardment, Napoleon and Empress Eugénie were on a four-day state visit to England, accompanied by a suite of civilian and military advisors. The purpose of the occasion was not only to reinforce the alliance but to work out a joint strategy for the campaign in Crimea. During the day, the War Council of ministers and generals huddled over conference tables awash in maps, charts and field reports; in the evening, the senior-most dined in elegance with the royal couples. Victoria gave herself over to the Emperor of the French, whom she had all along considered a common parvenu, but with whom she now had became quite enchanted.

A glittering military review was held at Windsor Castle – bands played, 'Loud and vivid were the cheers,' and Victoria and Eugénie 'looked remarkably well and pleased. They wore dresses of a light colour with dark scarves and veils, Her Majesty having on a green bonnet, and the Empress one of a blue colour.' In the evening, her majesty tendered a state dinner. 'The magnificent service of gold plate was used on this occasion,' with the 2nd Life Guards providing the music. A post-dinner party and then a departure for London. 'For the accommodation of the Queen's visitors, a special train in the Great Western Railway was provided . . . to convey Her Majesty's guests back to town,' departing from the Queen's private railway station.

On the following day, there was an afternoon reception for 1,200 people at the Guildhall. A 97-foot (29.5-metre) pavilion was especially erected for the occasion, with 'a beautiful ornamental device in cream colour bearing the following: "Alma, Baklava and Inkerman" '. There followed an excursion to the opera to see Beethoven's *Fidelio*, in the company of an assortment of Dukes and Duchesses, Princes and Princesses and 'the ladies and gentlemen of the household, the Imperial suite and a select party'. The West End streets were lit up: 'The illuminations in honour of the Imperial guests were highly general – some streets presenting one blaze of light. Their Imperial Majesties, on their way to the Royal Italian Opera, seemed very pleased at the splendid reception which greeted them from one of the most enthusiastic crowds ever witnessed.'

So it was. While those at home who bore the brunt of guilt for the start of the war revelled in glittering dinner parties and receptions, colourful reviews and illuminations, blameless unfortunates far away, who were expected to bring the senseless war to an end, suffered debilitating sickness and shortages, ghastly wounds and death.

The deliberations of the War Council during those four days, however, were fruitful. To their own surprise, the ministers and generals reached agreement on a fresh strategy for Sevastopol. With Turkish reinforcements, the supply routes into the city would be cut off, and an elaborate-planned three-pronged attack would be launched to destroy the Russian army and take the city. It was a simple offensive strategy, one that might well have worked had it been put into effect. The fresh plan, however, came to naught – Raglan and Canrobert were unconvinced of its merits, and nothing in the world could persuade them to press forward with it.

While the state visit was under way, the allies dispatched an amphibious invasion force to Kerch on Crimea's east coast, on the Sea of Azov. Its object was to take that lightly fortified port town and thus cut the supply route from the Don River. The initiative was Raglan's proposal, long in planning, agreed to by Canrobert with no enthusiasm – he was reluctant to withdraw 9,000 troops from the siege lines. No sooner had the allied fleet sailed out of Balaklava's harbour than word of the War Council's fresh plan of action was received via the recently-completed telegraph cable that had been laid between

Varna and Balaklava. New technology now permitted Paris and London to micro-manage more effectively the far-off campaign. A fast boat was dispatched from Balaklava to recall the expeditionary force.

The result of the muddled enterprise was a further deterioration of relations between the French and British. In addition, Canrobert's instruction from Paris now arrived by cable, but for whatever reason the British War Office continued to rely on hand-delivered communication – a two-weeks delay. Canrobert was ready to follow through on the three-pronged attacks, but with no orders to that effect, Raglan refused to act – tension between the two commanders became palpable. On the 17th, Canrobert requested to be relieved of his command to which Napoleon readily agreed, and the command was transferred to General Pélissier.

A second expedition to take Kerch was sent out three weeks later in an effort by Pélissier to placate Raglan. It was mostly manned by the French and Turks, with the British playing no more than a supporting role. The assault was successful; Kerch was taken, thereby giving the allies full control of the Sea of Azov. A colourful vignette from Roger Fenton on that particular occupation:

> We could see the French rushing through the plantations into the houses and coming out again laden with fowls, geese, looking-glasses, chairs, ladies dresses and everything useful or useless that they could lay their hands on. As they got to the contents of wine casks they got more outrageous, discharging their muskets right and left at fowls, pigs and birds . . . the disorder became greater, the stragglers were more drunk, the cries and shouts more savage, the firing of muskets and the whizzing of shot past our ears more continual, and it was evident that all control over the French army was gone.

The significance of the occupation of Kerch was that it forced the Russians to withdraw 30,000 troops from the immediate defences of Sevastopol in order to give protection to the remaining supply lines, particularly from the north – the garrison was thus further weakened. At the same time, allied forces had been strengthened by the infusion of 15,000 Italian troops under General de la Marmora. Six months earlier Camllio Cavour, the ambitious prime minister of the Italian state of Piedmont-Sardinia, had persuaded King Victor Emmanuel II to declare war against Russia. The wily statesman had anticipated the calling of a post-war peace conference, and he was determined to be at the table when the inevitable shuffle of territories took place and when spheres of political influence would be redefined. With the arrival of the Italians, total allied strength had grown to 225,000 men, with the French as the dominant force on the peninsula – for every British soldier on the ground, there were four Frenchmen, while the Turks outnumbered the British very nearly two to one.

By mid-June it was Pélissier who was really controlling the progress of the campaign – after all, the overwhelming majority of the forces were reporting directly to him. 'Raglan was under a shadow,' A.J. Barker points out. 'With a mood of dejection and humiliation prevailing in the British camps, the British commander-in-chief was a broken man in every sense of the word. Cholera and dysentery had again returned to the British army and in the week of 23 June the local death rate had risen to 35 per cent of the entire force.' Cholera knew no rank and had infected the commander-in-chief himself – the poor man additionally suffered from acute diarrhoea. After two bed-ridden days, the aged field marshal died. (He had been promoted seven months earlier.) The command of the British forces was passed to General Sir James Simpson.

17

THE FINAL CURTAIN

In the eleven-week period between Raglan's death and the evacuation of Sevastopol, two battles of significance were fought on Sevastopol's outskirts which generally are given short shrift in British history books. On 16 August, in a move to recapture the Fedioukine Heights, Gorchakov led a Russian attack on Traktir Bridge which spanned the Chernaya River. His forces numbered 60,000 infantry and artillery, supported by Don Cossack riflemen. The ground was the same as that of Balaklava, and it was from these same heights, now held by the allies, that Russian heavy guns at one time poured fire on the charge of the Light Brigade. To meet the Russians, 25,000 Frenchmen were in place, together with 15,000 Sardinians, 10,000 Turks, and twenty-four squadrons of British heavy cavalry. From the start, scepticism had beset many Russian commanders who felt that the attack plans had been sloppily formulated, and who had received orders that were simply unclear. On the eve of the battle, from one man's memoir:

> All the experienced Russian generals were absolutely certain that the next day would be a disaster. 'General Read [right-hand to Liprandi] has had a premonition that he will not survive tomorrow,' said his orderly. When Colonel Skyuderi, the commander of the Odessky regiment, heard it he said, 'Read has had the same premonition as we have. Mind you, many of us, myself and Bel'gard will be annihilated tomorrow.'

The next day was indeed a disaster for the Russians. Poorly communicated plans for the battle, including ambiguously worded instructions, combined to seal the fate of the Russians on that day. A snippet from a letter sent by Prince Sergei Obolensky, aide-de-camp to Gorchakov, to his father-in-law following the disaster – shades of orders received by Lord Cardigan before the start of the famous charge on that same field:

> At dawn the [commander-in-chief] was in the valley with the troops. General Read accordingly ordered the artillery, which was moved forward, to open fire on the Fedioukine Height. Despite the order not to advance until told to do so, the C-I-C sent his aide-de-camp to tell General Read to begin the action. When the aide-de-camp gave the order to General Read the artillery was already in action. General Read thought that this was the order to advance and attack Fedioukine Heights with the infantry. He asked his aide-de-camp if he understood the order of the C-I-C correctly. The aide-de-camp answered that he didn't know but he repeated word for word the order from the C-I-C 'to begin the action'. General Read then asked the chief of staff, General Veimann, how he interpreted it. The

latter said that, as he understood it, they ought to cross the river.

Attack, counter-attack; cavalry right, cavalry left; artillery fire up, artillery fire down. The battle that had started at 04:00 raged for an exhausting six hours and finally ended with a Russian withdrawal. Their losses were enormous – over 8,000 men, including 2,300 killed with the remainder wounded or taken prisoner. General Read's premonition had been realized – he was one of the earliest to die. The French suffered 1,800 casualties, and the Sardinians 250, of whom a mere 14 were killed. Dr Thomas Buzzard, an Englishman serving in the ranks of the Turks as a surgeon, afterwards toured the horrifying battlefield, which he describes:

On the banks of the aqueduct, on the bridge which crossed it, and also, but less frequently, in the water below, were heaps of Russian dead and wounded. The Tractir bridge, too, which is larger than the one over the aqueduct, was literally blocked with and for a time rendered impassable by a pile of corpses, numbers of dead and wounded also being strewn about the banks of the river, the water of which I could see in places running red with blood. Amongst the dead and dying were quantities of weapons – muskets, swords and bayonets – besides helmets or caps, crosses, icons and other religious emblems, and, perhaps not less pathetic, loaves of black bread scattered upon the ground or half exposed in the haversacks in which they had been carried by the weary soldiers during a very long night's march. Here and there some bottles were also to be seen.

In many classical paintings of battlefields that I have seen the dead soldier has been usually depicted lying on his back, with face upturned. I notice that in this tragic scene the dead in, I think, the majority of instances, lay on their faces, literally, to use the Homeric phrase, 'biting the dust'. These men had been shot whilst advancing up hill, and their bodies ceasing to be under the control of life would naturally fall in the direction in which they had been moving when struck.

Chernaya was a decisive turning point in the campaign for the Russians. It was their last effort to break the siege by launching an offensive action in the field; two-pronged column attacks against infantry equipped with Minié rifles had proven futile. A tragic lesson learned, and with a fresh bombardment of the city launched on the day after Chernaya, Gorchakov ordered that construction of a bridge be started across the bay to the north side. The city's position had become precarious and its evacuation appeared inevitable.

Within a fortnight of Chernaya, the final great battle was fought. It had become clear to the allies that for any successful assault on Sevastopol, the ground before the city's southern-most tip had first to be taken, and for that to happen Malakov and Little Redan had first to be taken, together with Great Redan. At one time a conspicuous stone tower had stood atop Malakov hill, but now it was barely recognizable for all the fortified earthworks that had been recently thrown up. The hill had been transformed into a major fortification with a semicircular battery and connecting trenches to the redans and the other flanking defensive structures. It bristled with guns.

On 8 September, the allies attacked these defences. As part of the plan, another bombardment of Sevastopol had been launched two days earlier, with 592 French guns and 183 British guns. Gorchakov felt what was coming; the final curtain on the Sevastopol drama was about to close. In the midst of the bombardment he wrote to his emperor:

The infernal fire, much of which is counter-bombardment, clearly indicates that the enemy intends to destroy or neutralize our guns and make an assault. It is impossible to repair the fortifications and the best that one can do is to try to keep the powder magazines and the shelters intact; the broken parapets are filling the ditches and we are keeping the embrasures clear. The losses among gun crews have been heavy and can hardly be replaced.

The plan for the attack called for the French to assail Malakov and the Little Redan, and for the British to strike against the Great Redan, a target they had previously failed to capture. It was a lop-sided division of responsibility, with the French pouring in 25,000 troops, supported by 5,000 Sardinians, and the British mustering only 3,000, of whom a half were being held in reserve. A small force was not the only disadvantage that hampered the British. They had failed beforehand to provide for themselves an adequate network of trenches leading to the redan, and therefore to get to it, they had first to sprint some 200 yards (180 metres) of open ground. The French, on the other hand, had so prepared their trenches that the attacking force was able to manoeuvre itself under cover to the very base of Malakov. One historian postulates, 'In all probability it was the British soldiers' incurable aversion to digging which contributed to the failure.'

The assaults were planned for noon, at a time when the Russians were normally at their midday meal and also changing their pickets – a deliberate deviation from the customary early-dawn attack. The surprise of the French attack was complete. So unprepared were the Russians, that by the time they fully realized what was happening, the leading Zouaves had clambered up the parapet into the fortification and, within ten minutes of quitting the trenches, had planted the tricolour atop the Malakov tower. The French left flank at the Little Redan, however, encountered considerable more difficulty, as attack and counter-attack melted into fierce hand-to-hand combat which lasted nearly six hours.

The raising of the French flag over Malakov's tower signalled the start of the British assault. Their four-point attack was met with fierce determination by the Russians who successfully pushed back the red line, and General Simpson was forced to retreat. It had been a miserable day for the British. 'Now I suppose the French will take it [the Great Redan] and we will have a double crow over us, and we may expect heartburnings and recriminations,' wrote Clarendon. 'We have cut a poor figure lately and I expect we shall continue to do so for as long as that worthy old gentlewoman, Simpson, is at the head of our affairs. I have a letter from Stratford today from headquarters saying that our army is living from hand to mouth and that we are even less prepared than last year for the winter while the French have vast resources of everything.'

By five o'clock, Malakov was firmly in French hands and the fighting in the area had become more of a mop-up operation than anything else. By then too it had become clear to Pélissier that the keys to Sevastopol were in his grasp. Gorchakov had much earlier come to the same sad realization, and, with no options remaining, had ordered the evacuation of the city. 'Gorchakov may not have been the greatest military genius – not that there were many in this tragic war anyway,' Fletcher correctly observes, 'but he was not that stupid that he did not recognize a lost cause when he saw one, and a prolonged defence of Sevastopol with Malakov in French hands was certainly a lost cause.' Everyone in the city was ordered to head for the recently completed pontoon bridge and for the ships that had been pressed into service as ferries. There would be a regrouping on the Severnaya side. It was the bitterest of pills for any defender to swallow, Pyotr Alabin among them:

> Everybody saw the necessity of leaving the southern part of the town. Everybody clearly knew that there was no other way out for us from the semi-circle in which we were put by the powers of circumstance. Our only was across the harbour. There, on the Severnaya side a glimmer of hope was still glowing for us . . . nonetheless, everyone took the news of the retreat with great sadness.
>
> How could we give up the sacred graves of our brothers to the enemy? How could we give them the fortifications, which were built by our heroic friends from dust soaked with their blood, the guns, and the piles of shells? You see, they will take all these with them as salvage to lay before the world as evidence of their triumph over Russia, which will never be defeated. And what of the houses and the large buildings? The enemy will make their homes in them; they will laugh at us and say, 'Russia prepared our winter houses for us!' But no, it will not be so! We cannot give trophies to the enemy; we will repeat the Moscow fire; we'll blow up everything that is of worth! Flame, smoke and ashes – that is what our enemy will find in Sevastopol!

The evacuation was handled brilliantly. Civilians had been evacuated earlier and now it was the fighting men's turn to funnel onto the bridge. Through it all a steady fire was maintained against the allies by the rear guard, and, as they retired, they blew up the magazines and batteries. Sailors scuttled the ships remaining in the harbour. After everyone had safely crossed the bridge, that too was blown up. The night sky was lit up by the fires and its stillness was broken by intermittent explosions. The allies thought twice about entering the city for fear that it may have been mined.

Tolstoy was one of those who crossed over the pontoon bridge with the massive crowd of the escaping. Soldiers and sailors, generals and sergeants; the bandaged, the crippled and the bleeding – all passed over the bridge. 'Each man,' he writes, 'on arriving at the other side of the bridge, took off his cap and crossed himself. But this feeling concealed another – draining, agonizing and infinitely more profound: a sense of something that was a blend of remorse, shame and violent hatred. Nearly every man, as he looked across from the North side at abandoned Sevastopol, sighed with a bitterness that could find no words, and shook his fist at the enemy forces.'

With the allies in possession of the city and the Russians on the Severnaya side, an unspoken truce seemed to have taken hold as a cloud of fatigue and despondency descended on both side of the bay. What next?

In September 1812, Napoleon I had boldly invaded Russia, routed its army and established himself in Moscow – put to the torch by its inhabitants. Forty-three years later, Napoleon III with his allies invaded Russia, pushed back its army, and by September was established in Sevastopol – blown up by its inhabitants. In 1812, Napoleon Bonaparte, threatened with hardships of rapidly advancing winter, impatiently awaited the surrender of the country. Four decades later, the armies of his nephew and the allies, threatened with hardships of rapidly advancing winter, impatiently waited for further orders from their respective governments. They had accomplished what they had set out to do. Their war seemed over. Indeed, what next?

'Sevastopol is not Moscow, the Crimea is not Russia,' Alexander wrote to Gorchakov. 'Two years after we set fire to Moscow, our troops marched in the streets of Paris. We are still the same Russians and God is still with us.' Trevor Royal points out, 'In military terms Gorchakov had merely made a tactical retreat into a new position which would continue to pose problems to the allies. The tsar also guessed correctly that his enemies had no intention of marching into Russia and that unless Gorchakov was defeated stalemate had returned to the Crimean peninsula.' Insofar as the Crimean Peninsula was concerned, it was indeed a stalemate.

But, at the time that the final chapter of the siege of Sevastopol was being brought to a close on the shores of the Black Sea, the Crimean War was firing up in the Caucasus, the land of the Chechens. Russia and Turkey at the time shared a 150-mile (240-kilometre) border that stretched from the Black Sea port of Batumi to Mount Ararat, near today's juncture of Turkey, Iran, Iraq and Armenia – a landmark more popularly remembered as the final resting place of Noah's ark. For decades, that part of the world had been suffering some form of warfare or another, with Russia at the centre and making no secret of its designs on the eastern provinces of Turkey, with an eye cast on Persia. The British, ever conscious of foreign encroachment on its commercial interests, took more than a passive interest in the goings on in that nook of the globe. By 1855, Russian supremacy in the Caucasus had been established through a series of military successes. With the Austrians occupying the Principalities, and with British, French and Sardinian armies attending to the war in Crimea, the Turks were free to focus attention on their Eastern empire. To help withstand further encroachment by the Russians, they fortified and provisioned the fortress of Kars in Armenia.

In June, a Russian force of 25,000 troops under General Muraviev moved towards Kars, urged on by Alexander 'to win decisive results'. In the previous year another Russian expedition under General Beboutov had engaged the Turks 20 miles (32 kilometres) south of Kars and had defeated them resound-

ingly, with the Ottomans retreating back to the city in a state
of disarray. At the time, however, Beboutov did not follow up
on his victory, which now was Muraviev's mission. Based on
the previous year's experience, the fresh expeditionary force
expected no formidable resistance by Turkish forces. Little was
Muraviev aware, however, that the quality of the Kars fighting
force had been transformed.

A couple of months after Beboutov's 1854 success, the
British sent a three-man mission to Kars to assess the situation.
Its specific orders were to evaluate the condition and morale of
Turkish forces and to liaise with whatever French mission
might happen by. Heading that mission was an artilleryman,
Colonel Fenwick Williams, a Canadian from Nova Scotia,
who had had plentiful experience in Asia Minor. At one time
he had been seconded to the Turkish army stationed in that
part of the world. He was to report back directly to Raglan.

What the mission found was appalling. Turkish forces had
been greatly reinforced by reluctant Armenian conscripts and
desertions were commonplace. Troops were indifferent and
left unpaid, recruits were untrained, and weapons were obsolete. Hospitals were non-existent and the care for the
wounded utterly primitive. The whole system was permeated
with inefficiency and graft. Absentee leadership was commonplace – commanding officers felt obliged to spend time schem-
ing in Constantinople in order to keep secure their positions.

Williams decided that the only way out would be for himself
to take control of the forces and of the defence. With the help
of the other members of his mission, another gunner and a
military physician, and supported by a number of foreign
officers in Turkish service, he energetically set about his task.
Additional military experts arrived from Constantinople to
lend a hand, particularly engineers. A training programme was
put into place, discipline was tightened, medical facilities

created, the walls and gun emplacements of Kars were strengthened. By spring, it was not only a substantially re-formed and efficient army, more spirited and motivated, but it was also a greatly strengthened city with a garrison of 17,000. Williams had wrought miraculous changes in a short time – truly, an unsung hero of the war.

By the 16th, General Muraviev's forces were at the walls of Kars and they made their assault. The columns of infantry and regiments of cavalry attacking the heights east of the city were at first repulsed. They regrouped and once more pressed forward, this time successfully pushing back the Turks and overcoming any resistance. The heights were taken and the principle supply road had been cut. Muraviev was so taken aback by the improved performance of the fighting Turk, above all by the ferocity of their resistance, that, rather than lose men unnecessarily, he decided to suspend further thrusts. He would now settle into besieging the city – a policy of blockade and starvation that lasted five months. Early in the siege, a certain Captain Thomas wrote home a rather pathetic report of conditions within Kars:

It is a most melancholy state of things . . . Constantinople appears to care nothing for General Williams's requisitions; we have not got siege ammunition for a week. The poor soldiers never get their full rations, and many of them are twenty-eight months in arrears of pay. While such things are going on, it is a wonder to me that the soldiers don't lay down their arms, or desert by the thousands; but strange to say that desertions are rare, and the men in the best of spirits. I think they are the finest soldiers (or stuff to make soldiers of) that the world can produce. Nothing comes amiss to them; they are literally in rags, and yet they never complain, although they are nearly always wet through. It would astonish you to see a regiment on parade. You could hardly pick out a worse lot from all the beggars in England.

Unless we get *English* or *French* reinforcements in a month or two, you may give up all chances of seeing my beloved countenance again, for there will not be a man of this army left alive. If the Russians don't kill us we shall die of starvation, which is not by any means a pleasing alternative.

Our communications are almost entirely cut off and the country swarms with Cossacks and Armenians (who are all hostile to us). Write me a letter soon, with nothing but *nonsense* in it and believe me ever yours . . .

By September, the Kars garrison was in wretched shape – cholera had struck, rations had run short, the weakest horses were slaughtered for food, desertions had become commonplace and mutiny was in the air – and there was no talk of outside reinforcements. Williams declared that Kars would collapse within two months. Captain Thomas in another letter:

We are placed in a very tenable position, but with a lamentable lack of all necessities of war. We are very badly off for ammunition, food, and clothing, and our army is in a sad state of discipline. The Russians are encamped on the other side of the valley in our front, about two miles and half at most, and are only I think prevented from attacking us by the heavy ground in the valley, caused by the almost incessant rain we have had for the last ten days. Our communications with our rear are almost cut off, and our last English post was captured by the Russians. General Muraviev very politely sent us our private letters but all newspapers and dispatches he has kept, bad luck to him!

The Russian army stubbornly maintained its siege position, making only the rare attack on one defensive position or another. Winter came and tents were replaced by primitive huts – the Russians seemed comfortably ensconced. Within the besieged garrison, however, the suffering continued amid the silence flowing from Constantinople – no hope for reinforcements. Months earlier, Omar Pasha at the Sevastopol front had informed Pélissier and Simpson of his desire to go to the rescue of Kars, but to do so he required the transport services of the Royal Navy. The proposal was summarily quashed by the commanders, at least initially – the sizeable Turkish contingent was required where it was. With fresh reports of the developing disaster at Kars, Omar once more approached the commanders. This time Simpson appeared more sympathetic to the proposal, but when Napoleon heard of it, he dismissed it angrily: 'The great objective was Sevastopol and not Kars.' Stymied again, the angry and frustrated Omar had to sit back and await further developments in Armenia. It must be noted that from the start of the Williams mission, the French maintained a suspicion that it was nothing more than a British ploy to gain strategic and commercial advantages at their expense.

On 25 November, with cholera, starvation, a dearth of supplies and the freezing cold to contend with, Williams capitulated – nothing further could be done, but to surrender Kars. Amid 'Hurrahs' and singing, the jubilant Russians marched in, and were immediately horrified to discover masses of men too weak to be evacuated, many of them in the throes of death. The following evening, Muraviev invited Williams and his senior officer to dine with him. In receiving the captive general, the Russian is reported to have greeted the Canadian with the following generous words: 'General Williams, you have made yourself a name in history, and posterity will stand amazed at the endurance, the courage and the discipline which the siege has called forth in the remains of the army.'

To the end Williams, embittered as he was by the lack of support he had received from Constantinople, remained loyal to his Turkish forces, to whom he paid a heartfelt tribute: 'They fell dead at their posts, in the tents, and throughout the camp, as brave men should who cling to their duty through the slightest glimmering of hope of saving a place entrusted to their custody.'

The war in Turkish Armenia was all but over with a couple of lesser engagements taking place at a distance from Kars. At the time that Sevastopol was evacuated, Omar Pasha succeeded in getting his forces to Turkish Armenia where he engaged the Russians at Mingrelia and Sukhum. The war in the Crimea had also concluded, save for a brief bombardment of Russian installations at the mouth of the Dnieper River east of Odessa.

By December 1855, the war had been raging for over two years, and, to put it bluntly, everyone had had enough, certainly those in the field – spirit had been drained from both sides, and the exhausted thought only of home. But tired or not, London continued to plot fresh offences – the lack of notable military success, particularly the failure to take the Great Redan, was a blotch on the British escutcheon and an affront to its pride. Paris, however, would have nothing of that. Napoleon III had attained his objective – with the success of Malakov and the fall of Sevastopol, he had established 'his new dynasty on a foundation of glory' – his uncle's long shadow had been gratifyingly shortened. The emperor made it clear that the French were no longer interested in pursuing the war, and could ill afford to do so in any case.

For Tsar Alexander, the commitment to the war begun by his father was no less a matter of national honour, but it was less of an emotional issue for him personally than it had been for Nicholas. Meanwhile, the horrendous costs of human and fiscal resources were unsustainable. His country alone had suffered 246,000 military casualties – to the allies combined 252,000. By one estimate, Russia had expended 142 million pounds sterling[22], a mere 15 per cent less than France and Britain together. Alexander's ambitions, furthermore, were focused more on liberal reform and the modernization of his vast country, rather than on territorial expansion, at the expense of the Ottomans or anyone else. For Russia and for everyone else, the time had come to end it all.

At this juncture, Austria appeared from out of the shadows. After three years of sitting on the sidelines of the various crises leading to the conflict and then the war itself, Francis Joseph now stepped forward to knock heads as it were. On the third day after Christmas 1855, Count Valentin Esterházy, Austrian ambassador to Russia, delivered an ultimatum in St Petersburg – its provisions having been previously agreed to by Paris and London. Accept the terms of the document and end the war, or Austria will join the allies in its further pursuit. Two years earlier, as the war clouds were gathering, Nicholas called Francis Joseph's failure to support Russia 'monstrous nonsense'. His infuriated son was now feeling the sting of the emperor's other hand. The portrait of Francis Joseph in the Winter Palace which the tsar had then turned to the wall remained hanging as it was with the words clumsily scribbled by the infuriated Nicholas clearly visible, '*Du Undankbarer*' – 'ingrate'.

The five demands of the ultimatum 1) Russian protectorate over the Danubian provinces to be surrendered, 2) freedom of navigation of the Danube River to be declared, 3) the Black Sea to be declared a neutral zone, open to ships of all nations, with the abolishment of all military and naval arsenals on its shores,

4) Russian claims of protectorate over Orthodox Christians in the Ottoman empire to be surrendered, and 5) the right of the allies to raise any other issues at a future peace conference to be assured.

In an all-night meeting with six of his key advisors, Alexander sorrowfully agreed to accept the Austrian ultimatum – there was no other reasonable choice. News of the decision spread quickly through St Petersburg, amid strongly divided opinion. Many were elated at last to be done with the war – it had been an excessive and purposeless drain on the suffering nation, and people were wholly fed up with it. Others, however, were in despair, feeling only bitterness at having to yield to foreign powers. Among the latter was Empress Maria Alexandrovna, who reportedly made this shockingly candid admission to a lady-in-waiting, Anna Fyodorovna Tytcheva:

> The tragedy is that we cannot tell our country that this war had begun in error on account to a tactless and unlawful incident – the occupation of the Principalities – that its conduct was weak, that the country was unprepared for it, that there were neither guns nor shells, that all sections of administration are badly organized, that our finances are depleted, that we have had flawed policies for some time and that all these resulted in the present situation. We cannot say anything. We can only keep silent.

On 25 February 1856, the Paris Peace Conference convened, and, five weeks later, after all the inevitable verbal skirmishing, divisions, changes and hidden agendas had played out, the Treaty of Paris was signed, which brought to a close 'the world's most curious and unnecessary struggle'.

APPENDIX:

ALEXIS SOYER'S CRIMEAN RECIPES

Soyer's Food, for one hundred men, using two stoves (for a regiment of 1,000, use 20 stoves):
Cut or chop 50 lbs of fresh beef in pieces of about lb each; put in the boiler, with 10 tablespoons of salt, two ditto of pepper, four ditto of sugar, onions 7 lbs cut in slices: light the fire now, and then stir the meat with a spatula, let it stew from 20 to 30 minutes, or till it forms a thick gravy, then add a pound and a half of flour; mix well together, put in the boiler 18 quarts of water, stir well for a minute or two, regulate the stove to a moderate heat, and let simmer for about two hours. Mutton, pork, or veal, can be stewed in a similar manner, but will take half an hour less cooking

Note: A pound of rice may be added with great advantage, ditto plain dumplings, ditto potatoes, as well as mixed vegetables.

Soyer's Salt Pork with Mashed Peas, for one hundred men:

Put in two stoves 50 lbs of pork each, divide 24 lbs in four pudding cloths, rather loosely tied; putting to boil at the same time as your pork, let all boil gently till done, say about two hours; take out the pudding and peas, put all meat in one cauldron, remove the liquor from the other pan, turning back the peas in it, add two teaspoonfuls of pepper, a pound of the fat, and with the wooden spatula smash the peas, and serve both. The addition of about half a pound of flour and two quarts of liquor, boiled ten minutes, makes a great improvement. Six sliced onions, fried and added to it, makes it very delicate.

Bill of Fare for London Suppers – lobster cutlets:

Cut a lobster in dice, letting the flesh weigh about half a pound; when done, put in a pan 2 oz of butter, 2 teaspoonfuls of chopped onions; put all on the fire, fry for a minute or two, add 1 teaspoonful of flour; mix well, stir in for a minute; add half a pint of milk; season with salt, pepper, and one salt-spoonful of cayenne, two teaspoonfuls of chopped parsley; let all boil for a minute or two, stirring all the time; add in your lobster, give it a boil; add two yolks of eggs; mix quick, put on a dish to cool. When quite cool and firm, divide in six parts, giving each the shape of a small cutlet; egg and breadcrumb twice. Put a piece of the very small claw to the end of each cutlet, so as to form a bone; fry for a few minutes, like you would a sole, in plenty of fat; lay on a cloth, and serve on a napkin, with plenty of fried parsley; you may adopt any shape you choose, if cutlets are too troublesome, as you would a croquette. No sauce is requisite.

Note: The lobsters for the preceding receipts may be prepared, shaped, and bread-crumbed hours before wanted.

Pierce's Claret and Champagne Cup à la Brunov:
To three bottles of claret, take two-thirds of a pint of Curaçao, one pint of sherry, half ditto of brandy, two wine-glasses of ratafia, three oranges and one lemon, cut in slices; some springs of green balm, ditto of borage, a small piece of rind of cucumber, two bottles of German-Seltzer-water, three ditto of soda-water; stir this together, and sweeten with capillaire or pounded sugar until it ferments, let it stand one hour, strain it, and ice it well; it is then fit for use.

The same for Champagne Cup – Champagne instead of claret; noyeau instead of ratafia.

This quantity is for an evening party of forty persons. For a smaller number reduce the proportions.

REFERENCES

CHAPTER 1 – 1844 and the Straits

1 'There is no feature': Argyll, I, 448
2 'We have to decide': Martens, 412
3 'A brilliant diplomatic victory': Tatischev, 'Diplomatitschesky' 95
4 'My beloved Uncle': Victoria, 14
5 'I got to know': ibid, 16.

CHAPTER 2 – Nicholas and Victoria

1 'In my lessons': cited in Grünwald, 42
2 'His system was': Jomini, I, 39
3 'God is Master': cited in Grünwald, 42
4 'The barbarians of the North': O'Meara, 138
5 'Never before and never': Argyll, I, 436
6 'The heroic courage': de Tocqueville, 288
7 'The meanness and improvidence' Fortescue, VIII, 18
8 'The only cooking utensils': Woodward, 257
9 'If ever there is': cited in Barker, 24
11 'He thought it was very': cited in Woodham-Smith, *The Reason Why*, 30

12 'Let us sit down': Stockmar, II, 104
13 'Louis Philippe has meant': ibid, 126
14 'Turkey is a dying man': ibid, 126
15 'What will France require?': ibid, 127
16 'By land Russia': ibid, 128
17 'To provide against': Parliamentary Papers (F.O.-Russia), 424
18 'I know I am taken': Tatischev, 'Diplomatitschesky', 22
19 'Years ago Lord Durham': Martens, 237
20 'Turkey must fall': Stockmar, 107
21 'I do not want Constantinople': Goryainov, 98; cited in Puryear, *England, Russia*, 48
22 'We cannot now stipulate': Stockmar, 108; Tatischev, 584
23 'Trophies to British valour': *Illustrated London News* (15 June 1844)
24 'The weather was glorious': Argyll, 436

CHAPTER 3 – The Crimean War – What was it?

1 'The Russian diplomats': cited in Dowty, 74
2 'Relations with the leading': ibid, 74
3 'His Majesty has as': ibid, 74
4 'We desire most sincerely': Golder, 'Purchase of Alaska'
5 'The American people': Dulles, 52
6 'Typical of the Irish': Dowty, 88
7 'Aggressive policy of the': *Illustrated London News*
8 'When the boat': Golder, 'Russian-American relations', 474
9 'Headlands, lines of coast': cited in Chesney, 42
10 'Was it possible that American prejudices': Alexander, 126
11 'I knew that Miss Nightingale': Soyer, 139
12 'We must not blind ourselves': cited in Chesney, 40
13 'The program of Fourtier's': ibid 42
14 'A curious experiment': ibid Chesney, 42
15 'MacIntosh's Portable Buoyant': ibid Chesney, 42
16 'The swan song of the old': *Historical Outlook*, 344
17 'Stout, spectacled, whiskered': Fisher, III, 946
18 'It is extremely fortunate': Victoria, II, 20

CHAPTER 4 – 'Some Fatal Influence at Work'

1 'The Crimean War was the result': Henderson, 257
2 'The War and its causes': Engels, 532
3 'Too small for the things': Thompson, 109

4 'The great object of the': Puryear, *England, Russia*, 91
5 'Infinite riches of this': ibid, 110
6 'A more determined': ibid, 183
7 'Battle of civilization': cited in Seaton-Watson, 327
8 'I myself and the entire': Horvath, 'Origins of the Crimean War'
9 'The principle responsibility': Puryear, *England, Russia*, 304

CHAPTER 5 – Stratford and the Hungarians

1 'Lord Stratford wishes this': Lane-Poole, 55
2 'When he began his': ibid., 56
3 'Destruction will not come': cited in Lane-Poole
4 'Hot! Hot! Hot!' (notes): ibid.
5 'Nothing is unimportant which': Lane-Poole, 58
6 'The thought of the Sovereignty': Lane-Poole, 58
7 'His fierce temper': Kinglake, I, 119
8 'When the set face': Lane-Poole, 61
9 'High words he spoke': ibid., 61
10 'Mohammed in condemning': ibid., 92
11 'By the mere presence': ibid., 101
12 'It was hard to resist': Kinglake, I, 120
13 'The question of extradition': Temperley, *England and the Near East*, 263
14 'A part at least of Her Majesty's Mediterranean squadron': Sproxton, 121
15 'It will be necessary to give the Sultan': ibid., 123
16 'If they want us': ibid., 129
17 'Sufficiently were limited': Puryear, *England, Russia*, 158
18 'If powers pretended': Sproxton, 133
19 'This direct appeal': Temperley, *England and the Near East*, 268
20 'While the Porte remains': Puryear, *England, Russia*, 158
21 'Under present circumstances': Phillimore, III, 579

CHAPTER 6 – Napolean III and Jerusalem

1 'He says he has been': Simpson
2 'A weaver oppressed': Kinglake, I, 228
3 'Insignificant quarrel between': Grünwald, 344
4 'The miserable satisfaction': Parker, 537
5 'From Lake Baikal': Temperley, *England and the Near East*
6 'The closest likeness': Kinglake, I, 45
7 'The Latins are dissatisfied': Temperley, *England and the Near East*, 286
8 'An instrument for opening': Nesselrode, 234
9 'If it depended on me': Temperley, England & Near East, 289
10 'The question of the Holy Places': Tarlye, I, 136

11 'Conveying successfully her mass artillery': Temperley, *England and the Near East*, 295
12 'What is the meaning': Thouvenal, 12
13 'In the month of December': Kinglake, I, 53

CHAPTER 7 – The Sick Man of Europe

1 'Frail, narrow-chested': Barber, 138
2 'Enfeebled early in': Barber, 138
3 'Declaration or opinion': Puryear, *England, Russia*, 227
4 'Perhaps your Majesty': *American Register*, 253
5 'Oh! but you must understand': ibid., 253
6 'The Principalities are, in fact': Kinglake, I, 95
7 'Induce your government', :ibid., I, 96
8 'The Emperor is very irritated': Parliamentary Papers I (1854)
9 'The man who shone so brilliantly': Grünwald, 263
10 'Even in the capacity': Tarlye, 157
11 'Very gentlemanlike and agreeable': Grünwald, 263
12 'It was understood that': Kinglake, I, 103
13 'Menshikov understood that': Tarlye, 158
14 'Often had received the most': Parliamentary Papers (F.O. France)
15 'We did quite right in showing': ibid.
16 'In the event of a single': ibid.
17 'If Russia, in contempt': *The Times* (26 March 1853)
18 'Would be incompatible': Parliamentary Papers (F.O. Russia)
19 'Uphold the Turkish Empire': ibid.
20 'In these uncertain times': ibid.
21 'Long before noon the voyage': Kinglake, I, 128
22 'He had to carry the affair': cited in Temperley
23 'That the crisis is one': Lane-Poole, 234
24 'Be very careful in preparing': Walpole, *Russell*, II, 178
25 'Your Excellency will in such case'; Kinglake, I, 127
26 'Implicates for us': *American Register*, 261
27 'The *firman* respecting': Parliamentary Papers
28 'My own impression is that': Parliamentary Papers
29 'In the event of imminent danger': Parliamentary Papers
30 'The order in itself': Kinglake, I, 168
31 'A dry and categorical': Tarlye, 187

CHAPTER 8 – War Fever Rises

1 'The causes of his discomfiture': Kinglake, I, 188
2 'I feel the five fingers': ibid., 189
3 'If a statesman': Kinglake, I, 185

4 'Indispensable to take measures': ibid., I, 197
5 'At that time there were': Walpole, *Russell* 180
6 'While the ship of state': ibid., 180
7 'By the grace of God': *American Register*, 273
8 'It is easy to bring war': Grünwald, 204
9 'You will see': Tarlye, 236
10 'The current disagreements': ibid., 238
11 'Nicholas has practised': cited in Puryear, *England, Russia*, 269
12 'As proof of the understanding': Parliamentary Papers
13 '*Les invectives des journaux*': Tarlye, 239
14 'Wait before entering': cited in Puryear, *England, Russia*, 276
15 'A formidable fleet kept': Temperley, 333
16 'In the condition': Kinglake, I, 193
17 'A colossus without arms': Marx
18 'It was hard to preach peace': Temperley, 339
19 'Words may be properly answered': Walpole, *Russell* II, 283
20 'The question of peace': cited in Grünwald, 271
21 'The maintenance of its independence': Kinglake, 209
22 'Hitherto supposed to be': Kinglake, I, 211
23 'As much ink was spilled'; La Gorce, 186
24 'The Emperor has accepted our Note': Russell, *Expedition*, 184
25 'Fully guarded the principle': Parliamentary Papers, 374
26 'I called the attention': Kinglake, I, 375
27 'For on that day': Temperley, 346
28 'Work began anew': Rousset, 44
29 'The Note emphasized rather': Temperley, 345
30 'The real blame for the rejection': Schmitt, 63
31 'Landing troops on the coasts': Lane-Poole, II, 292
32 'The governments of all the four': Kinglake, I, 372
33 All correspondence extracts are taken from Maxwell, 18–21
34 'I love the Emperor of Austria': Grünwald, 271
35 'As matters have now been arranged': Victoria, II, 456
36 'It is evident that': *Cambridge Diplomatic History*, 353
37 'I am resolved to put': Nesselrode
38 'For thirty years I have imposed': Grünwald, 270
39 'This son of a Catholic': ibid., 270
40 'The contradiction between': ibid, 270
41 'Are we to remain as I': Goryainov
41 'The intentions of Your Majesty': Victoria, II, 563
42 'Russia is challenged to fight': *American Register*, 297
43 'The situation, altogether of an expectant': Nesselrode

CHAPTER 9 – First Blood

1 'Irritated Russia just as': Temperley, 369
2 'They were a murderous and inchoate': Vulliamy, 79
3 'The Turks took revenge': Tarlye, I, 293
4 'Under cover of fire': ibid., 284

5 'I report to Your Excellency': ibid., 284
6 'Sinope was in flames'; *American Register*, 299
7 'With hearty joy I request': cited in Chambers, 60
8 'The feelings of honour which this': *American Register*, 301
9 'No longer compatible': cited in Temperley, 375
10 'Strike down the aggressor': ibid., 375
11 'Prepared, should it become': Temperley, 377
12 'To prevent the recurrence': *American Register*, 309
13 'The combined fleets will require': *American Register*, 309
14 'The Emperor shook hands with each of us': cited in Chesney
15 'If England and France will fix': Parliamentary Papers
16 'Neither the diplomatic communications': Goryainov
17 'Receive Austrian approval': Kinglake, II, 115
18 'In very pressing language': ibid., 116
19 'To avoid a conflict, I': ibid., 118
20 'Her Majesty feels called': Chambers 71
21 'England and France have sided with': Chambers, 70

CHAPTER 10 – The Armies: Allied and Russian

1 'In this respect he was': Gooch, 69
2 'A generation had sprung up in England': Fortescue, 33
3 'Perhaps it ought to be': Kinglake, II, 56
4 'When war is carried on against': cited in Gooch, 58
5 'The British Army under the French command': Gooch, 59
6 'But when he found no demand': ibid., 21
7 'I am happy, known, appreciated': St Arnaud, II, 162
8 'A more common willingness': Kinglake, II, 153
9 'I had all the apertures': cited Kinglake, II, 160
10 'It would be impossible to': Pemberton, 181
11 'Whether he talked to a statesman': Kinglake II, 173
12 'The tragedy of Raglan': Pemberton, 180
13 'He could not have been ignorant': *Fraser's Magazine* (July, 1853)
14 'To pick whatever prestige': Gooch, 60
15 'The amazing degree in which the': ibid., 60
16 'Each as proud as Lucifer': Russell, *Expedition*, 320
17 'What a thing war is': Paget, 57
18 'Our arrangements have been infamous': Lysons, 15
19 'Why a defensive position': Bapst, II, 94
20 'A wretched collection': Russell, 27
21 'Gone up the Dardanelles': ibid., 23
22 'Why was this? Because': ibid., 27
23 'A tremendous storm': ibid., 50
24 'A splendid spectacle': ibid., 54
25 'The thing was well done': ibid., 55
26 'There were present some three': ibid., 54

27 'Poorly clothed, poorly mounted': St Arnaud, II, 425
28 'Any other factor than having': Gooch, 66
29 'Crushing all effectively and': ibid. 85
30 'In 1855 an officer': ibid., 237
31 'For the Russian soldier': ibid., 244
32 'To teach and to beat': ibid, 242
33 'Broke open during drill, exposing': ibid., 241
34 'Cast off in winter to a': cited in Curtiss, *The Russian Army,* 195
35 'Crossed themselves, many uttered': Alabin, II, 178
36 'Is true to the holy oath': cited in Curtiss, op. cit. 260
37 'The Russian soldier always goes': Alabin, I, 25
38 'The Russian soldier is an': cited in Curtiss, op. cit., 269
39 'Their brilliant moral qualities': ibid., 269
40 'Seventy were so badly rusted': ibid., 125
41 'With us troops having this': cited in ibid., 120
42 'The rifleman, in the confusion': ibid., 120
43 'We rehearsed manoeuvres exactly': ibid., 132
44 'If it were not for the [Russian]': Lysons, 131
45 'I think they are': cited in Curtiss, op. cit., 149
46 'Such were the formidable defences': Deldafield, 26

CHAPTER II – Silistria and Debate

 1 'After a few days at Aladyn': Russell, 62
 2 'The whole plain around Varna': ibid., 69
 3 'Either Silistria will be left': Tarlye, I. 452
 4 'Prince Bragation with': ibid., 476
 5 'We cannot occupy the': ibid., 458
 6 'Paskevich at Silistria wanted': ibid. 453
 7 'The soldiers worked with': ibid., 454
 8 'In the event that the batteries': cited in Tarlye, 455
 9 'I cannot recover from the shock': St Arnaud, 307
10 'In order to sooth their': Russell, 69
11 'There they are': Marx, 451
12 'Very fine to look at': cited in Gooch, 91
13 'The objectives for which': Kinglake, II, 221
14 'I repeat now what we have': Victoria, III, 170
15 'England had become so eager': Kinglake, II, 223
16 'A good cannonade': Bosquet, IV, 178
17 'The result of this expedition': Russell, 78
18 'Cholera declared itself': ibid., 78
19 'If Sweden joins us': Balfour, 216
20 'Stupendous naval and military establishment': Kinglake II, 241
21 'In the first place it would': Argyll, 474
22 'It is very curious that neither': Greville, 225
23 'An attack on Sevastopol': Fortescue, 40
24 'I remember that when you spoke': cited in Gooch
25 'Day after day in that month': Kinglake II, 245

26 'It was the habit of ministers': Argyll, 475
27 'It was mid-Summer': ibid., 477
28 'In this way, after many': ibid., 475

CHAPTER 12 – On the Crimea

1 'The doctors thought a pound of meat': Russell, 71
2 'Served out of the Varna bakeries': ibid., 71
3 'Live in their uniform, while everybody': ibid., 48
4 'The poor women are most': Sterling
5 'Their morality seems to have': Vulliamy, 74
6 'Only a mile or two from the' (notes): Thomas, 225
7 'You ask how I really endure': Tisdall, 54
8 'We buried three this morning': ibid., 56
9 'Suffered even more acutely': Wood, *Midshipman*, 17
10 'Men sent in there with': Russell, 84
11 'Horrors occurred here every day': ibid., 89
12 'After a time the corpses': Hamley, 9
13 'Drilling and tight stocking': Russell, 85
14 'They might be seen lying drunk': ibid.,80
15 'Tired with the monotony of life': ibid., 82
16 'Earlier Dundas had refused': Gooch,
17 'I will make them go': Quatrelles, II, 385
18 'Sevastopol was intended': Russell, *Todleben,* 26
19 'One battery was known': Vulliamy, 118
20 'Clarity and precision of language': Cited in Gooch, 113
21 'Soldiers you have just given': Chambers, 105
22 'It was a vast armada': Russell, 98

CHAPTER 13 – The War on the Baltic

1 'Lads, war is declared with a common and bold enemy': quoted in Clowes, VI, 397
2 'Daily did we practise at the target': quoted in Royle, 153
3 'If every Captain when detached chose to throw': Bonner-Smith, 81
4 'Soldiers have the habit of moaning': Greenhill and Gifford, 276
5 'The shock of the surprise was fearful': quoted in Royle, 162
6 'We are always reminded that the Russians': quoted in Clowes, VI, 427
7 'I should consider myself unfit for the command': quoted in Royle, 164
8 'The guns were shortly dismounted, and the battery:' Cowes, 422

CHAPTER 14 – First Crimean Steps

1 'Common, sensible, fanciful men – men wise': Kinglake, II, 323
2 'Of those who only this morning ascended': Kinglake, 346
3 'A gig or a cutter, pulled by eight or twelve sailors': Russell, *Expedition*, 86
4 'The beach is a vast and crowded camp': quoted in Royle, 204
5 'His whole camp gave signs': Kinglake, II, 349
6 'Thus marched the strength of the Western powers': Kinglake, II, 373
7 'The pain of weariness had begun; few spoke': Kinglake, II, 375
8 'They approached him respectfully, but without submissiveness': Kinglake, II, 350
9 'As it became dark, we could plainly see': Hodasevich, 55
10 'Is generally fordable for troops': quoted in Warner, 28
11 'With governed features, restraining': Kinglake, III, 24
12 'The Russian officers had been accustomed': Kinglake, III, 41
13 'God does not abandon the righteous': quoted in Royle, 217
14 'Our hearts pounded at the sight of the endless mass': Seaton, 83
15 'Up to the river we rushed and got ready': Gowing,
16 'The mass of English troops, notwithstanding our': quoted in Fletcher, 90
17 'Driving the Russian skirmishers and riflemen': Calthorpe,
18 'Then a small child-like youth ran forward': Kinglake, III, 123
19 'We had re-topped the Heights, routing them': Gowing
20 'The French continued their onset': Kinglake, III, 166
21 'On arriving at the brow': quoted in Fletcher, 112
22 'The scene was so agonizing and sorrowful': quoted in Fletcher, 111
23 'On the more distant heights now occupied by the British': Calthorpe
24 'Going over the field of battle was a dreadful sight': Calthorpe

CHAPTER 15 – On to Sevastopol

1 'But of one fact there is no doubt': Kinglake, III, 382
2 'The English, intrepid and indefatigable in action': Bazancourt, I, 270
3 'Lord Raglan desired to press forward': Kinglake, III, 305
4 'It must be that God did not abandon Russia': Tarle, II, 124
5 'Had the enemy acted with decisiveness': ibid
6 'The blows dealt by this Christian woman fell thick': Kinglake
7 'The ground flees beneath [Russian] horses' feet': Russell
8 'Some of the Russians seemed to be rather astonished': Franks
9 'Lord Raglan's orders are that the cavalry should attack': Kinglake, V, 202
10 'It is difficult, if not impossible to do justice to the feat': Seaton, 149

CHAPTER 16 – The First Winter

1 'And now commenced the bloodiest struggle ever': *New York Times*, 5 November 1854
2 'About 10 o'clock a body of French artillery': *New York Times,* ibid.
3 'On our part it was a confused and desperate struggle': Hamley, 109
4 'In the Quarry Ravine I saw a terrible picture': quoted in Fletcher, 245
5 'Were aware now of having to commit to a long': Fletcher, 268
6 'Not even in the time of ancient Greece': Tolstoy
7 'Now, if ever you have nerve strong enough, go through': Tolstoy
8 'This is the fourth day of the second bombardment': quoted in Ponting
9 'How true that 'War' is usually a series of mistakes' Windham
10 'The illuminations in honour of the Imperial guests': *Illustrated London News*, 21 April 55
11 'We could see the French rushing through the plantations': quoted in Ponting, 267
12 'Raglan was under a shadow. With a mood of dejection': Barker, 255

CHAPTER 17 – The Final Curtain

1 'All the experienced Russian generals were absolutely': quoted in Fletcher, 435
2 'At dawn the [commander in chief] was in the valley': ibid., 436
3 'On the banks of the aqueduct, on the bridge'
4 'The infernal fire, much of which is counter-bombardment': Seaton, 209
5 'The assaults were planned for noon': Fletcher, 460
6 'Now I suppose the French will take it': Fletcher, 267
7 'Everybody saw the necessity of leaving the southern': Alabin
8 'Each man on arriving at the other side': Tolstoy, 184
9 'Sevastopol is not Moscow, the Crimea is not Russia': quoted in Royle, 58
10 'In military terms Gorchakov had merely made': Royle, 435
11 'It is a most melancholy state of things': quoted in Warner, 190
12 'We are placed in a very tenable position': quoted in Warner, 189
13 'General Williams, you have made yourself a name': quoted in Royle, 431
14 'They fell dead at their posts, in the tents': quoted in Royle, 432
15 'The tragedy is that we cannot tell our country': quoted in Fletcher, 525

BIBLIOGRAPHY

Adolenko, C.R. *Histoire de l'Armée Russe*. Paris: Flammarion, 1967.

Alabin, P.V. *Pohodnyia Zapiski v Voinye, 1853–1856 Godov*. Vols I and II. Viatka, 1861.

Alexander, Z. & Dewjee, A. *Wonderful Adventures of Mrs. Seacole in Many Lands*. London: Falling Wall Press, 1984.

American Register

Anderson, Olive. *A Liberal State at War, English Politics and Economics During the Crimean War*. London: Macmillan and Co., 1967.

Annual Register, 1853, 1854, 1855

Argyll, Duke of. *Autobiography and Memoirs*. (Edited by Dowager Duchess of Argyll.) Vol. I. New York: E.P. Dutton, 1906.

Ashley, Evelyn. *The Life and Correspondence of Henry John Temple, Viscount Palmerston*. Vol. II. London: Richard Bentley and Son, 1879.

Askenazy, S. 'Russia', *The Cambridge Modern History*. Vol. X. Cambridge: The University Press, 1934.

Balfour, Lady Frances. *The Life of George, 4th Earl of Aberdeen*. Vol. II. London: Hodder & Stoughton, 1922.

Bapst, Edmund. *Les Origines de la guerre de Crimée*. Paris: 1912.

Barber, Noel. *The Sultans*. New York: Simon & Schuster, 1973.

Barker, A.J. *The War Against Russia*. New York: Holt, Rinehart and Winston, 1970.

Baumart, Winfred. *The Crimean War*. Arnold: London, 1989

Bazancourt, C.L. *Cinq mois devant Sévastopol: L'Expédition de Crimée jusqu'à la prise de Sebastopol*. Ed. Amyot. Paris, 1856

Bentley, Nicholas (ed.). *Russell's Dispatches from the Crimea, 1854–56*. London: Andre Deutsch, 1966.

Bestuzhev, I.V. 'Sevastopol Defense of 1854–55', *The Modern Encyclopedia of Russian and Soviet History*. (Edited by J.L. Wiecznski.) Florida: Academic International Press, 1983

Blackwood, Lady Alicia. *A Narrative of a Residence on the Bosphorus During the Crimean War*. London, 1856.

Bolshoya Sovietskaya Encyclopedia (2nd Edition). Vol. XXXII. 1956.

Bonner-Smith, D. & Dewar, A.C. (ed.). *Russian War, 1854 – Baltic and Black Sea Official Correspondence*. London: Naval Records Society, 1943.

Bosquet, P.F.J. *Lettres du Maréchal Bosquet à sa mère, 1829–1858*. Pau: 1877–79.

Bourgeois, Emile. 'The Orleans Monarchy', *The Cambridge Modern History*. Vol. X. Cambridge: The University Press, 1934.

Brunn, Geoffrey. 'The Nineteenth Century, 1815–1914', *The European Inheritance*. Vol. III. Barker, Clark, Vaucher (ed.) London: Oxford University Press, 1954.

Calthorpe, Somerset. *Letters from Headquarters by an Officer on the Staff*. London: J. Murray, 1856

Chesney, K. *Crimean War Reader*. London: Frederick Miller Ltd., 1960.

Clowes, W.L. *The Royal Navy: A History from the Earliest Times to the Death of Queen Victoria*. Vol. 6. London: Sampson Low, Marston and Company. 1901

Craig, G. 'The System of Alliances and the Balance of Power', *The New Cambridge Modern History*. Vol. X. (Edited by J.P.T. Bury.) Cambridge: The University Press, 1867.

Curtiss, J.S. *The Russian Army under Nicholas I, 1825–1855*. Durham, North Carolina: Duke University Press, 1965.

Curtiss, J.S. *Russia's Crimean War*. Durham, North Carolina: Duke University Press, 1979.

Dansette, Adrien. 'Louis-Napoléon à la conquête du pouvoir', *Histoire du Second Empire*. Vol. I. Paris: Librairie Hachette, 1961.

Deldafield, R. *Report on the Art of War in Europe*. Washington: House of Representatives, 36th Congress, 1861.

Dewar, A.C. (ed.). *Russian War, 1855 – Black Sea Official Correspondence*. London: Naval Records Society, 1945.

Dobrovin, N.F. *Materialy dlya istorii Krymskoy voinyi oborony Sevastopolya*. St Petersburg: 1871

Dodd, George. *Pictorial History of the Russian War*. London: W. & R. Chambers, 1856.

Donaldson, D.C. 'Relations of the Hudson's Bay Company with the Russian-American Company on the Northwest Coast, 1829–1867', *British Columbian Historical Quarterly*. Vol. V, no.1.

Donaldson, D.C. 'The War Scare of 1854', *British Columbia Historical Quarterly*. Vol. V, no.4.

Douglas, Sir G.B. & Ramsey, G.D. *The Panmure Papers, Being a Selection from the Correspondence of Fox Maule, 2nd Baron of Panmure*. London: Hodder & Stoughton, 1908.

Dowty, Alan. *The Limits of American Isolation: The United States and the Crimean War*. New York: New York University Press, 1971.

Dulles, Foster R. *The Road to Teheran*. Princeton: Princeton University Press, 1944.

Eardley-Wilmot, S. *Life of Vice Admiral Edmund, Lord Lysons*.

Ffrench Blake, R.L.V. *The Crimean War*. London: Leo Cooper, 1971

Fisher, H.A.L. *A History of Europe*. Vol. III. London: Eyre & Spottiswoode, 1905.

Fletcher, I. and Ishchenko, N. *The Crimean War: A Clash of Empires*. Staplehurst: Spellmount Ltd., 2004

Fortescue, The Hon. J.W. *A History of the British Army*. Vol. XIII, London: Macmillan & Co., 1930.

Franks, Sergeant-Major Henry, *Leaves from a Soldier's Notebook*. 1904
Fraser's Magazine, London: July, 1863.
Gibbs, Peter. *Crimean Blunder*. London: Frederick Muller, Ltd, 1960.
Gibbs, Peter. *The Battle of the Alma*. London: Weidenfeld & Nicolson, 1963.
Golder, Frank A. 'Russian-American Relations during the Crimean War', *American Historical Review*. Vol. 31, no.3. 1925–26.
Golder, Frank A., 'The Purchase of Alaska', *American Historical Review*. Vol. 25. 1919–20.
Gooch, B.D. *The New Bonapartist Generals in the Crimean War*. The Hague: Martinus Nijhoff, 1959.
Gooch, G.P. *The Second Empire*. London: Longmans, Green & Co., 1960.
Goryainov, Serge. 'The Secret Agreement of 1844 between Russia and England', *The Russian Review*. Vols I, III, IV. University of Liverpool.
Gough, B.M. *The Royal Navy on the Northwest Coast of North America, 1810–1910*. Vancouver: University of British Columbia Press, 1969.
Gouttman, Alain. *La Guerre de Crimée, 1853–1856*. Perrin: Paris, 2003.
Gowing, Timothy. *A Soldier's Story, or a Voice from the Ranks*. Nottingham, 1883.
Greenhill, B. and Gifford, A. *The British Assault on Finland*. London: Naval Institute Press, 1988.
Grenville, Henry. *Leaves from the Diary of Henry Grenville*. (Edited by Viscountess Enfield.) London: Smith, Elder & Co., 1933.
Grünwald, Constantine de. *Tsar Nicholas I*. London: Douglas Saunders, 1954.
Guedalla, Philip. *Palmerston, 1784–1865*. New York: G.P. Putnam's Sons, 1927.
Hamley, Sir Edward. *The War in the Crimea*. London: Seeley & Co, 1891.
Heamshaw, F.J.C. 'European Revolution and After, 1848–1854', *The Cambridge History of British Foreign Policy, 1783–1919*. *Vol.* II. Cambridge: The University Press, 1923.
Henderson, G.B. *Crimean War Diplomacy*. Glasgow: 1947.
Historical Outlook. Vol. XV, no.8. November, 1924.
Hodasevich, Captain R. *A Voice from Within the Walls of Sevastopol: A Narrative of the Campaign in the Crimea and the Events of the Siege*. London, 1856
Horvath, E. 'Origins of the Crimean War', *South Eastern Affairs*. Vol. VII (1937), VIII (1938).
Higginson, Sir G. *71 Years of a Guardsman's Life*. London: Smith, Elder & Co., 1916.
Illustrated London News. Vols 23, 24, 25.
Jomini, Baron Henri. *Diplomatic Study of the Crimean War*, London: W.H. Allen & Co., 1882.
Kinglake, A.W. *The Invasion of the Crimea*. Vols I, II, III. London: William Blackwood & Sons, 1885.
La Gorce, Pierre de. *Histoire du Second Empire*. Vol. I. Paris: Plon Nourrit et Cie, 1908.
Lane-Poole, S. *The Life of Stratford Canning*. London: Longmans, Green, 1888.
Lavisse, Ernest. *Histoire de France Contemporaine*. Vol. VI. Paris: Librairie Hachette, 1921.
Lincoln, Bruce W. *Nicholas I, Emperor and Autocrat of All the Russias*. DeKalb: Northern Illinois University Press, 1989. *New York Times*, 5 November 1854.
Lysons, Sir Daniel. *The Crimean War From First to Last*.
MacMunn, Sir George. *The Crimea in Perspective*. London: G. Bell & Sons, Ltd., 1935.

Manning, C.A. *Russian Influence on Early America*. New York: Library Publishers, 1953.

Martens, F. *Recueil des traités conclus par la Russie avec les puissances étrangères*. Vol. XI. St Petersburg: 1895.

Martin, Theodore. *The Life of His Highness the Prince Consort*. London: Smith, Elder & Co., 1880.

Marx, Karl. *The Eastern Question, 1853–56*. London: Sonnenschein, 1897.

Maxwell, Sir H. *Life and Letters of George William Frederick, 4th Earl of Clarendon*. London: Edward Arnold, 1913.

Molènes, Paul de. *Les Commentaires d'un Soldat*. Paris: Ancienne Maison Michel Lévy Frères, 1877.

Mosse, W.E. *The Rise and Fall of the Crimean System, 1855–71*. London: Macmillan & Co., 1963.

Napier, Sir Charles. *The History of the Baltic Campaign of 1854, from Documents and Other Materials* furnished by Vice Admiral Sir C. Napier, K.G.B. (Edited by Sir W.F.P. Napier.) 1857.

Nesselrode, A. de. *Lettres et Papiers du Chancelier Comte de Nesselrode, 1760–1856*. Paris: Lahure, 1904–12.

Nikolai Mihailovich, Grand Duke. *Znamenytya Rossiyany XVIII–XIX Vekov*. St Petersburg: Lenizdat, 1996.

Olga Nikolavna, Grand Duchess. 'Syon Yunostye', no.7, *Voyennoye Historitscheskaya Biblioteka*. Paris.

O'Meara, Barry E. *Napoleon in Exile, or a Voice from St Helena*, London: W. Simpson & R. Marshall, 1822.

Paget, George. *The Light Cavalry Brigade in the Crimea*. London: 1881.

Parker, J.W. *The Holy City*. Vol. II. London: 1869.

Parliamentary Papers (Eastern Papers), 1854. *Correspondence Relating to the Affairs of the Levant*. Vol. VI.

Pemberton, W.R. *Battles of the Crimean War*. London: R.T. Batsford, Ltd., 1962.

Phillimore, Vice Admiral Augustus. *Life of Sir William Parker*. Vol. III. London: 1876.

Ponting, Clive. *Crimean War: The Truth Behind the Myth*. London: Chatto & Windus, 2004.

Puryear, Vernon J. *England, Russia and the Straits Question*. Hamden, Connecticut: Archon Books, 1965.

Puryear, Vernon J. 'New Light on the Origins of the Crimean War', *The Journal of Modern History*. Vol. III. June, 1931.

Quatrelles, l'Epine. *Le Maréchal de Saint Arnaud, 1798–1854*. Vol. II.

Ranken, George. *Canada and the Crimea*. London: Longman, Green and Longman, 1862.

Reddaway, W.F. 'The Crimean War and the French Alliance, 1853–1858', *The Cambridge History of British Foreign Policy, 1783 1919*. *Vol.* III. Cambridge: The University Press, 1923.

Rousset, Camille. *Histoire de la Guerre de Crimée*. Paris: Librairie Hachette et Cie., 1894.

Royle, Trevor. *Crimea: The Great Crimean War, 1854–1856*. London: Little, Brown and Company, 1999.

Russell, W.H. *General Todleben's History of the Defense of Sebastopol, 1854–55*. London: Tinsley Brothers, 1865.

Russell, W.H. *The British Expedition to the Crimea*. London: G. Routledge & Co., 1858. *Russkaya Staryna*. No.7.

Saint-Arnaud, A.J. *Lettres du Maréchal de Saint Arnaud, 1832–1854.* Vol. II. Paris: Ancienne Maison Michel Lévy, 1895.

Saul, Norman E. *Distant Friends: The United States and Russia, 1763–1867.* Lawrence, Kansas: University Press of Kansas, 1991.

Schmitt, B.E. 'The Diplomatic Preliminaries of the Crimean War', *American Historical Review.* Vol. XXV. October, 1919.

Seaton, Albert. *The Crimean War: A Russian Chronicler.* London, 1977

Seaton-Watson, R.W. *Britain in Europe, 1789–1914, a Survey of Foreign Policy.* Cambridge: The University Press, 1938.

Selby, John. *Balaclava, Gentlemen's Battle.* New York: Antheneum, 1970.

Seymour, H.D. *Russia on the Black Sea.* London: John Murray, 1855.

Simpson, F.A. *Louis Napoleon and the Recovery of France (1848–56).* London: Longmans, Green, 1923.

Slade Sir Adolphus. *Turkey and the Crimean War.* London: Smith, Elder & Co., 1867.

Soyer, Alexis. *Soyer's Culinary Campaign.* London: G. Routledge & Co., 1857.

Sproxton, Charles. *Palmerston and the Hungarian Revolution.* Cambridge: The University Press, 1919.

Stearns, P.N. *1848: The Revolutionary Tide in Europe.* New York: W.W. Norton & Co., 1974.

Sterling, A. *The Story of the Highland Brigade in the Crimea.* London: Remington & Co., 1895.

Stockmar, Baron von. *Memoires.* Vol. II. London: Longman, Green, 1873.

Tarlye, E.V. *Krymskya Voyna.* U.S.S.R.: Academya Naouk, 1950.

Tatischev, S.S. 'Imperator Nicholay y Ynostranye Dvory', *Historychesky Vestnik.* Vol XXXV. St Petersburg: 1889.

Tatischev, S.S. 'Diplomatitschesky Razriv Russiya s Tourtzii', *Historychesky Vestnik.* Vol. 47. St Petersburg.

Tatischev, S.S. 'Raskaze ob Nicholaya Pervovo', *Historychesky Vestnik.* Vol. 68. St Petersburg.

Temperley, H.W.V. *England and the Near East – the Crimea.* London: Frank Cass & Co., 1964.

Temperley, H.W.V. 'Stratford de Redcliffe and the Origins of the Crimean War', *English Historical Review.* Vol. 48, October, 1933.

Temperley, H.W.V. *The Unpublished Diary and Political Sketches of Princess Lieven.* London: Jonathan Cape Ltd., 1925.

The Story of the War by Collated Passages. London: 1857.

The London Times. 1853.

Thomas, Albert. 'Napoleon III and the Period of Personal Government, 1852–59', *The Cambridge Modern History.* (Edited by Lord Acton.) Vol. XI. Cambridge: The University Press, 1934.

Thomas, Donald. *Charge! Hurrah! Hurrah! A Life of Cardigan of Balaclava.* London: Routledge & Kegan Paul, 1974.

Thompson, J.M. *Louis Napoléon and the Second Empire.* New York: Noonday Press, 1955.

Thouvenel, L. *Nicholas Ier et Napoléon III – Les Préliminaires de la Guerre de Crimée.* Paris: 1891.

Tisdall, E.E.P. *Mrs. Duberly's Campaign.* London: Jarrolds Publishers (London) Ltd., 1963.

Tolstoy, Leo. *The Sevastopol Sketches.* London: Penguin Books, 1986.

Tocqueville, Alexis de. *Recollections of Alexis de Tocqueville*, New York: Macmillan, 1896.

Valsecchi, Franco. *Il Risorgimento e l'Europa; L'Alleanza di Crimea*. Firenze: Vallecci Editore, 1968.

Victoria. *The Letters of Queen Victoria*. (Edited by A.C. Benson & Viscount Esher.) London: John Murray, 1907.

Vulliamy, C.E. *Crimea, the Campaign of 1854–56*. London: Jonathan Cape, 1939.

Walpole, Spencer. *The Life of Lord John Russell*. Vol. II. London: Longman, Green & Co., 1889.

Walpole, Spencer. 'Great Britain in the Crimean War, 1852–56', *The Cambridge Modern History*. Vol. XI. (Edited by Lord Acton.) Cambridge: The University Press, 1934.

Warner, Philip. *The Crimean War: A Reappraisal*. Taplinger Publishing: New York, 1973

Williams, R.L. *The Mortal Napoléon III*. Princeton: Princeton University Press, 1971.

Wood, Sir Evelyn. *From Midshipman to Field Marshal*. Vol. I. London: Methuen & Co., 1906.

Wood, Sir Evelyn. *The Crimea in 1854 and 1894*. London: Chapman & Hall Ltd., 1895.

Woodham-Smith, C.B. *Florence Nightingale*. London: Collins, 1951.

Woodham-Smith, C.B. *The Reason Why*. London: Constable, 1953.

Woodward, E.L. *The Age of Reform, 1815–1870*. Oxford: The Clarendon Press, 1938.

Yevaldye, A.V. 'Roskazye ob Imperatora Nicholya Pervovo'. *Historychesky Vestnik*. Vol. 65. 1896.

Zaïontchkovsky, A.M. *Vostochnaia Voina, 1853–56, v Sviazi s Sovremenoy ei Politicheskoy Obstanovkoy*. St Petersburg: 1908.

NOTES

1 Details concerning the tsar's last days, his death and the mysterious aftermath are the subject of an earlier work by the author: *Imperial Legend: The Mysterious Disappearance of Tsar Alexander I.*

2 As the war drew to a close, the condition and quality of forces in Crimea improved through hastily wrought reforms, and continental opinion of the British army changed. With the suppression of the Indian Mutiny (1857), the prestige associated with Waterloo was substantially restored.

3 In 1812 a general court martial could order an unlimited number of lashes, although a regimental court martial was limited to 300 lashes. By 1850 the maximum number of lashes had been limited to 50, and in 1867 flogging was entirely forbidden except in time of war.

4 Michael Crichton wryly comments on the charge. Ineptitude in Crimea culminated in 'Lord Cardigan's Charge of the Light Brigade, a spectacular feat of heroism which decimated three-quarters of his forces in a successful effort to capture the wrong battery of enemy guns'.

5 'When the boat was completed and named *America*, it hoisted the Star and Stripes and set sail for the Pacific by way of Cape Horn. On the way it put into Rio Janeiro and while there an English warship threatened to seize it as a Russian vessel and probably would have done so had not the American naval officer come to the rescue.' (F.A. Golder)

6 Samples of Soyer's recipes may be found in the Appendix.

7 In arguing for the actual invasion of Crimea, Palmerston astutely reasoned in June 1854: 'Austria has, as usual, been playing a shabby game. When she thought the Russians likely to get on, and while she fancied England and

France needed hastening, she bragged of her determination to be active against Russia. As soon as she found our troops at Varna, she changed her tone, and according to a dispatch which Clarendon had in his hand yesterday, she now says she shall not enter the Principalities, and the Russians must be driven out by the Turks and the English and the French. She can hardly think us simple enough to do her work for her; but the best way to force her to act would be to send our troops off to Crimea. This is my vote.

8 Some vignettes from Stratford's pen at the time: 'Hot! Hot! Hot! Most horribly hot! . . . the Secretary of State was seen one morning at an early hour floating down the Potomac with a black cap on his head and a pair of goggles on his eyes . . . [Pennsylvania Avenue was] the only thing approximating to our notion of a street . . . chewing and spitting appear on the decline; indoor spitting is also less common . . . the diplomatic body at Washington ought really to be reckoned amongst the labouring classes . . . life is one of privation and restraint . . .'

9 The Straits Convention was signed by the great powers, who jointly agreed to demilitarize the Bosphorus and the Dardanelles. So long as Turkey remained at peace, these passages were permanently closed to all warships. The sultan might, however, permit the passage of 'small vessels of war, which, in conformity with usage, are employed in the service of Ambassadors of friendly Powers'.

10 En route to New York, Kossuth stopped in London and addressed a number of massed meetings, speaking in the English which he had gleaned from reading the Bible and Shakespeare while in prison. Eventually, he moved to Italy, where in 1894 he died, infirm, impoverished and lonely. In death, he became the symbol of Hungarian aspiration for independence, and his body was received home amid nationwide mourning.

11 Britain, more than any other nation, would have been justified in not admitting to 'NIII' in as much as Britain had consistently refused to recognize Napoleon I. Lord Derby, however, felt it prudent not to rile the newly-crowned Emperor of the French.

12 Article VII of the treaty actually made rather vague stipulations: 'The Sublime Porte promises constant protection to the Christian religion and to the Churches of this religion. She allows the Minister of the Imperial Court to make, at all times, representation to the Porte, either for the church built at Constantinople, of which mention shall be made in Article XIV, or for the ministering in it, and she promises to pay heed to these observations as coming from a person of importance and helping to a neighbouring and sincerely friendly Power.'

13 'The Principalities' – Moldavia and Wallachia – were united in 1859 to form Romania, still remaining under the sultan's suzerainty until 1873, at which time the country was declared independent.

14 Some thirty years earlier, Napoleon Bonaparte, from his exile on St Helena, prophesied: 'In the course of a few years, Russia will have Constantinople . . . almost all the cajoling and flattering which Alexander practises towards me was to gain my consent to effect this object . . . the only hypothesis that France and England may ever be allied with sincerity will be to prevent this.' (B.E. O'Meara, *A Voice From St Helena,* vol II, 69)

15 The Russian Imperial Naval ensign was the blue cross of St Andrew on a field of white.

16 On 29 March, Clarendon lamented: 'The die is cast and war was declared yesterday. We are already beginning to taste the fruits of it. Every species of

security has rapidly gone down, and everybody's property in stocks, shares, etc. is depreciated already from twenty to thirty per cent. I will be as heartily sick of it as they are now hot upon it.' Within months of the declaration, the public was bemoaning the rise of income tax from 7 pence to 1 shilling 2 pence in the pound, a 100 per cent increase.

17 A quarter of a century earlier Emperor Nicholas was warned that should he elect to gather strength at Sevastopol, he might have to reckon with the British navy. 'Although it may not be probable that we shall see an English fleet in the Black Sea, it would be prudent to make Sevastopol very secure against attack from the sea. If ever England were to come to a rupture with us, this is the point to which she would direct her attacks, if only she believed them possible.' (Count Pozzo di Borge to Nicholas, 28 November, 1828)

18 In his later years, some of Lord Aberdeen's actions and thoughts were peculiar, morose and hard to explain. He stubbornly refused, for example, to rebuild a chapel on his estate but delegated the task to his son as part of his inheritance. After his death, there were found in Aberdeen's belongings numerous scraps of paper each with the same message in his hand: 'And David said unto Solomon, My son, as for me, it was in my power to build an house unto the name of the Lord my God. But the word of the Lord came to me, saying Thou has shed blood abundantly and hast made great war: thou shalt not build an house unto my name, because thou hast shed much blood upon the earth in my sight.' [*Chronicles* xxii, 7–8. Taken from Temperley]

19 In October 1854, Lord Cardigan's yacht, the *Dryad*, arrived on the harbour of Balaklava. There 'only a mile or two from the great camp of hungry and exhausted men, lay the trim pleasure craft, equipped as though for the Cowes Regatta, with its comfortable saloon and cabins; its running water and elegant furnishings; its French chef and its cases of champagne. Cardigan was granted permission by Raglan to use this ship and now retired to the *Dryad*, where he dined and slept, returning to command his Brigade after breakfast.'

20 Napier failed to obtain a formal enquiry into this behaviour and by way of protest he refused promotion to the highest class of the Order of Bath. In 1855, he was elected to Parliament for Southwark, where he continued unsuccessfully his dispute with the Admiralty from the floor of the House of Commons.

21 It would appear that the piece was submitted by an Englishman, since the word 'we' is used throughout. The United States, it will be remembered, exercised benign neutrality throughout the war in favour of Russia.

22 In terms of today's purchasing power, an estimated £ 8.606 billion.

INDEX